The Story of London

Henry B. Wheatley

Alpha Editions

This edition published in 2024

ISBN : 9789362926401

Design and Setting By
Alpha Editions
www.alphaedis.com
Email - info@alphaedis.com

As per information held with us this book is in Public Domain.
This book is a reproduction of an important historical work. Alpha Editions uses the best technology to reproduce historical work in the same manner it was first published to preserve its original nature. Any marks or number seen are left intentionally to preserve its true form.

Contents

PREFACE ....- 1 -

CHAPTER I Introduction: Early History of London to the Norman Conquest.........................- 3 -

CHAPTER II The Walled Town and its Streets..- 16 -

CHAPTER III Round the Town with Chaucer and the Poets of his Time ....- 49 -

CHAPTER IV The River and the Bridge ....- 62 -

CHAPTER V The King's Palace—The Tower ....- 74 -

CHAPTER VI *Manners* ....- 90 -

CHAPTER VII *Health, Disease and Sanitation*[125] ....- 110 -

CHAPTER VIII The Governors of the City..- 147 -

CHAPTER IX Officials of the City ....- 176 -

CHAPTER X Commerce and Trade..................................- 184 -

CHAPTER XI The Church and Education ....- 218 -

CHAPTER XII London from Mediæval to Modern Times .... - 245 -

FOOTNOTES: .... - 263 -

PREFACE

'History! What is history but the science which teaches us to see the throbbing life of the present in the throbbing life of the past.'—JESSOPP'S *Coming of the Friars*, p. 178.

THERE can be no doubt that our interest in the dim past is increased the more we are able to read into the dry documents before us the human character of the actors. As long as these actors are only names to us we seem to be walking in a world of shadows, but when we can realise them as beings like ourselves with the same feelings and aspirations, although governed by other conditions of life, all is changed, and we take the keenest interest in attempting to understand circumstances so different from those under which we live.

The history of London is so varied and the materials so vast that it is impossible to compress into a single volume an account of its many aspects.

This book therefore is not intended as a history but as, to some extent, a guide to the manners of the people and to the appearance of the city during the mediæval period.

An attempt is here made to put together some of the ample materials for the domestic history of the city which have been preserved for us.

The City of London possesses an unrivalled collection of contemporary documents respecting its past history, some of which have been made available to us by the late Mr. H. T. Riley, and others are being edited with valuable notes by Dr. Reginald Sharpe.

The Middle Ages may be considered as a somewhat indefinite period, and their chronology cannot be very exactly defined, but for the purposes of this book the portion of the mediæval period dealt with is that which commences with the Norman Conquest and ends with the Battle of Bosworth.

It is impossible to exaggerate the enormous influence of the Norman Conquest. The Saxon period was as thoroughly mediæval as the Norman period, but our full knowledge of history begins with the Conquest because so few historical documents exist before that event. Moreover, the mode of life in Saxon and Norman London was so different that it would only lead to confusion to unite the two in one picture.

In order, however, to show the position of the whole mediæval period in the full history an introductory chapter is given which contains a short notice of some of the events during the Saxon rule, and a chapter at the end is intended to show what remains of the mediæval times were left when Shakespeare lived and Johnson expressed his opinion of the pre-eminent position of London.

It is necessary for the reader to bear in mind that London means the city and its liberties up to the end of the eighteenth century. The enlarged idea of a London in the north and the south, the east and the west, is a creation of the nineteenth century.

The City of London is still the centre and heart of London, and the only portion of the town which has an ancient municipal history.

Other cities have shifted their centres, but London remains as it always was. The Bank, the Royal Exchange and the Mansion House occupy ground which has been the 'Eye of London' since Roman times.

There is no greater mistake than to suppose that things were quiescent during the Middle Ages, for these pages at least will show that that was a time of constant change, when great questions were fought out.

The first seven chapters of this book refer to life in the Old Town. Here we see what it was to live in a walled town, what the manners of the citizens were and what was done to protect their health and morals. The following five chapters deal with the government of the city. Some notice is taken of the governors and the officials of the Corporation, the tradesmen and the churchmen.

The subject of each chapter is of enough importance to form a book by itself, and it is therefore hoped that the reader will not look for an exhaustive treatment of these subjects. There is more to be said in each place, but I have been forced to choose out of the materials that which seemed most suitable for my purpose.

During the editing of this volume a vivid picture of the mediæval life has ever been before my mind, and I can only regret that it has been so difficult to transfer that picture to paper. I can only hope that my readers may not see the difference between the conception and the performance so vividly as I do myself.

In the preparation of these pages I have received the kind assistance of more friends than I can mention here, but I wish especially to thank Mr. Hubert Hall, Mr W. H. St. John Hope, Mr. J. E. Matthew, General Milman, C.B., Mr D'Arcy Power, Sir Walter Prideaux, Sir Owen Roberts, Mr. J. Horace Round, Dr Reginald Sharpe and Sir William Soulsby, C.B.

CHAPTER I

Introduction: Early History of London to the Norman Conquest

THE question as to the great antiquity of London has formed a field for varied and long-continued disputes. An elaborate picture of a British London, founded by Brut, a descendant of Æneas, as a new Troy, with grand and noble buildings, was painted by Geoffrey of Monmouth. The absurdity of this conception, although it found credence for centuries, was at last seen, and some antiquaries then went to the opposite extreme of denying the very existence of a British London.

The solid foundation of facts proving the condition of the earliest London are the waste, marshy ground, with little hills rising from the plains, and the dense forest on the north—a forest that remained almost up to the walls of the city even in historic times, animal remains, flint instruments, and pile dwellings. All the rest is conjecture. We must call in the aid of geography and geology to understand the laws which governed the formation of London. The position of the town on the River Thames proves the wisdom of those who chose the site, although the swampiness of the land, caused by the daily overflowing of the river before the embankments were thrown up, must have endangered its successful colonisation. When the vast embankment was completed the river receded to its proper bed, and the land which was retrieved was still watered by several streams flowing from the higher ground in the north into the Thames.

Animal remains, very various in character, have been found in different parts of London. Examples of mammoth, elephant, rhinoceros, elk, deer, and many other extinct as well as existing species are represented. Of man, the mass of flint instruments in the 'Palæolithic floor' which prove his early existence is enormous.

General Pitt Rivers (then Colonel Lane Fox) in 1867 made the discovery of the remains of pile dwellings near London Wall and in Southwark Street. The piles averaged 6 to 8 inches square, others of a smaller size were 4 inches by 3 inches, and one or two were as much as a foot square. They were found in the peat just above the virgin gravel, and with them were found the refuse of kitchen middens and broken pottery of the Roman period. There is reason to believe that the piles were sunk by the Britons rather than by the Romans, and General Pitt Rivers was of opinion that they are the remains of the British capital of Cassivellaunus, situated in the marches, and, of necessity, built on piles.[1] Dr. Munro, however, who alludes to this discovery in his book on Lake Dwellings, believes that these piles belong to the post-Roman times, and supposes that in the early Saxon period these pile dwellings were used in the low-lying districts of London.[2]

The strongest point of those who disbelieve in a British London is that Julius Cæsar does not mention it, but this negative evidence is far from conclusive.

We learn from Tacitus that in A.D. 61 the Roman city was a place of some importance—the chief residence of merchants and the great mart of trade—therefore we cannot doubt but that to have grown to this condition it must have existed before the Christian era. The Romans appear to have built a fort where the Tower of London now stands, but not originally to have fortified the town. London grew to be a flourishing centre of commerce, though not a place capable of sustaining a siege, so the Roman general, Paullinus Suetonius, would not run the risk of defending it against Boadicea. Afterwards the walls were erected, and Londinium took its proper position in the Roman Empire. It was on the high road from Rome to York, and the starting-point of half the roads in Britain.

Bishop Stubbs wrote: 'Britain had been occupied by the Romans, but had not become Roman.' Probably few Romans settled here. The inhabitants consisted of the Governor and the military officers and Romanised Britons. When the Roman legions left this country Londinium must have had a very mixed population of traders. There were no leaders, and a wail went up from the defenceless inhabitants. In the year 446 we hear of 'The groans of the Britons to Aetius, for the third time Consul,' which took this form of complaint: 'The savages drive us to the sea, and the sea casts us back upon the savages; so arise two kinds of death, and we are either drowned or slaughtered.'[3]

In this place, however, we have not to consider the condition either of British or Roman London, for the Middle Ages may be said to commence with the break up of the Roman Empire. Saxon London was a wooden city, surrounded by walls, marking out the same enclosure that existed in the latest Roman city. We have the authority of the Saxon Chronicle for saying that in the year 418 the Romans collected all the treasures that were in Britain, and hid some of them in the earth.

From the date of the departure of the Roman legions to that of the Norman Conquest nearly six centuries and a half had elapsed. Of this long period we find only a few remains, such as some articles discovered in the river, and some entries in that incomparable monument of the past—the

Saxon Chronicle. All we really know of Saxondom we learn from the Chronicle, Bede's *Ecclesiastical History*, and the old charters. The history of England for the greater portion of this time was local and insular, for the country was no longer a part of a great empire.

Professor Earle tells us that the name London occurs fifty times in the Chronicle, and Londonburh thirteen times, but we do not know whether any distinction between the two names was intended to be indicated.

The Chronicler tells us of the retreat of the Roman legions, and how Hengist and Horsa, invited by Vortigern, King of the Britons, landed in Britain. Then comes the ominous account of the Saxons, who turned against the friends that called upon them for succour and totally defeated the British at Crayford in Kent:—

'457. This year Hengist and Æsc, his son, fought against the Britons at the place which is called Crecganford, and there slew four thousand men; and the Britons then forsook Kent, and in great terror fled to Lundenbyrg.'

Then for a century and a half there is no further mention of London in the Chronicle. We are not told what became of the fugitives, nor what became of the city; as Lappenberg says: 'No territory ever passed so obscurely into the hand of an enemy as the north bank of the Thames.'

It is as difficult to suppose what some have supposed—that the city was deserted and remained desolate for years—as to imagine that trade and commerce continued in the city while all around was strife. There may have been some arrangement by which the successful Saxon who did not care to live in the city agreed that those who wished to do so should live there. But all is conjecture in face of this serious blank in our history.

If there had been a battle and destruction of the city we should doubtless have had some account of it in the Chronicle. Gradually the Saxons settled on the hithes or landing places on the river side, and at last overcame their natural repugnance to town life and settled in the city. When London is again mentioned in the Chronicle it appears to have been inhabited by a population of heathens still to be converted. Under the date 604 we are told:—

'This year Augustine consecrated two bishops; Mellitus and Justus. He sent Mellitus to preach baptism to the East Saxons, whose King was called Sebert, son of Ricole, the sister of Ethelbert, and whom Ethelbert had then appointed King. And Ethelbert gave Mellitus a bishop's See in Lundenwic, and to Justus he gave Rochester, which is twenty-four miles from Canterbury.'

The Christianity of the Londoners was of an unsatisfactory character, for after the death of Sebert, his sons, who were heathens, stirred up the multitude to drive out their bishop. Mellitus became Archbishop of Canterbury, and London again relapsed into heathenism. In this, the earliest period of Saxon London recorded for us, there appears to be no relic left of the Christianity of the Britons which at one time was well in evidence. Godwin recorded a list of sixteen ecclesiastics, styled by him Archbishops of London, and Le Neve adopted the list in his *Fasti Ecclesiæ Anglicanæ*, on the authority of Godwin.

The list begins with Theanus during the reign of Lucius, King of the Britons in the latter half of the second century. The second is Eluanus, who was said to have been sent on an embassy to Eleutherius, Pope from A.D. 171 to 185. The twelfth on the list is Restitutus, whose name is found on the list of prelates present at the Council of Arles in the year 314.

Perhaps the answer to the question as to the extinction of British Christianity in London is to be found in Geoffrey of Monmouth's statement that when the Saxons drove the British fugitives into Wales and Cornwall, Theon, the sixteenth and last on this list of British bishops, fled into Wales with the Archbishop of Caerleon, the Bishop Thadiac of York, and their surviving clergy. The traditional date of this flight is A.D. 586, not many years before the appearance of Mellitus. Geoffrey of Monmouth is not a very trustworthy authority, but there is no reason to doubt his belief in his own story, and it is interesting to note that he specially mentions Theonus. At all events, we know from other sources that there were Bishops of London during the Roman period.

The bold statement that King Lucius founded the Church of St. Peter, Cornhill, can scarcely be said to find any credence among historians of the present day, but a reference to the doings of this ancient King will be found imbedded in the Statute Book of St. Paul's Cathedral:—'In the year from the Incarnation of the Lord one hundred and eighty-five, at the request of Lucius, the King of Greater Britain, which is now called England, there were sent from Eleutherius the Pope to the aforesaid King two illustrious doctors, Fagnus and Dumanus, who should incline the heart of the King and of his subject people to the unity of the Christian faith, and should consecrate to the honour of the one true and supreme God the temples which had been dedicated to various and false deities.'[4]

To return from the wild statements of tradition to the facts of sober history, we find that London, after the driving out of Mellitus, remained without a bishop until the year 656, when Cedda, brother of St. Chad of Lichfield, was invited to London by Sigebert who had been converted to Christianity by Finan, Bishop of the Northumbrians. Cedda was consecrated Bishop of the East Saxons by Finan about 656, and held the See till his death on the 26th October 664. The list of bishops from Cedda to William, who is addressed in the Conqueror's Charter, is a long one, and each of these bishops apparently held a position of great importance in the government of the city.

In the seventh century the city seems to have settled down into a prosperous place and to have been peopled by merchants of many nationalities. We learn that at this time it was the great mart of slaves. It was in the fullest sense a free trading town; neutral to a certain extent between the kingdoms around, although the most powerful of the Kings successively obtained some authority over it, when they conquered their feebler neighbours.[5] As to this there is still more to be said. During the eighth century, when a more settled condition of life became possible, the trade and commerce of London increased in volume and prosperity. A change, however, came about towards the end of the century, when the Scandinavian freebooters, known to us as Danes, began to harry our coasts. The Saxons had become law-abiding, and the fierce Danes treated them in the same way that in former days they had treated the Britons. Freeman divided the Danish invasions into three periods:—

1. 787-855. A period when the object was simply plunder.

2. 902-954. Attempts made at settlement.

3. 980-1016. During this period the history of England was one record of struggle with the power of Denmark till Cnut became undisputed King of England.[6]

We still have much to learn as to the movements of the Danes in this country, and when the old charters are more thoroughly investigated we shall gain a great accession of light. Thus we learn from an Anglo-Saxon charter, printed in De Gray Birch's *Cartularium Saxonicum* (Nos. 533, 534), that in the year 872 a great tribute was paid to the Danes which is not mentioned in the Chronicle. London was specially at the mercy of the fierce sailors of the North, and the times when the city was in their hands are almost too numerous for record here.

Even when Alfred concluded with Guthrun in 878 the Treaty of Wedmore, as it is still commonly called,[7] and by which the country was divided between the English and the Danes, London suffered much.

With the reign of Alfred we come to the consideration of a very difficult question in the history of London. It has been claimed for this King that he rebuilt London. Mr Loftie expresses this view in the very strongest terms. He writes:—

'So important, however, is this settlement, so completely must it be regarded as the ultimate fact in any continuous narrative relating to the history of London, that it would be hardly wrong to commence with some such sentence as this; "London was founded exactly a thousand years ago by King Alfred, who chose for the site of his city a place formerly fortified by the Romans, but desolated successively by the Saxons and the Danes." '

There is certainly no evidence for so sweeping a statement. Nothing in the Chronicle can be construed to contain so wide a meaning. The passage upon which this mighty superstructure has been formed is merely this:—

'886. In the same year King Alfred restored (*gesette*) London, and all the Angle race turned to him that were not in the bondage of the Danish men, and he then committed the burgh to the keeping of the Alderman Æthered.'

The great difficulty in this passage is the word *gesette*, which probably means occupied, but may mean much more, as founded or settled. Some authorities have therefore changed the word to *besaet*, besieged.

Professor Earle proposed the following solution of the problem, which seems highly probable. London was a flourishing, populous and opulent city, the chief emporium of commerce in the island, and the residence of foreign merchants. Properly it had become an Angle city, the chief city of the Anglian nation of Mercia, but the Danes had settled there in great numbers, and they had many captives whom they had taken in the late wars. Thus the Danes preponderated over the free Angles, and the latter were glad to see Alfred come and restore the balance in their favour. It was of the greatest importance for Alfred to secure this city, not only the capital of Mercia, but able to do what Mercia had not done, to bar the passage of pirate ships to the Upper Thames. Accordingly, Alfred in 886 planted the garrison of London, *i.e.*, introduced a military colony of men, and gave them land for their maintenance, in return for which they lived in and about a fortified position under a commanding officer. Professor Earle would not have *Lundenburh* taken as merely an equivalent to London. Alfred therefore founded not London itself but the burh of London.[8]

Under Athelstan we find the city increasing in importance and general prosperity. There were then eight mints at work, which shows great activity and the need of coin for the purposes of trade. The folkmoot met in the precincts of St. Paul's at the sound of the bell, which also rang out when the armed levy was required to march under St. Paul's banner. For some years after the decisive Battle of Brunanburh (937) the Danes ceased to trouble the country. But one may affirm that fire was almost as great an enemy as the Dane. Fabyan, when recording the entire destruction of

London by fire in the reign of Ethelred (981), makes this remarkable statement: 'Ye shall understande that this daye the cytie of London had most housynge and buyldinge from Ludgate toward Westmynstre, and lytell or none wher the chief or hart of the citie is now, except [that] in dyvers places were housyng, but they stod without order.'[9]

The good government of Athelstan and his successors kept the country free from foreign freebooters, but when Ethelred II., called the Unready (or rather the Redeless), came to the throne, the Danes saw their opportunity. In 991 he tried to bribe his enemies to stay away, and was the first English King to institute the Danegelt, which was for so many years a severe tax upon the resources of the country. The bribe was useless, and the enemy had to be bought off again. A Danish fleet threatened London in 992, and in 994 Olaf (or Anlaf) Trygwason (who appears first as harrier of English soil in 988), with Sweyn, the Danish King, laid siege to London, but failed to take it. They then harried, burned and slew all along the sea coasts of Essex, Kent, Sussex and Hampshire. The English paid £10,000 to the Danes in 991, and in 994 they had to produce the still larger sum of £16,000 in order to purchase peace. Olaf then promised never again to visit England, except in peace. Subsequently Ethelred brought disaster upon himself and his country by his treachery. In 1002 he issued secret orders for a massacre of all the Danes found in England, and in this massacre Gunhild, sister of Sweyn, was among the victims. In consequence of Ethelred's conduct the Danes returned in force to these shores and had to be bought off with a sum of £36,000. They came again and made many unsuccessful assaults upon London, upon which the Chronicler remarks: 'They often fought against the town of London, but to God be praise that it yet stands sound, and they have ever fared ill.'

In 1010 Ethelred took shelter in London, and in 1013 Sweyn again attacked the city without success, but having conquered a great part of England the Londoners submitted to him, and Ethelred fled to Normandy. After Sweyn's death, in 1014, Ethelred was invited to return to England, as the country was not willing to receive Sweyn's son Cnut as its King. When Ethelred returned to England he was accompanied by another Olaf (Anlaf Haroldson) who succeeded by a clever manœuvre in destroying the wooden London Bridge, and taking the city out of the hands of the Danes. The story is told in Snorro Sturleson's *Heimskringla* (The Story of Olaf the Holy, the son of Harold): 'Olaf covered the decks of his ship with a roof of wood and wicker work to protect them from the stones and shot which were ready to be cast at them by the Danes. King Olaf and the host of the North-men rowed right up under the bridge, and lashed cables round the poles that upheld the bridge, and then they fell to their oars and rowed all the ships down stream as hard as they might. The poles dragged along the ground, even until they were loosened under the bridge. But inasmuch as an host under weapons stood thickly arrayed on the bridge, there were on it both many stones and many war-weapons, and the poles having broken from it, the bridge broke down by reason thereof, and many of the folk fell into the river, but all the rest thereof fled from the bridge, some into the city, some into Southwark. And after this they made an onset on Southwark and won it. And when the towns-folk saw that the River Thames was won, so that they might not hinder the ships from faring up into the land, they were afeard, and gave up the town and took King Ethelred in.'[10]

The later life of Olaf was one of adventure. He was driven by Cnut from his kingdom of Norway, and took shelter in Sweden. Here he obtained help, and in the end regained his throne. At the Battle of Sticklestead he was defeated and slain (1030). His body was hastily buried, but was afterwards taken up, and, being found incorrupt, was buried in great state in a shrine at Drontheim. He was canonized, and several English churches are dedicated to him. There are four parishes bearing the name of St. Olave in London, one of the churches is in Tooley Street which also preserves the name of St. Olave in a curiously corrupted form.

After this Ethelred succeeded in driving Cnut out of England back to Denmark. Of this success Freeman enthusiastically wrote: 'That true-hearted city was once more the bulwark of England, the centre of every patriotic hope, the special object of every hostile attack.'[11]

There was, however, little breathing space, for Cnut returned to England in 1015, and Ethelred's brilliant son, Edmund Ironside, prepared to meet him. Edmund's army refused to fight unless Ethelred came with them, and unless they had 'the support of the citizens of London.' Before, however, Cnut arrived Ethelred died, England was in the hand of the Dane, and London only remained free. Edmund was elected King by the Witan, united with the inhabitants of the city, and thus the Londoners first asserted the position which they held to for many centuries—of their right to a voice in the election of the King.

Cnut was determined now to succeed, and he at once sailed up the Thames. He was, however, unable to pass the bridge, which had been rebuilt. He therefore dug a trench on the south side of the river, by which means he was enabled to draw some of his ships above the bridge. He also cut another trench entirely round the wall of the city. In spite of his clever scheme, the determined resistance of our stubborn forefathers caused it to fail.[12]

Edmund Ironside was successful in his battles with Cnut till his brother-in-law, Eadric, Alderman of Mercia, turned traitor, and helped the Danish King to vanquish the English army at Assandun (now Assenton in

Kent). Edmund was now forced to agree to Cnut's terms, and it was therefore settled that Edmund should retain his crown, and take all England south of the Thames, together with East Anglia, Essex and London, Cnut taking the rest of the kingdom. On the 30th November 1016 Edmund died, and Cnut became King of the whole of England. His reign was prosperous, and he succeeded in gaining the esteem of his subjects, who appreciated the long-continued peace which he brought them. Dr. Stubbs describes him as one of the 'conscious creators of England's greatness.' He died in November 1035 at the early age of forty.

We may now pass over some troubled times, caused by the worthless successors of Cnut, and come to the period when the West Saxon line was restored in the person of Edward the Confessor, who, being educated at the Norman Court, became more a Norman than an Englishman, and prepared the way for the Conqueror's success. The Confessor was but an indifferent King, although he holds a more distinguished place in history than many a more heroic figure as the practical founder of Westminster Abbey, where his shrine is still one of its most sacred treasures. When Edward died, the Witan which had attended his funeral elected to succeed him, Harold, the foremost man in England, and the leader who had attempted to check the spread of the far too wide Norman influence.

After conquering his outlawed brother, Tostig, and Harold Hardrada, King of Norway, at Stamford Bridge, he had to hurry back to meet William Duke of Normandy, which he did on a hill on the Sussex Downs, afterwards called Senlac. He closed his life on the field of battle, after a reign of forty weeks and one day. Then the Conqueror had the country at his mercy, but he recognised the importance of London's position, and moved forward with the greatest caution and tact.

The citizens of London were possibly a divided body, and William, knowing that he had many friends in the city, felt that a waiting game was the best for his cause in the end. His enemies, led by Ansgar the Staller, under whom as sheriff the citizens of London had marched to fight for Harold at Senlac, managed to get their way at first. They elected Edgar Atheling, the grandson of Edmund Ironside, as King, but this action was of little avail.

When William arrived at Southwark the citizens sallied forth to meet him, but they were beaten back, and had to save themselves within the city walls. William retired to Berkhamsted,[13] and is said to have sent a private message to Ansgar asking for his support.[14] In the end the citizens, probably led by William the Bishop, who was a Norman, came over to the Conqueror's side, and the best men repaired to Berkhamsted. Here they accepted the sovereignty of William, who received their oath of fealty.

Thus ends the Saxon period of our history, and the Norman period in London commences with the Conqueror's charter to William the Bishop and Gosfrith the Portreeve, supposed to be the elder Geoffrey de Mandeville.

In the foregoing pages the main incidents of the history of Saxon London are recited. These are, I fear, rather disconnected and uninteresting, but it is necessary to set down the facts in chronological order, because from them we can draw certain conclusions as to the condition of London before the Norman Conquest. Unfortunately our authorities for the Saxon period do not tell us much that we want to know, and, in consequence, many of the suggestions made by one authority are disputed by another. Still we can draw certain very definite conclusions, which cannot well be the subjects of contention.

The first fact is the constant onward march of London towards the fulfilment of its great destiny. Trouble surrounded it on all sides, but, in spite of them all, the citizens gained strength in adversity, so that at the Conquest the city was in possession of those special privileges which were cherished for centuries, never given up, but increased when opportunity occurred. Patient waiting was therefore rewarded by success, and London by the endeavours of her men grew in importance and stood before all other cities in her unique position.

The Governor who possessed the confidence of Londoners, although all the rest of the country was against him, needed not to despair, while he who had the support of the rest of the country, but was opposed by London, could not be considered as triumphant.

The so-called Heptarchy was constantly changing the relative positions of its several parts, until Egbert, the King of Wessex, became 'Rex totius Britanniæ' (A.D. 827). The seven kingdoms were at some hypothetical period

1. Kent,
2. Sussex,   ⎯South of the Thames.
3. Wessex,

4. Essex,
5. East Anglia,   ⎯North of the Thames.
6. Mercia,

7. Northumbria |—North of the Humber,
  (including Deira   and as far north as the
  and Bernicia),   Forth.

    The walled city of London was a distinct political unit, although it owed a certain allegiance to one of the kingdoms, which was the most powerful for the time being. This allegiance therefore frequently changed, and London retained its identity and individuality all through.

    Essex seems seldom to have held an independent position, for when London first appears as connected with the East Saxons the real power was in the hands of the King of Kent. According to Bede, Wini, being expelled from his bishopric of Wessex in 635, took refuge with Wulfhere, King of the Mercians, of whom he purchased the See of London. Hence the Mercian King must then have been the overlord of London. Not many years afterwards the King of Kent again seems to have held some jurisdiction here. From the laws of the Kentish Kings, Lhothhere and Eadric, 673-685, we learn that the Wic-reeve was an officer of the King of Kent, who exercised a jurisdiction over the Kentish men trading with or at London, or who was appointed to watch over their interests.[15]

    There is a very interesting question connected with the position of the two counties in which London is situated. It is necessary to remember that London is older than these counties, whose names, viz., Middlesex and Surrey, indicate their relative position to the city and the surrounding country. We have neither record of their settlement nor of the origin of their names. Both must have been peopled from the river. The name Middle Saxons clearly proves that Middlesex must have been settled after the East and West Saxons had given their names to their respective districts.

    There has been much discussion as to the etymology of Surrey, more particularly of the second syllable. A once favourite explanation was that Surrey stood for South Kingdom (A.S. *rice*), but there is no evidence that Surrey ever was a kingdom, and this etymology must surely be put aside.

    In Elton's *Origins of English History* there is the following note, p. 387: 'Three Underkings concur in a grant by the King of Surrey.—Cod. Diplom. 987.' This is a serious misstatement, for the document cited says: 'Ego Frithuualdus prouinciae Surrianorum subregulus regis Wlfarii Mercianorum ... dono concedo,' etc.

Frithwald is here described as 'subregulus' (under-king), subject to the King of the Mercians; and in the attestation clause it is added: 'Et isti sunt subreguli qui omnes sub signo suo subscripserunt.' Their names are Fritheuuold, Osric, Wigherd and Ætheluuold. Each is described as 'testis' merely. This does not seem to imply concurrence; but, even if it does, the title 'subregulus' does not mean an independent sovereign. In the description of the boundaries of the granted land, which is in Anglo-Saxon, the grantor is certainly described as 'Fritheuuold King,' but this cannot mean king in the full sense, and the Anglo-Saxon clause in the charter could not have been intended to contradict the Latin, which designates Frithwald as 'subregulus' throughout.

Dr. Stubbs (*Constitutional History*, vol. i. p. 189), after describing the gradual disappearance of the smaller sovereignties, and pointing out that 'the heptarchic King was as much stronger than the tribal King as the King of United England was stronger than the heptarchic King,' wrote: 'In Wessex, besides the Kings of Sussex, which has a claim to be numbered among the seven great States, were Kings of Surrey also.' The note to this, however, only refers to Frithewold, 'subregulus or ealdorman of Surrey,' and no mention is made of any ruler who was capable of making Surrey into a kingdom.

The form of the name used by Bede, 'in regione Sudergeona' (*Hist. Eccles.*, iv. 6), may suggest a derivation quite different from any yet suggested.

Surrey was originally an integral part of Kent, and when it was severed from that county it became apparently an independent district, a sort of republic under its own alderman. In later times it became subject to the neighbouring kingdoms. At the date of this charter it was under Mercia. It was never reckoned as a separate member of the heptarchy.

London fought an uphill fight with Winchester for the position of chief city of Southern England. Under Egbert London grew in importance, but Winchester, the chief town of Wessex, was still the more important place politically. In the trade regulations enacted by Edgar in the tenth century London took precedence of Winchester: 'Let one measure and one weight pass such as is observed at London and at Winchester.' In the reign of Edward the Confessor London had become the recognised capital of England.

Some dispute has arisen respecting the position of the lithsmen, who appear at the election in Oxford of Cnut's successor, and subsequently. Freeman (*Norman Conquest*, vol. i. p. 538) describes them as 'seafaring' men of London, while Gross (*The Gild Merchant*, vol. i. p. 186) writes: 'The lithsmen (shipowners) of London, who, with others, raised Harold to the throne, were doubtless such "burg-thegns." '

Another important point to be noted is the prominent political position of the bishop. As early as A.D. 900 'the bishop and the reeves who belong to London' are recorded as making in the name of the citizens laws which were confirmed by the King, because they had reference to the whole kingdom. Edward the Confessor greeted William Bishop, Harold Earl, and Esgar Staller. So that William the Conqueror followed precedent when he addressed his charter to Bishop and Portreeve.

Foreigners in early times occupied an important position in London, but there were serious complaints when Edward the Confessor enlarged the numbers of the Normans. The Englishman always had a hatred of the foreigner, and this dislike grew as time went on, and the English tried to obtain the first place and succeeded in the attempt.

Other points, such as government by folkmoots and gilds, which will be discussed in the following chapters, find their origin in the Saxon period. The government of London under the Saxons was of a simple character, approximating to that of the shire, and so it continued until some years after the Conquest. When the Commune was extorted from the Crown a fuller system of government was inaugurated, which will be discussed in a later chapter.

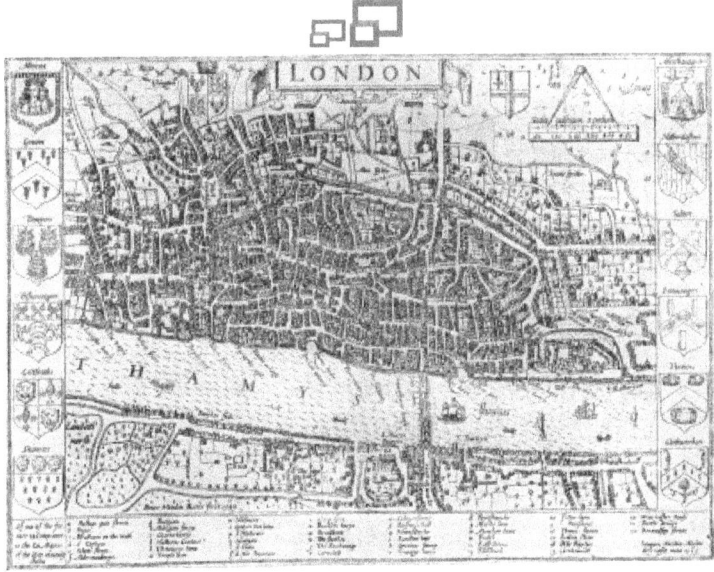

CHAPTER II

The Walled Town and its Streets

IN the mediæval city the proper protection of the municipality and the citizens largely depended upon the condition of the walls and gates. The government of town life was specially congenial to the Norman, and the laws he made for the purpose were stringent; while the Saxon, who never appreciated town life, preferred the county organisation. Thus it will be found that, as the laws of the latter were too lax, those of the former were too rigorous.

Riley, referring to the superfluity of Norman laws, describes them as 'laws which, while unfortunately they created or protected few real valuable rights, gave birth to many and grievous wrongs.' He proceeds to amplify this opinion, and gives good reason for the condemnation he felt bound to pronounce: 'That the favoured and so-called *free* citizen of London, even—despite the extensive privileges in reference to trade which he enjoyed—was in possession of more than the faintest shadow of liberty, can hardly be allowed, if we only call to mind the substance of the ... enactments and ordinances, arbitrary, illiberal and oppressive: laws, for example, which compelled each citizen, whether he would or no, to be bail and surety for a neighbour's good behaviour, over whom it was perhaps impossible for him to exercise the slightest control; laws which forbade him to make his market for the day until the purveyors for the King, and the "great lords of the land," had stripped the stalls of all that was choicest and best; laws which forbade him to pass the city walls for the purpose of meeting his own purchased goods; laws which bound him to deal with certain persons and communities only, or within the precincts only of certain localities; laws which dictated, under severe penalties, what sums and no more he was to pay to his servants and artisans; laws which drove his dog out of the streets, while they permitted "genteel dogs" to roam at large: nay, even more than this, laws which subjected him to domiciliary visits from the city officials on various pleas and pretexts; which compelled him to carry on a trade under heavy penalties, irrespective of the question whether or not it was at his loss; and which occasionally went so far as to lay down rules at what hours he was to walk in the streets, and incidentally, what he was to eat and what to drink.'[16]

We see from this quotation that the position of the inhabitant of a walled town was not a happy one. Still he was more favoured than his neighbour who lived in the country. A few examples will show us what the city life was, and these specific instances are necessary, for so many centuries have passed since Englishmen lived in a walled town that without them it is barely possible for us to conceive what this life of suspicion and fear of danger was really like.

The one thing which we do see distinctly is the gradual emancipation of the Englishman from the wearing thraldom of his position. He went on gradually in his course, always bearing towards the light, and he gained freedom long before the citizens of other countries. In the fifteenth century we find that galling laws here in England were allowed to fall into desuetude in favour of freedom, while the same rules were retained in foreign countries. Some of our countrymen objected to this, and English merchants were irritated to find that while the regulation enjoining every alien merchant during his residence in London to abide in the house of a citizen assigned to him as a host by the magistrates had fallen into abeyance, the restriction was rigidly enforced abroad. The writer of the remarkable *Libelle of Englyshe Polycye* (1437) alludes to this feeling:—

'What reason is't that we should go to host in these countries and in this English coast they should not so, but have more liberty than we ourselves?'[17]

The citizens had to put up with constant surveillance. The gates were closed early in the evening, and at curfew all lights, as well as fires, had to be put out. Night-walkers, male and female, and roysterers generally had a bad time of it, but probably they were very ill-behaved, and in many cases they doubtless deserved the punishment they received. In the year 1100 Henry I. relaxed these stringent regulations, and restored to his subjects the use of lights at night. The streets were first lighted by lanterns in 1415.

London within the walls was a considerable city in the Middle Ages, although it only contained the same area that was walled in during the later Roman period. The relics of this wall, continually renewed with the old materials, are so few, and the old area is so completely lost sight of in the larger London, that it is necessary to point out the line of the walls before dealing further with the habits of the Londoners. It was long supposed that the Ludgate was the chief entrance to the city from the west, but, in spite of its name, there can be little doubt that for some centuries the great western approach was made through Newgate. We will therefore commence our walk round the walls with that gate.

Although there can be no doubt that here was a gate in the Roman period, we have little or no record of its early history. One of its earlier names was Chamberlain's Gate. The 'new' gate was erected in the reign of Henry I., and in a Pipe Roll of 1188 it is mentioned as a prison. In 1414 the prison was in such a loathsome condition that the keeper and sixty-four of the prisoners died of the prison plague. In consequence of this it was decided to rebuild the gate. Richard Whittington was the moving spirit in this rebuilding, and it is supposed that he paid the expenses. In the course of excavations made in 1874-1875 for the improvement of the western end of Newgate Street, the massive foundations of Whittington's gate were discovered several feet below the present roadway.

The wall passed north through the precincts of Christ Church (Christ's Hospital), formerly occupied by the Grey Friars (or Franciscans). The town ditch, which was outside the walls, and arched over about the year 1553, ran through the Hospital grounds. The wall then turned round to the north of Newgate Street, and passed into St. Martin's-le-Grand, where, in 1889, the foundations of several houses on the west side were exposed while the excavations for the latest addition to the General Post-Office were being proceeded with.

The great bell of the Collegiate Church of St. Martin's tolled the curfew hour when all the gates of the city were to be shut. The great gates were shut at the first stroke of the bell at St. Martin's and the wickets opened; at the last stroke the wickets were to be closed, and not to be opened afterward that night unless by special precept of the Mayor. The ringing of the curfew of St. Martin's was to be the signal for the ringing 'at every parish church, so that they begin together and end together.'[18] In an Ordinance (37 Edward III., 1363) the bell at the Church of our Lady at Bow was substituted for that at St. Martin's.

Outside the walls were Smithfield, where the tournaments were held, and Giltspur Street, where the knights bought their spears, and armour might be repaired when tournaments were going on.

Within the gate were the Grey Friars, Stinking Lane (now King Edward Street), and the Butchers' Shambles in Newgate Street.

St. Paul's had its enclosed churchyard, so that the main thoroughfare for centuries passed round it from Newgate Street to Cheapside. The name of Cheap tells of the general market held there, and the names of several of the streets out of Cheapside tell of the particular merchandise appropriated to them, as Friday Street (Friday's market for fish), Milk Street and Bread Street. At the west end of Cheapside was the Church of St. Michael le Querne (or at the Corn), which marked the site of the Corn Market. It was destroyed in the Great Fire. At the east end of this church stood the Old Cross, which was taken down in the year 1390, and replaced by the Little Conduit, which is described as standing by Paul's gate. There is an engraving of this church and the conduit, with the water-pots of the water-carriers dotted about.

The wall passed north along the side of St. Martin's-le-Grand till it came to Aldersgate, close by the Church of St. Botolph. The exact spot is marked by No. 62 on the east side of the street. Stow's etymologies of London names are seldom very satisfactory, but he never blundered worse than when he explained Aldgate as old gate and Aldersgate as the older gate; but his explanation has been followed by many successive writers, who do not seem to have seen the impossibility of the suggestion. One of the earliest forms of the name is Aldredesgate, showing pretty conclusively that it was a proper name.

The wall proceeds east to Cripplegate, with an outpost—the Watch-Tower or Barbican. The Rev. W. Denton has explained the name of Cripplegate as due to the covered way between the postern and the Barbican or Burgh-kenning (A.S., *crepel*, *cryfle* or *crypele*, a burrow or passage under ground). The name occurs also in the Domesday of Wiltshire, where we read: 'To Wansdyke, thence forth by the dyke to Crypelgeat.'[19] If this etymology be accepted, we have here the use of the word gate as a way. In the north this distinction is kept up, and the road is the gate, while what we in the south call the gate is the bar. For instance, at York, Micklegate is the road, and the entrance to the wall is Micklegate bar.

It may be noted that St. Giles was the patron saint of Cripples, but the first church was not built until about 1090 by Alfune, the first Hospitaller of St. Bartholomew's, so that the dedication may have been owing to a mistaken etymology at that early date. In the churchyard is an interesting piece of the old wall still in position. The course of the wall to the east is marked by the street named London Wall, from Cripplegate to Bishopsgate Street. Here it bore south to Camomile and Wormwood Streets, where stood till 1731 the gate.

The distance between Cripplegate and Bishopsgate is not great, and much of the space outside the walls was occupied by Moorditch. Still, in 1415, Thomas Falconer, then Mayor, opened a postern in the wall, where Moorgate Street now is, for the benefit of the hay and wood carts coming to the markets of London. He must also have made a road across the morass of Moorfields, for that place was not drained until more than a century afterwards. The site of Bishopsgate is marked by two tablets on the houses at the corners of Camomile and Wormwood Streets respectively (Nos. 1 and 64 Bishopsgate Street Without), inscribed with a mitre, and these words, 'Adjoining to this spot Bishopsgate formerly stood.'[20]

Bishopsgate was named after Erkenwald, Bishop of London (d. 685), son of Offa, King of Mercia, by whom it was erected. At first the maintenance of the gate was considered to devolve upon the Bishop of London, but after an arrangement with the Hanse Merchants it was ruled that the bishop 'is bound to make the hinges of Bysoppsgate; seeing that from every cart laden with wood he has one stick as it enters the said gate.' The liability was limited to the hinges, for after some dispute it was (1305) 'awarded and agreed that Almaines belonging to the House of the Merchants of Almaine shall be free from paying two shillings on going in or out of the gate of Bishopesgate with their goods, seeing that they are charged with the safe keeping and repair of the gate.' The line of the wall bears southward to Aldgate, and is marked by the street named Houndsditch.

The earliest form of the name Aldgate appears to have been Alegate or Algate, and, therefore, has nothing to do with Old, the *d* being intrusive. Within the walls was the great house of Christ Church, founded by Queen Maud or Matilda, wife to Henry I., in the year 1108, and afterwards known as the Priory of the Holy Trinity within Aldgate. In 1115 the famous Cnichtengild, possessors of the ward of Portsoken (which was the soke without the port or gate called Aldgate), presented to the priory all their rights, offering upon the altars of the church the several charters of the guild. The King confirmed the gift, and the prior became *ex officio* an alderman of London. This continued to the dissolution of the religious houses, when the inhabitants of the ward obtained the privilege of electing their own alderman. Stow tells us that he remembered the prior riding forth with the Mayor as one of the aldermen. 'These priors have sitten and ridden amongst the aldermen of London, in livery like unto them, saving that his habit was in shape of a spiritual person, as I myself have seen in my childhood.'

The old name of Christ Church is retained in St. Katherine Cree or Christ Church, on the north side of Leadenhall Street, which was built in the cemetery of the dissolved priory. This church was taken down in 1628, and the present building erected in 1630.

The wall led south by the line of the street now called the Minories to the Tower, thus dividing Great Tower Hill, which was within the wall, from Little Tower Hill, which was outside. The Abbey of Nuns of the Order of St. Clare, which was situated outside the city walls, gave its name of Minoresses to the street. When William the Conqueror built the Tower he encroached upon the city ground, a proceeding which was not popular with his subjects. Near Tower Hill, that is out of George Street,

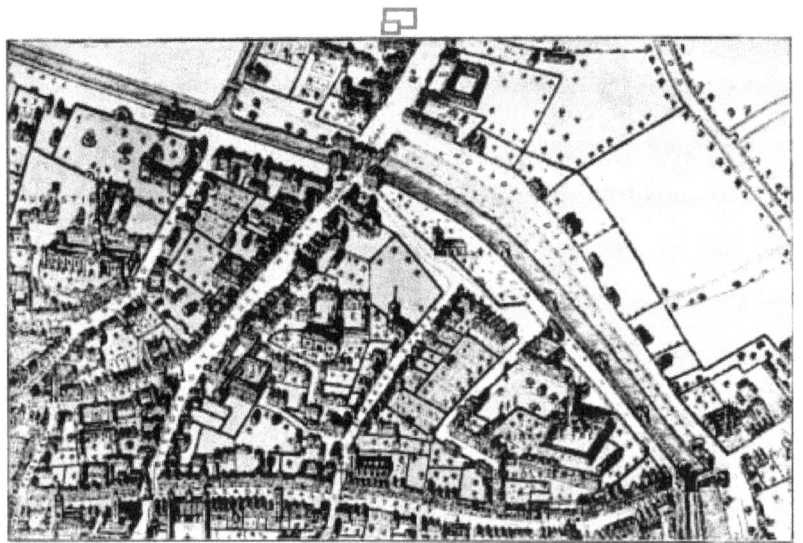

ALDGATE AND PRIORY OF THE HOLY TRINITY.
(From Newton's Map of London.)

Trinity Square, there is a fine fragment of the old London wall.

We must now turn westward and follow the course of the river from the Custom House to the Blackfriars, as this forms the southern boundary of the city.

A little to the west of the Tower gate was Galley Quay, where, according to Stow, 'the gallies of Italie and other parts were used to unlade and land their merchandises and wares.' These strangers, inhabitants of Genoa and other parts, lodged, says Stow, in Galley Row, near Mincing Lane. They 'were commonly called galley-men, as men that came up in the galleys, brought up wines and other merchandises, which they landed in Thames Street, at a place called Galley Key; they had a certain coin of silver amongst themselves which were halfpence of Genoa, and were called galley halfpence; these halfpence were forbidden in the 13th of Henry IV., and again by Parliament in the 4th of Henry V.... Notwithstanding in my youth I have seen them pass current, but with some difficulty, for that the English halfpence were then, though not so broad, somewhat thicker and stronger.' Next Galley Quay was Bear Quay, appropriated chiefly to the landing and shipment of corn.

The first Custom House of which we have any account was built by John Churchman, Sheriff of London in 1385, and stood on 'Customer's Key,' to the east of the present building, and therefore much nearer Tower Wharf. Another and a larger building was erected in the reign of Elizabeth, and burnt in the Great Fire of 1666. Wren designed the third building, which was completed in 1671 and destroyed by fire in 1718. Ripley's building, which succeeded this, was destroyed in the same way in 1814. The present is therefore the fifth building devoted to the customs of the country.

Billingsgate must be of great antiquity, but it has not always held its present undisputed position. In early times Queenhithe and Billingsgate were the chief city wharfs for the mooring of fishing vessels and landing their cargoes. The fish were sold in and about Thames Street, special stations being assigned to the several kinds of fish. Queenhithe was at first the more important wharf, but Billingsgate appears to have gradually overtaken it, and eventually to have left it quite in the rear, the troublesome passage of London Bridge leading the shipmasters to prefer the below-bridge wharf. Corn, malt and salt, as well as fish, were landed and sold at both wharfs, and very strict regulations were laid down by the city authorities as to the tolls to be levied on the several articles, and the conditions under which they were to be sold.[21]

In 1282 a message was sent from Edward I to the Serjeants of Billingsgate and Queenhithe commanding them 'to see that all boats are moored on the city side at night'; and in 1297 the order was repeated, but it was now directed to the warden of the dock at Billingsgate, and the warden of Queenhithe, who were 'to see that this order is strictly observed.'

Opposite to Billingsgate, on the north side of Lower Thames Street, the foundations of a Roman villa were discovered in 1847 when the present Coal Exchange was built. A spring of clear water which supplied the Roman baths was found running through the ruins at the time of the excavations. This was the spring which supplied the boss, fountain or jet by the corner of an opening, of old called Boss Alley, where a reservoir was erected by Sir Richard Whittington, or his executors, expressly for the use of the inhabitants and market people.

We now come to London Bridge, the great southern approach to London, and the most important strategical position, as when that was fortified the inhabitants were safe from attack on the south. Passing westward from the bridge we come to the Old Swan Stairs, the Steelyard, Coldharbour, Dowgate and the Vintry, and then we come to Queenhithe, said to have been named after Eleanor, widow of Henry II., to whom it belonged. It was previously known as Edred's hithe. Passing Paul's Wharf, we come to the vast building known as Baynard's Castle, built by Humphry, Duke of Gloucester, in 1428. This mansion had an eventful history until it was destroyed in the Great Fire. A previous Baynard's Castle was situated on the Thames nearer the Fleet River, and was named after Ralph Baynard, one of the Norman knights of William the Conqueror. It afterwards came into the possession of Robert Fitzwalter, chief bannerer or castellan of the city of London. When the Dominicans or Black Friars removed from Holborn to Ludgate they swallowed up in their precincts the Tower of Mountfichet and Castle Baynard, which were the strongholds built at the west end of the city. Edward I. allowed the friars to pull down the city wall and take in all the land to the west as far as the River Fleet. Moreover, the King intimated to the Mayor and citizens his desire that the new wall should be built at the cost of the city. We here pass up to Ludgate, which does not appear to have been a gate of much importance until the beginning of the thirteenth century. The idea that it is named after a mythical King Lud is, of course, exploded now, and there are at present two etymologies to choose from. Dr. Edwin Freshfield supposes the name to be derived from the word lode, a cut or drain into a large stream. The main stream of the Fleet passes from the Thames to the foot of Ludgate Hill, but a short branch went in a north-eastward direction to Ludgate, joining there the town ditch. Mr. Loftie explains Ludgate as a postern, and supposes it to have existed in the Saxon period as a postern gate.

All along the river front of London originally there was a wall, remains of which have been found at various times. Fitz-Stephen, writing in the twelfth century, says: 'London formerly had walls and towers ... on the south, but that most excellent river the Thames, which abounds with fish, and in which the tide ebbs and flows, runs on that side, and has in a long space of time washed down, undermined and subverted the walls in that part.'[22]

Outside Ludgate the road to the west was not much frequented. Fleet Street and the Strand were not the important thoroughfares during the Middle Ages that Holborn was. The roads were much neglected, and no one traversed them who could travel by boat on the Thames, which was literally the Silent Highway of London.

When the gates of London were closed at eight o'clock at night, and the inhabitants were ruled with an iron hand, it was somewhat a sign of reproach to live outside the walls. This feeling continued for centuries, and the name of 'suburbs' was long held in little respect. In spite of this stigma, the main avenues leading to the several gates became inhabited, and in course of time were added to the city of London as liberties. The extent of these liberties was marked by bars—thus outside Ludgate was Temple bar, outside Newgate, Holborn bars, outside Aldersgate, Aldersgate bars, outside Bishopsgate, Bishopsgate bars, and outside Aldgate, Aldgate bars. After this arrangement the liberties were no longer suburbs, and the disreputable neighbourhood was therefore pushed farther out. The suburbs outside Cripplegate were unlike those of any of the other gates. There was no main road straight north, but a village with a church and a Fore Street grew up outside the walls.

There is a great deal of information respecting the protection of the walls and the city gates in the important series of 'Letter Books' preserved among the city archives and in Riley's *Memorials*. The authorities were allowed by the King to levy a tax called Murage from time to time on goods entering the city to enable them to keep the wall and gates in a state of efficiency. In 1276 Edward I. called upon the citizens to devote a portion of the dues to the rebuilding of the city wall by the house of the Blackfriars, and eight years after the grant of murage was renewed to the Mayor and citizens on condition that they built this wall, so that for some years the city gained no particular advantage from the King's license. The Hanse Merchants were freed from payment of murage on account of their engagement to keep Bishopsgate in order.

In 1310 a royal writ was issued for the punishment of those who injured the city walls, gates and posterns.[23] Two years before this date special orders were issued as to the guard of the gates. The Wards adjoining each gate had to supply a certain number of men-at-arms. Newgate was supplied with 26 men; Aldgate, Bishopsgate, Ludgate and Bridgegate with 24 each; Cripplegate and Aldersgate with 20 each.

The authorities were often very parsimonious, and we find in Riley this curious entry under the date of 1314: 'Removal of an elm near Bishopsgate and purchase of a cord for a ward hook with the proceeds of the sale thereof.'

Some of the gates were let as dwelling-houses, Chaucer's tenancy of Aldgate being a familiar instance; but this practice was found to be very inconvenient and objectionable, and in 1386 an enactment was issued forbidding the grant in future of the city gates or of the dwelling-houses there.[24]

There must have been accommodation at the gates (even when let as dwelling-houses) for the serjeants who performed the duty of opening and closing the gates. One of the orders that these serjeants had to carry into effect was to prevent the admission of lepers into the town. Money was collected at the gates for the repair of the roads, a charge which was in addition to murage. The serjeants had also to see that a fugitive bondman did not enter the city, because if one gained admittance and resided in a chartered town for a year and a day he obtained freedom and was entitled to the franchise. In small towns it was easier to keep out the fugitive, but in a large city like London he could often escape notice, although the authorities might be against him. In Letter Book A we read this notice: 'Pray that the said fugitives may not be admitted to the freedom of the city';

and Pollock and Maitland write: 'The townsmen were careful not to obliterate the distinction between bond and free, and did not admit one of servile birth to the citizenship.'[25] There can be little doubt that there was much laxity in keeping the gates at various times, and in cases where there was fear of invasion the King sent special orders to the Mayor to see to the protection of the city.

In spite of the singular freedom of England from invasion the English have constantly been overwhelmed with panic, fearing the worst which never came. In 1335 an alarm was raised of a French invasion. The King at the beginning of August wrote to order all men between sixteen and sixty to be arrayed, and a Council to be immediately held in London. Leaders of the Londoners were appointed who were to defend the city in case the enemy landed. Again in 1370 preparations were made for an expected attack upon the city, and in 1383 false reports were circulated from the war in Flanders, for the circulation of which an impostor was punished.[26] Three years later the citizens were in great terror on account of a widespread report that the French King was about to invade England. There seems to have been something in the report, because Harry Hotspur believed it, and having waited impatiently for the French King to besiege Calais, returned to England to meet him here. Stow, however, was very satirical about the English fears. He wrote: 'The Londoners, understanding that the French King had got together a great navie, assembled an armie, and set his purpose firmly to come into England, they trembling like leverets, fearefule as mise, seeke starting holes to hide themselves in, even as if the citie were now to bee taken, and they that in times past bragged they would blow all the Frenchmen out of England, hearing now a vaine rumour of the enemies comming, they runne to the walles, breake downe the houses adjoyning, destroy and lay them flat, and doe all things in great feare, not one Frenchman yet having set foote on shipboard, what would they have done, if the battell had been at hand, and the weapons over their head.'[27]

No improvement in the condition of houses in London appears to have taken place until long after the Conquest, and the low huts, closely packed together, which filled the streets during the Saxon period, were continued well into the thirteenth century. These houses were wholly built of wood, and thatched with straw, or reeds.

All mediæval cities were fatally liable to destruction by fire, but London appears to have been specially unfortunate in this respect. In the first year of the reign of Stephen a destructive fire spread from London Bridge to the Church of St. Clement Danes, destroying St. Paul's in the way. This fire caused some improvements in building, but special regulations were required, and one of the early works undertaken by the newly established 'Commune' was the drawing up, in 1189, of the famous Assize of Building, known by the name of the first Mayor as Fitz-Ailwyne's Assize.

In this document the following statement was made: 'Many citizens, to avoid such danger, built according to their means, on their ground, a stone house covered and protected by thick tiles against the fury of fire, whereby it often happened that when a fire arose in the city and burnt many edifices, and had reached such a house, not being able to injure it, it there became extinguished, so that many neighbours' houses were wholly saved from fire by that house.'[28]

Various privileges were conceded to those who built in stone, and these privileges are detailed in the Assize of 1189. No provision, however, was made as to the material to be used in roofing tenements. This Assize, which has been described as the earliest English Building Act, is of the greatest value to us from an historical point of view, and much attention is paid to it in Hudson Turner's *Domestic Architecture*, where a translation of the Assize is printed. Turner points out that it is evident from this specimen of early civic legislation that although citizens might, if it so pleased them, construct their houses entirely of stone, yet they were not absolutely required to do more than erect party walls 16 feet in height, the materials of the structure built on such walls being left entirely to individual choice, and there can be no doubt that in the generality of houses it was of wood. This assumption is justified by the fact that, in deeds of a much later period, houses constructed wholly of stone are frequently named as boundaries, without any further or more special description than that such was the substance of which they were built. Turner adds that it is obvious such a description would have been vague and insufficient in a district where houses were generally raised in stone, and he therefore supposes that the Assize of 1189 had no more direct effect than in regulating the method of constructing party walls, and then only in cases where individuals were willing to build in stone.[29]

There can be no doubt that the Assize had but little effect, for in 1212 a still more destructive fire occurred which destroyed part of London Bridge—then a wooden structure—and the Church of St. Mary Overy, Southwark. It raged for ten days, and it is calculated that 1000 persons—men, women and children—lost their lives in the fire.

This fire had a striking effect upon the authorities, for at once they set to work to enact a new ordinance which introduced certain compulsory regulations. This is known as Fitz-Ailwyne's Second Assize, 1212; and thus the first Mayor, about whom little else is known, is associated with two important Acts, one issued at the beginning and the other near the end of his long mayoralty. Thenceforth everyone who built a house was strictly charged not to cover it with reeds, rushes, stubble or straw, but only with tiles, shingle boards, or lead. In future, in order to stop a fire, houses could be pulled down in case of need with an alderman's hook and cord. For the speedy removal of burning houses each ward was to provide a strong iron hook, with a wooden handle, two chains and two strong cords, which were to be left in the charge of the bedel of the ward, who was also provided with a good horn, 'loudly sounding.' It was also ordered that occupiers of large houses should keep one or two ladders for their own house and for their neighbours in case of a sudden outbreak of fire. Also, they were to keep in summer a barrel or large earthen vessel full of water before the house, for the purpose of quenching fire, unless there was a reservoir of spring water in the curtilage or courtyard.[30]

Ancient lights are not provided for, and chimneys are not mentioned. They were not general in Italian cities in the fourteenth century, but in London they were comparatively common by the year 1300. In the *Rotuli Hundredorum*, date 1275, a chimney is mentioned as built against a house in St. Mary-at-Hill made of stone, a foot or more in breadth, and projecting into the street.

Most of the houses consisted of little more than a large shop and an upper room or solar. The latter was often merely a wooden loft. When an upper apartment was carried out in stone it was described in deeds as *solarium lapideum*. In the fourteenth century houses were built of two and three storeys, and in some cases each storey was a distinct freehold. This seems to have caused a large number of disputes. It is an interesting fact that at a certain period there was the possibility of London becoming a city of flats. One cannot but feel that it is strange that flats should be general abroad and in Scotland, while it is only lately that they have become at all popular in England. Some reason for this diversity of custom must exist if we could only find it out. Cellars were entered from the street; and possibly, in those cases where separate floors belonged to different tenants, the upper storeys were entered by stairs on the outside.

Sometimes a householder was allowed to encroach upon the road, and in Riley's *Memorials* we find patents of leave for building a *hautpas*, that is, a room or floor raised on pillars and extending into the street. Such a grant was made to Sir Robert Knolles and his wife Constance in the year 1381. Penthouses are frequently mentioned in the city ordinances, and they were to be at least 9 feet in height, so as to allow of people riding beneath. It was enacted, for the benefit of landlords, that penthouses once fastened by iron nails or wooden pegs to the timber framework of the house should be deemed not removable, but fixtures, part and parcel of the freehold.[31]

Shops were open to the weather, and the need of a better place of protection for certain property was felt, which caused the erection of selds—sheds or warehouses—which were let out in small compartments for the storing of cupboards or chests. These served in their day the purpose fulfilled in ours by Safe Deposit Companies.

Several of these selds are mentioned in the city books; thus there was the Tanner's Seld, in or near St. Lawrence Lane, and Winchester Seld, near the Woolmarket of Woolchurch, also another in Thames Street. In the Hustings Roll we hear of the 'Great Seld of Roysia de Coventre in the Mercery,' known as the Great or Broad Seld. In 1311 we find tenants surrendering to Roysia, wife of Henry de Coventre, space for the standing of a certain chest in the seld called 'La Broselde,' in the parish of St. Pancras, in the ward of Cheap.

Windows are mentioned in the Assize, but glass was only used by the most opulent. The windows of the citizens in the reign of Richard I. were mere apertures, open in the day, crossed, perhaps, by iron stanchions, and closed by wooden shutters at night. Glass is mentioned as one of the regular imports into this country in the reign of Henry III., and in the time of Edward III. glaziers (*verrers*) are mentioned as an established gild.[32]

The buildings were constantly improved as time passed, and there is reason to believe that London was much in advance of continental cities as to comfort and cleanliness, in spite of some unflattering pictures that have come down to us. We have reason to believe that the standard idea of Englishmen as to comfort and decency was always higher than that of his neighbours. This point, however, will be more fully considered in the seventh chapter on Sanitation.

It took some time to establish the principle that an Englishman's house is his castle, and some of our Kings tried hard to override the rights of the faithful citizens. Mr. Riley makes the following remarks on this point: 'In the times of our early Kings, when they moved from place to place, it devolved upon the Marshal of the King's household to find lodgings for the royal retinue and dependants, which was done by sending a billet and seizing arbitrarily the best houses and mansions of the locality, turning out the inhabitants and marking the houses so selected with chalk, which latter duty seems to have belonged to the Serjeant-Chamberlain of the King's household. The city of London, fortunately for the comfort and independence of its inhabitants, was exempted by numerous charters from having to endure this most abominable annoyance at such times as it pleased the King to become its near neighbour by taking up his residence in the Tower. Still, however, repeated attempts were made to infringe this rule within the precincts of the city.'

Henry III. instituted some specially tyrannical proceedings in the year 1266, which naturally gave great offence. The particulars are related in Stow's Chronicle: 'Henry III. came to Westminster, and there gave unto divers of his householde servants about the number of threescore householdes and houses within the city, so that the owners were compelled to agree and redeem their houses, or else to avoyde them. Then he made Custos of the city Sir Othon, Constable of the Tower, who chose Bayliffs to be accountable to him. After this the King tooke pledges of the best men's sons of the city, the which were put in the Tower of London, and there kept at the costs of their parents.'

To meet such violations of the liberties of the city an enactment was promulgated apparently in the reign of Edward I. to the effect 'that if any member of the royal household or any retainer of the nobility shall attempt to take possession of a house within the city, either by main force or by delivery [of the Marshal of the royal household]; and if in such attempt he shall be slain by the master of the house, then and in such case the master of the house shall find six of his kinsmen who shall make oath, and himself making oath as the seventh, that it was for this reason that he so slew the intruder, and thereupon he shall go acquitted.'

In spite of this, Edward II. tried to carry out a similar piece of tyranny, but he was thwarted by John de Caustone, one of the sheriffs, who proved himself a stalwart leader of the citizens. Alan de Lek, serjeant-harbourer (provider of lodgings), prosecuted John de Caustone, and said 'that whereas his lordship the King, with his household, on the Monday next after the Feast of the Translation of Saint Thomas the Martyr, in the nineteenth year of the said King then reigning, came to the Tower of London, there at his good pleasure to abide; and the said Alan, the same day and year, as in virtue of his office bound to do, did assign lodgings unto one Richard de Ayremynne, secretary to his said lordship the King, in the house of the aforesaid John de Caustone, situate at Billyngesgate, in the city of London, and for the better knowing of the livery so made, did set the usual mark of chalk over the doors of the house aforesaid, as the practice is; and did also place men and serjeants, with the horses and harness of the said Richard, within the livery so made as aforesaid.'

The sheriff knowing this to be an illegal exercise of royal privilege, boldly rubbed out the obnoxious marks and turned the King's men and serjeants out of his house. When he was brought to trial the Mayor and citizens appeared for him and pleaded the rights of the city. Caustone successfully defended himself before the Steward and Marshal of the King's household sitting in the Tower in judgment upon him, and he came off scot-free.[33]

When we consider the smallness of the houses in the early period of the Middle Ages and the insufficient accommodation for families we see that the greater part of the population must of very necessity have constantly filled the streets, and the Londoners appear, from accounts that have come down to us, to have been rather a turbulent body.

The watch and ward arranged for the protection of the city was efficient enough in quiet times, but when the inhabitants were troublesome it was quite insufficient. The regulations were strict, but the streets were crowded, as more than half of them were used as market-places, and every moment occasions for quarrelling arose, of which the young bloods were only too ready to avail themselves.

Punishments and fines were frequent. Cheats and fraudulent tradesmen were promptly punished, and those who had a sharp tongue soon found that the free use of it was dangerous. The authorities, who had the making of the laws, had no fancy for being maligned. Such entries as these are frequent in Riley's *Memorials*: Process against Roger Torold for abusing the Mayor, 1355; Punishment or imprisonment for reviling the Mayor, 1382; Pillory and whetstone for slandering the Mayor, 1385; Pillory for slandering an alderman, 1411; Punishment for insulting certain aldermen; Pillory for insulting the Recorder, 1390. The pillory was freely used for cheats, users of false dice, false chequer boards (1382), swindlers, forgers of title-deeds, bonds, papal bulls, etc., impostors pretending to be dumb, etc. False measures, false materials and unwholesome food were confiscated and publicly burnt. Dishonest tradesmen appear to have been very reckless, and punishment was constantly awarded for the sale of putrid fish, food and meat. Enhancers of the price of wheat were specially obnoxious to the citizens, and some of the cheats connected with bread-making were curious, such as inserting iron in a loaf to increase the weight (1387), and stealing dough by making holes in the baker's moulding-boards (1327). The seller of unsound wine was punished by being made to drink it (1364). Night-walkers (male and female) were very summarily treated, but they must have been mostly connected with the dangerous classes, for we read of notorious persons with swords and bucklers and frequenters of taverns after curfew, 'contrary to peace and statutes.' We may presume that quiet, inoffensive persons, who were known to be law-abiding citizens, were not necessarily hauled up for being in the streets after regulation hours. Mr. Riley, in his valuable Introduction to the *Liber Albus*, makes special reference to these night-walkers: 'It being found that the houses of women of ill-fame had become the constant resort of thieves and other desperate characters, it was ordered by royal proclamation, *temp.* Edward I., that no such women should thenceforth reside within the walls of the city under pain of forty days' imprisonment. A list, too, was to be taken of all such women by the authorities, and a certain walk assigned to them. The Stews of Southwark are once, and only once, alluded to in this volume, and the result of this enactment was no doubt to drive the unfortunates thither.' Ordinances of later date appear to have been still more stringent. The Tun, a round-house or prison on Cornhill, was so called from its having been 'built somewhat in fashion of a tun standing on the one end.' It was built in 1282 for the special reception of night-walkers.

In spite of stringent regulations the streets were seldom free from rioting of some kind, and the watch were kept fully employed. There is a record of inquests or trials by juries (the jury consisting of no less than four representatives from each of the wards), held in 1281 upon a number of offenders 'against the King's peace and the statutes of the city.' The offences for the most part comprise night-walking after curfew, robbery with violence, frequenting taverns and houses of ill-fame, and gambling.[34]

In 1304 there was an Inquisition as to persons rioting and committing assaults by night,[35] and in 1311 a similar Inquisition and Delivery made in the time of Sir Ricker de Repham, Mayor, as to misdoers and night-walkers.[36]

Women of bad repute were restricted to a certain garb.[37] It was enacted by royal proclamation of Edward I. that none of them should wear minever (spotted ermine) or cendale (a particular kind of thin silk), on her hood or dress, and if she broke the law in this respect the city serjeant was allowed to seize the minever or cendale and retain it as his perquisite. At later periods it was enacted 'that no common woman shall wear a vesture of peltry or wool,' and again, that she shall not wear 'a hood that is furred, except with lambs' wool or rabbit skin.' From the Letter Books we learn that, in the middle of the fourteenth century, most of these women were Flemings by birth.[38]

The prisons mentioned in the *Liber Albus* are Newgate and Ludgate, the Tun and the Compters. They could none of them have been pleasant places, but it is probable that they were not so intolerable as they afterwards became. It is impossible that they could have been in a worse condition than the grossly mismanaged prisons of the eighteenth century.

It is not easy to understand what was the level of morality in the mediæval cities and towns. In truth, we can only draw inferences from the facts, and as most of the documents that have come down to us relate to those who have broken the laws, we are too apt to take a low view of the morality of the mass. Laws are not made for the law-abiding, except for their protection, and we have reason to know that this class is by far the most numerous.

Comfort, as we understand it, could not have existed in the Middle Ages, but the life seems to have been fairly agreeable to those who lived it, and it is only fair to give credence to such witnesses as Fitz-Stephen, who knew 'the noble city of London' well, and could only write of it in terms of hearty praise. He commences with these words, and then proceeds to substantiate the several points mentioned: 'Amongst the noble and celebrated cities of the world, that of London, the capital of the kingdom of England, is one of the most renowned, possessing, above all others, abundant wealth, extensive commerce, great grandeur and magnificence. It is happy in the salubrity of its climate, in the profession of the Christian religion, in the strength of its fortresses, the nature of its situation, the honour of its citizens, and the chastity of its matrons; in its sports, too, it is most pleasant, and in the production of illustrious men most fortunate.'

The people must have been closely packed in some parts of London, but gardens and open spaces within the walls were not uncommon. The statistics of the Middle Ages are not to be relied upon, as they largely consisted of the wildest guesses. Kings and Parliaments were continually deceived as to the produce of a tax, owing to the impossibility of knowing the number of the people upon whom it was to be levied.

During the latter part of the Saxon period the numbers of the population of the country began to decay; this decay, however, was arrested by the Norman Conquest. The population increased during ten peaceful years of Henry III., and increased slowly until the death of Edward II., and then it began to fall off, and it continued to decrease during the period of the Wars of the Roses until the accession of the Tudors.

A calculation has been made of the population of England and Wales in the last years of the reign of Edward III. (1372), which fixed the number at two and a half millions. Macpherson adopted this as a correct guess, but it probably errs more on the side of excess than of deficiency. Of this population it has been estimated that those employed in agriculture were in proportion to townspeople as eleven to one, but, according to another estimate, it was as fifteen to one.

It is not easy to arrive at a satisfactory calculation of the approximate population of London at different periods. At the end of the twelfth century Peter of Blois, Archdeacon of London, in a letter to Pope Innocent III., calculates the population at 40,000, and this is a quite probable calculation, although Francis Drake maintains that London was less populous than York about the time of the Conquest. York, however, could not then have had anything like 10,000 inhabitants. Fitz-Stephen greatly exaggerated the population of London. He wrote: 'The city is ennobled by her men, graced by her arms, and peopled by a multitude of inhabitants, so that in the wars under King Stephen there went out to a muster of armed horsemen, esteemed fit for war, twenty thousand, and of infantry sixty thousand.' Hallam agrees generally with Peter of Blois' calculation, for he supposes London to have had a population in John's reign of at least 30,000 or 40,000.

In 1377 the population, reckoned by the poll tax, was 44,770; the number taxed (consisting of males and females above fourteen years of age) being 23,314. We see from these numbers how greatly the population of London was in excess of the other great towns. From the same source we find the population of the towns next in size were:—

York,   7248

Bristol,   6345

Plymouth,   4837

Coventry,   4817

Norwich,   3952

Londoners were fortunate in not having suffered from any severe attack upon their fortifications, and therefore we are unable to tell how London would have stood a prolonged siege. We know, however, that at some periods it was very insecure. The most portentous event in England during the Middle Ages in respect to the changed conditions of life caused by it was the Peasants' Rising of 1381, the turning-point of which is entirely connected with the history of London. For four days the very existence of the city was in the direst peril. It is styled a rising, but it was really a revolution, and it is only lately that the full history of the movement has been presented to us in Mr. G. M. Trevelyan's valuable book, *England in the Age of Wycliffe* (1899).

There are two particular incidents in the history of mediæval London which are of the first importance as illustrations of the life of the inhabitants of a walled city. They stand alone, for no other internal occurrences fraught with such possible evil consequences are to be found in our history; and it is well to compare their likenesses and distinguish their unlikenesses. For this purpose it is not necessary to enter at all fully into the respective causes and effects of Wat Tyler's and Jack Cade's Rebellions.

The consideration of these points belongs to the history of the country, but a fairly full account of the proceedings of the few days in which the city was given over to the lawless violence of the followers of Wat Tyler and Jack Cade respectively seems to be necessary here.

In both insurrections the mob had their own way entirely at the beginning of the outbreaks. The insurgents were allowed to enter the city through the sympathy of many of the citizens, and in both cases the insurgents were worsted in the end, one hardly knows how, except we explain the cause as due to the inherent weakness of an undisciplined mob. Both insurrections occurred owing to widespread discontent. In the case of Wat Tyler's, from social ills of the most serious character; while in that of Jack Cade's the evils complained of were purely political. Again the movement in the earlier rebellion came from below, while in the later one the prime movers were the squires.

In Wat Tyler's Rebellion the King and Court were present at all the great events, but in Jack Cade's the King marched off to Kenilworth and left the city to take care of itself. Other likenesses and unlikenesses will be evident in the notices of the respective insurrections.

In order to understand the doings in London from Wednesday, June 12th, to Saturday the 15th inst., 1381, it is necessary to take some measure of the movement as a whole. Most of the chroniclers naturally write in strongly condemnatory terms of Wat Tyler's Rebellion, but Stow in his Chronicle attempts to be just, although he describes John Ball as 'a wicked priest.' He had the advantage of consulting a manuscript account of the Rising in 1381, written in Old French apparently by an eye-witness.[39]

The different descriptions are full, but they vary greatly in details, so that, though it is possible to make a complete record of events, we cannot be sure that we are altogether correct. At this distance of time from the occurrences we ought to be able to consider the sequence of events with a judicial mind. Both sides in the duel are to a great extent outside our sympathies. The rebels were exorbitant in their demands and violent in their methods, while the Court, being completely at the mercy of the mob, promised everything demanded, with no intention of carrying out their pledges. They had, however, this excuse, that the only way to save the city and its inhabitants was to get the mob into the open country by any possible means available.

The vast concourse of persons who demanded entrance into the city was composed of a heterogeneous mass of discontented men with different aims to forward and different grievances calling for redress. The poll tax, although it gave great dissatisfaction to the nation, was not the cause of the outbreak; the great object of the majority was to obtain the abolition of serfdom. Had this been the only demand the sympathies of the country would have been entirely with the insurgents, but, in order to increase the number of their followers, the leaders had gathered around them all the disaffected persons they were able to get together, and Wat Tyler, to enhance his importance, formulated a number of revolutionary and socialistic demands.

It is not necessary here to discuss these demands, for their number sufficiently condemns them. We may allow that the masses have a right to demonstrate and urge upon their rulers a change of so fundamental a nature as serfdom, which affected them all more or less, but an evil which the rulers were very remiss in attempting to redress. At the same time no government can exist if mob law is triumphant and if an irresponsible mass of people is allowed to demand changes which require much consideration by a legislative body, as Wat Tyler's followers did. It is instructive to find that although the demands were first agreed to by the King, and then the promise revoked, the serfs were gradually freed while the other demands were quite overlooked. Serfdom was out of date, and the change could no longer be postponed.

Richard II., a boy of ten years, came to the throne in 1377, and few sovereigns have had to take up a more troubled inheritance. The whole country was distressed, and the agricultural population had been driven to the verge of rebellion. Revolutionary views, supported from the writings of Wyclyf and Langland, had taken root among large masses of the people. Doubtless the reformer and the poet had great influence on the people, and although they were not themselves sowers of sedition, their burning words were quoted with effect by the leaders of the revolutionary movement. John Ball's democratic preaching caused the insurrection, but he gave way to the more practical Wat Tyler, as the leader of the rebels.

The area of the risings extended over part of the Midlands south of Yorkshire, and the whole of the South. There was a reign of terror on all sides. The manor houses were broken open and sacked by mobs, and it was said that every attorney's house in the line of march was destroyed. Lawyers were exposed to the special hatred of the rebels, who exhibited an ignorant hatred of legal documents. The University of Cambridge suffered severely from the lawlessness of the mob. The University chest was robbed, and a large number of documents were ruthlessly destroyed. Many of the colleges also suffered.

The mob that marched on London and besieged it were mostly from Kent and Essex, and their march was marked by murder and pillage. The authorities were paralysed, and when the mob arrived at the walls of London no preparations had been made, save the strengthening of the gates, so the King and the Court were cut off from communication with all outside London. It is remarkable that we are able to record the daily proceedings of the mob which took place more than six centuries ago; still we can be fairly certain that the events which dovetail into one another are to a great extent correctly reported. The chief difficulty arises when we consider the speeches of the several actors. Chroniclers like John Stow are very picturesque in their descriptions, and often put words into the mouths of their puppets which are evidently written for the purposes of effect. Even when the words are probably historical there is some doubt as to whether they have not been attributed to the wrong persons.

On Monday, June 10th, Canterbury had been overrun, and on Wednesday, the 12th, the main body of the rebels from Kent were crowded together on Blackheath. John Ball preached to them from the text which has come down to us in the familiar couplet—

'Whan Adam dalf and Eve span,
Wo was thanne a gentilman,'

and he kept his audience enthralled with his eloquence.

Messengers were sent by the King to demand the cause of the rising, and brought back the answer that the Commons were gathered together for the King's safety. The King's mother—Joan, Princess of Wales, and widow of Edward, the Black Prince, who had been on a pilgrimage to the shrines of Kent—was allowed by the rebels to enter the city.

Mr. Trevelyan tells us how a conference was proposed: 'The rebels invited the King to cross the river and confer with them at Blackheath. He was rowed across in a barge accompanied by his principal nobles. At Rotherhithe, a deputation from the camp on the moor above was waiting on the bank to receive them. At the last moment prudence prevailed, and Richard was persuaded not to trust himself on shore. The rebels, shouting their demands across the water, professed their loyalty to Richard, but required the heads of John of Gaunt, Sudbury, Hales, and several other ministers, some of whom were at that moment in the boat. The royal barge put back to the Tower.'[40]

Stow tells us that the watchword of the peasants was 'With whom hold you?' and the answer was 'With King Richard and the true Commons.' The Chronicler adds: 'Who could not that watchward, off went his head.'

Mr. James Tait, the author of the excellent life of Wat Tyler in the *Dictionary of National Biography*, mentions 'a Proclamation in Thanet Church, on the 13th June, [which] ran in the names of Wat Tyler and John Rackstraw, but the St. Albans insurgents who reached London on Friday the 14th were divided as to which was the more powerful person in the realm, the King or Tyler, and obtained from the latter a promise to come and shave the beards of the abbot, prior and monks; stipulating for implicit obedience to his orders.'

The men of Essex were outside Aldgate in great numbers, and as the day advanced the leaders became fearful as to their condition. They had no means of breaking into the city, and if they remained long where they were they would inevitably have been starved.

'Walworth guarded the bridge, and sent to the peasants, bidding them, in the name of the King and the city, come no nearer to London.'[41] If there had been no treachery it would have been easy to keep the rebels outside till they were forced by hunger to desist from their endeavours to enter, for time was on the side of the besieged, but the peasants had friends and well-wishers within, and the city being divided against itself, fell.

Mr. Trevelyan writes: 'A committee of three aldermen rode out to Blackheath to deliver [Walworth's] message. Two of them, Adam Carlyll and John Fresh, faithfully performed their mission. But the third alderman, named John Horn, separated himself from his two colleagues, conferred apart with the rebel leaders, and exhorted them to march on London at once for they would be received with acclamation into the city. After this treachery he did not fear to return to the city, and brought some of the peasants with him and lodged them in his house. He even advised Walworth to admit the mob.'[42]

The rioters burnt the Marshalsea prison, situated in the High Street, Southwark, and set the prisoners free. Others gutted Lambeth Palace to show their hatred of the archbishop, but he was not there.

On Thursday morning, 13th June, Horn, the disaffected alderman, rode out to Blackheath to confer with the rebels, and he urged them to come to the bridge, where they would find friends. He had an ally in Walter Sybyle, alderman of Bridge Ward, who in virtue of his office took command on the bridge, and he announced that he would let the rebels in by the bridge gate in spite of all opposition. Then Walworth, the Mayor, finding that he was powerless, gave leave to Wat Tyler's followers to enter the city on condition that they paid for everything they took, and did no damage.

The Kentish rebels poured into the city over the bridge, and at the same time the men of Essex were let in at Aldgate. The first cry of the mob as they entered the city—their defiant answer to the Mayor's condition—was 'To the Savoy! To the Savoy!' the house of John of Gaunt, outside the city liberties and by the riverside, which was burnt and entirely destroyed. In the accounts of the Savoy for 1393-1394 mention is made of the annual loss of £4, 13s. 4d.—'the rent of fourteen shops belonging lately to the manor of the Savoy annexed, for each shop by the year, at four terms, 6s. 8d., the accomptant had nothing, because they were burnt at the time of the insurrection, and are not rebuilt.' In these accounts the Rising of 1381 is referred to as 'The Rumor.'

Sir Robert Hales, the Treasurer, was a marked man, and his manor house at Highbury was burnt and utterly destroyed. Jack Straw's Castle, which was built on the site of Highbury Castle, retained the name of the second leader of the revolt almost to our own time. Later in the same day the Priory of the Order of St. John at Jerusalem, at Clerkenwell, of which Hales was prior, was burnt by the men of Essex, who in their march to London had previously attacked the Priory of the Order at Cressing, Essex.

Stow informs us that the Commons passed through the city and did no harm, they took 'nothing from any man, but bought all things at a just price, and if they found any man with theft they beheaded him.' This, however, was soon changed; first they were joined by the dangerous classes in the city who were glad of an opportunity of punishing their enemies the Flemings by the riverside and the lawyers of the Temple; then the prisons of Fleet, Newgate and Westminster were broken open, and hordes of rascality were added to those contributed by the Marshalsea. To add to these elements of disorder the men became drunk with wine supplied by the rich citizens, and we hear no more of restraints. Gross outrages against property and life now follow one another rapidly. Much damage was done in Fleet Street and the Temple. The rolls and records of the lawyers were burned or otherwise destroyed. The royal account books suffered in the same way. Stow relates that the insurgents 'determined to burne all Court-rolles and old muniments, that the memory of antiquities being taken away, their lords should not be able to challenge any right on them from that time forth.' Not content with destroying the documents, they desired to destroy the producers of documents. Again Stow tells us that 'they took in hand to behead all men of law, as well apprentises as utter-barristers and old justices, with all the jurers of the country whom they might get into their hands, they spared none whom they thought to be learned, especially if they found any to have pen and ink they pulled off his hood, and all with one voice crying, "Hale him out and cut off his head." '

The only place of safety was the Tower, and here the young King watched the flames in several parts of the city, and listened to the turbulent cries of the mob on all sides of him. Just beneath, on the east side near St. Katherine's Hospital, was an encampment of the rebels who clamoured for the murder of the Chancellor and others who had taken refuge in the Tower. This was an eventful day for all, crowded with actions more than enough to terrify a boy suddenly called upon to act.

The Council were hurriedly called together, and after considering the serious dangers which surrounded them, agreed to a policy of concession. The rebels, however, were invited to meet the King at Mile End on the following day.

On Friday, the 14th June, the King and his Court went to Mile End to hear the demands of Wat Tyler and his followers. We learn from the Stow MS. (referred to above), that when they arrived the Commons came to the King, and all knelt to him, saying, 'Be welcome, our lord King Richard, if it please you, and we will not have any other King than you; and Wat Tighler, master and leader of them, praying to him (the King), on the part of the Commons, that he would suffer them to take and have all traitors that were against the King and the law.' The demands are recited as follows in the manuscript:—

'That no man should be a serf by birth, nor do homage or any manner of suit to any lord.

'No man should be a serf to any man except by his own will, and by covenant duly indentured.

'To give fourpence for an acre of land.'

Stow gives the demands in fuller detail:—

'The first, that all men should be free from servitude and bondage, so as from thenceforth there should be no bondmen.

'The second, that he should pardon all men of what estate soever, all manner actions and insurrections committed, and all manner treasons, fellonies, transgressions and extortions by any of them done, and to grant them peace.

'The third, that all men from thenceforth might be enfranchised to buy and sell in every country, city, borough town, fair, market and other place within the realm of England.

'The fourth, that no acre of land holden in bondage or service should be holden but for fourpence, and if it had been holden for less aforetime, it should not hereafter be enhanced.'

Stow adds: 'These and many other things they required. Moreover, they told him [the King] he had been evilly governed till that day, but from that time he must be governed otherwise.'

After consultation with his courtiers the King conceded everything asked by Wat Tyler. They agreed that serfage should be abolished, and that all servile dues should be commuted for a rent of fourpence per acre, and a general pardon was pronounced on all. Clerks were set to work to draw up charters of liberation and pardon in proper legal form for every village and manor, as well as for every shire.[43]

While these arrangements were going on, the soldiers, who could have kept the Tower with ease, were ordered or at least permitted, to let in the mob. This appears to have been part of the agreement, and we cannot but brand it as a wicked compact, as it was clearly the duty of the Court to protect its servants.

The unfortunate Leg, the farmer of the poll tax, was murdered, and a learned friar, the friend and adviser of John of Gaunt, was torn in pieces as a substitute for his patron. In the chapel, Archbishop Sudbury and Hales were torn from the altar and hurried to Tower Hill, where their heads were struck off and straightway placed on London Bridge.

John Ball was said to be among the first who entered the Tower, and to have directed the outrages. The mob suffered the Princess of Wales to escape by boat, when she went to the Queen's Wardrobe, which had been given to Queen Philippa, and was afterwards called the Tower Royal in the Vintry Ward. In some accounts it is said that she went to the Wardrobe in Carter Lane, but this is a mistake. The King, after his return from Mile End, joined his mother at the Queen's Wardrobe.

On Friday and Saturday, as they received their charters, the bulk of the insurgents left London and returned to their homes, leaving the residue and more dangerous masses behind them.

Mr. Trevelyan relates how the King and his nobles rode out from the Queen's Wardrobe through Ludgate and Temple Bar, passed along the Strand by the smouldering ruins of the Savoy to Westminster. This was on Saturday the 15th of June. The royal party was met at the doors of the Abbey by a sorrowful procession of monks in penitential garb, bearing the Cross before them. The King dismounted and kissed the Cross. The nobles, the courtiers and men-at-arms entered the church and performed with unusual fervour the acts of piety. The reason why the monks were in this subdued condition was owing to the fact that a violation of sanctuary had just occurred.[44]

The insurgents had marched on Westminster, broken open the Exchequer, destroyed the books and records, and violated the sanctuary. Richard or John Inworth, warden of the Marshalsea, after the destruction of that prison, had fled for refuge to Westminster Abbey. On their arrival the mob found him at the shrine of Edward the Confessor, and having torn him away carried him back to the city, where his head was struck off on the block in Cheapside.

Stow gives a vivid account of the King's visit to the Abbey: 'The same day (June 15), after dinner, about two of the clock, the King went from the Wardrobe called the Royal, in London, toward Westminster, attended only by the number of 200 persons, to visit Saint Edward's shrine, and to see if the Commons had done any mischief there. The abbot and convent of that Abbey, with the chanons and vicars of Saint Stephen's Chappell, met him in rich copes with procession, and led him by the charnel-house into the Abbey, then to the church, and so to the high altar, where he devoutly prayed and offered. After which he spake with the anchore [anchoret], to whom he confessed himself; then he went to the chapel called Our Lady in the Pewe, where he made his prayers.' Froissart tells us that the figure of the Virgin in this chapel was renowned for its many virtues, and that the Kings of England had much faith in the miracles performed at this shrine. When Richard left Westminster he 'made proclamation that all the Commons of the country that were in London should meet him in Smithfield.'[45]

In the Stowe MS. there is a very full and clear record of the subsequent proceedings: The King went to the house of the canons of Saint Bartholomew, 'and then the Mayor of London, William Walworth, came to the King, who commanded him to go to the Commons to make their chieftain come to him, and when he was called by the Mayor, Wat Tighler of Maidstone by name, he came to the King with great countenance mounted on a small horse, so as to be seen by the Commons, and dismounted, carrying a dagger in his hand, which he had taken from another man; and when he was dismounted he took the King by the hand, half kneeling, and shook his arm sharply and strongly, saying to him: "Brother, be of good comfort," ... and the King said to the said Wat, "Why will you not go to your country?" and the other replied with a great oath, that he and his companions would not go unless they had their charter such as they wished to have.'[46]

The points are then set forth in fuller particularity than they were in the previous meeting at Mile End. Such demands as were not mentioned previously are as follows:—

'That there should be no law outside the law of Winchester.

'That no outlawry should be by any process of law made henceforth.

'That the goods of Holy Church should not be in the hands of men of religion, nor of the parsons and vicars, nor of others of Holy Church, but the "avantés" should have their sustenance easily, and the remainder of the goods should be divided among the parishioners, and no bishop should be in England except one ... and all the lands and tenements of the possessors should be taken from them and parted among the Commons, saving to them their reasonable sustenance.

'To this the King replied easily, and said that he [Wat] should have all this that he [the King] could properly grant, saving to him the rights of his crown, commanding him [Wat] to go to his hold without more delay.'

From this point there are differences in the accounts, and it is difficult to be quite certain about the sequence of events which bought about Wat Tyler's death. Stow accuses the leader of a deep-laid scheme for which there does not appear to be any special authority. He writes: 'Wat Tyler being a crafty fellow, of excellent wit, but lacking grace, answered that peace be offered, but with conditions to his liking, minding to feed the King with fair words till the next day, that he might in the night have compassed his perverse purpose, for they thought the same night to have spoiled the city, the King first being slain, and the great lords that cleaved to him, to have burnt the city by setting fire in four parts thereof.'[47]

We have now to co-ordinate the different accounts of the end of Wat Tyler. Some of these take no notice of the causes that led to Walworth's action, but Stow's description seems in the main to make the whole scene clear, although he does not produce a consecutive narrative, but rather relates incidents out of their proper order.

The great open space of Smithfield, the favourite meeting-place on the north of London, and the chosen site for the tournaments and jousts, was crowded on all sides. Near the gate of St. Bartholomew's Priory were the King and his Court, and farther to the west were the ranks of the Commons set in order of battle. There had been some conference between the leaders, but no agreement had been come to, and naturally the state of tension was profound.

Wat Tyler threatened the King, and took umbrage at the position of Sir John Newton or Newentone, keeper of Rochester Castle, who bore the King's sword. He treated with much disrespect the knight, who remarked that he recognised in the rebel leader the greatest thief and robber of his country. This so enraged Wat Tyler that he first ordered his followers to behead Newentone, and then attempted to strike him with his dagger. At this Walworth came forward and requested the King to allow him to arrest Wat, who struck at him, but without effect, as Walworth's armour protected him. The Mayor then, in self-defence, attacked Wat, and wounded him in the neck, and gave him a blow on the head. John Cavendish (or, as some say, Ralph Standish) then came forward in support of the Mayor and wounded Wat in several places. The chieftain spurred his horse and cried to the Commons to avenge him. After riding some thirty yards he fell off his horse, half dead, and was taken to the Hospital of St.

Bartholomew's, where he died. What purports to be the dagger with which Walworth struck Wat Tyler is in the possession of the Fishmongers' Company.

The suspense at this crisis must have been intense. The rebels prepared their bows, but the arrows were not let fly, for the King spurring his horse, rode forward across the square to the host, and cried out, 'Will you shoot your King? I am your captain and leader, follow me.' This brilliant display of courage by the beautiful boy of fourteen, who had the misfortune to be King, had its effect, and the Commons followed him peaceably into the fields of Clerkenwell.

Walworth raised a body of loyal citizens, and these marched out under the command of Sir Robert Knolles and surrounded the rebels, who surrendered and asked for pardon. The host was divided into companies and sent to their respective homes under proper escort.

Now that the authorities were triumphant, the leaderless rebels fared badly. On July 2nd the charters were revoked. John Ball fled to the Midlands, and, according to Froissart, he was taken prisoner at Coventry in an old ruin. On the 15th of July he was drawn, hanged and quartered, just one month after the death of Wat Tyler. On December 13th the King proclaimed a general pardon.

A contemporary account of the insurrection was drawn up and inserted in the City 'Letter Book H' (fol. cxxiii.). A translation of this is printed in Riley's *Memorials* (pp. 449-451). It is of great interest, but naturally no attempt at a judicial statement is made. The events are described as 'among the most wondrous and hitherto unheard-of prodigies that ever happened in the city of London,' and it is stated that 'hardly was there a street in the city in which there were not bodies lying of those who had been slain.' The traitors who let in the mob are described as 'perfidious Commoners within the city.' The whole account is written with spirit, and the ending of the fearful days is graphically described: 'Therefore our Lord the King returned into the city of London with the greatest glory and honour, and the whole of this profane multitude in confusion fled forthwith for concealment in their affright.' 'Our Lord the King, beneath his standard in the said field, with his own hands decorated with the order of knighthood the said Mayor [William Walworth], and Sir Nicholas Brembre and Sir John Philipot, who had already been Mayors of the said city, as also Sir Robert Lamb.'

Thus ended the Peasants' Rising, which, although it ended in total defeat to its promoters, exercised an enormous influence on the course of English history.

The insurrection of Jack Cade was not so important an event as that of Wat Tyler, but it must not by any means be considered merely as an outbreak of the lower classes.

Fabyan, the alderman and sheriff, has left us particulars of the insurrection, and some further details have been discovered by Dr. James Gairdner, C.B., who has given a connected account in the Preface to his authoritative edition of the *Paston Letters*, and also in the *Dictionary of National Biography*. It is almost impossible to understand the characters of the men who held responsible positions in the reign of Henry VI. The uncles of the King quarrelled among themselves, and their respective followers were hunted down by their enemies.

William De la Pole, fourth Earl and first Duke of Suffolk, a distinguished leader in the French wars, but a politician in later life, was the chief opponent of Humphrey, Duke of Gloucester, the leader of the warlike party. Suffolk was an active agent for peace. Apparently the English people were then very much like what they have been in later time. Peace after a successful war has usually been unpopular, and the unfortunate Suffolk was howled at for having given back the Provinces to France.

'By thee Anjou and Maine were sold to France;
The false, revolting Normans thorough thee
Disdain to call us lord; and Picardy
Hath slain their governors, surpris'd our forts,
And sent the ragged soldiers wounded home.'[48]

The Londoners were strongly antagonistic to Suffolk, who was generally accused of maladministration and malversation without definite charges. His friends could not protect him against his enemies, and when trying to escape to France he was intercepted in the Straits of Dover, put in a little boat, and murdered. His body was thrown on the beach near Dover. It was afterwards buried by order of the King. His death did not satisfy the discontented, and other courtiers succeeded to his place in the disfavour of the people.

Whole districts of the counties of Kent, Surrey and Sussex rose in arms to the extent of 30,000 men, clamouring for the redress of grievances. The masses received assistance from some of the best families of these counties. The Chronicler Gregory says that the Captain 'compassed all the gentles to arise with him.'

A man who called himself John Mortimer, and affirmed that he was a cousin of the Duke of York, was chosen to be leader. His real name was believed to be Cade. He was an Irishman, who had had some experience in war, and showed himself a strong leader.

On the 1st of June 1450 a considerable army marched on London and encamped at Blackheath, where they formed a regular encampment.

On hearing of this Henry VI. came from Leicester to London, where he arrived on the 6th inst. He took up his quarters at the Hospital of St. John's, Clerkenwell, and with him were 20,000 troops. The King sent to know the cause of the rising, and was answered thus: 'To destroy traitors being about him, with other divers points.' A message was then sent by the King, and proclamation was made that loyal men should immediately quit the field. Upon the night after all the insurgents were gone, and the insurrection seemed to have come to an end.

On the 11th June the King proceeded to Blackheath, and he found that the rebels had withdrawn in the nighttime. Instead of leaving well alone, it was decided to pursue the insurgents, and a detachment of the royal army, under Sir Humphrey Stafford and his brother William, were sent in pursuit. A battle took place on the 18th at Sevenoaks, in which both the Staffords were killed and the rest of the party completely routed. The followers of the King in the royal camp were dismayed, and many of them threatened that if justice was not done on certain traitors who had resisted the King they would go over to the Captain of Kent. One of the chief of these unpopular courtiers was James Fiennes, Lord Saye and Sele, a follower of Suffolk, and to please the disaffected he was sent to the Tower.

The King withdrew to Greenwich and the whole of the army dispersed. He returned to London by water and made preparations for removal to Kenilworth. The Mayor and Commons beseeched him to remain in London, offering to live and die with him and to pay half the cost of his household, but he would not consent. The city authorities did not know what to do, and a party among them opened negotiations with the insurgents. Alderman Cooke passed to and fro under the safe conduct of the Captain.

Stow prints in his Chronicle 'The safeguard and sign manual of the Captain of Kent sent to Thomas Cocke, draper of London, by the Captain of the great Assembly in Kent.' He also gives 'the Complaint of the Commons of Kent,' and 'the Requests by the Captain of the great Assembly in Kent.' These are differently worded from the 'Proclamation made by Jack Cade,' which has been printed from a MS. in the handwriting of Stow,[49] but the sentiments and complaints in all the documents are essentially the same. They contain a remarkable expression of the feelings of general unrest among the people, although they are doubtless very unjust to the character of the Duke of Suffolk and his followers.

On the 1st of July the insurgents entered Southwark, and Jack Cade made the White Hart Inn his headquarters. According to Fabyan, while the Commons of Kent settled themselves in Southwark, the rebels of Essex made 'a field upon the plain of Mile End' their resting-place. On the 2nd of July a court was held by the Mayor for the purpose of considering the best means of resisting the entry of the rebels into the city. It was found, however, that the majority were in their favour, so that Alderman John Horne was committed to Newgate for opposing the views of the malcontents. In the afternoon, about five o'clock, the insurgents were admitted into the city and passed over London Bridge, Cade cutting the ropes of the drawbridge with his sword. Cade then issued proclamations in the King's name against robbery and forced requisitions, and rode through the streets, taking the city under his complete control. When he came to the London Stone in Cannon Street he struck it with his sword, and said: 'Now is Mortimer Lord of this city.' This was a circumstance of the greatest interest in the history of London, for it shows that some special virtue was supposed, in the popular mind, to be connected with London Stone.

Cade now gave orders to the Mayor, and returned to Southwark for the night.

On Friday, the 3rd of July, he returned to the city, and sent for Lord Saye and ordered him, after a mock trial, to be beheaded at the Standard in Cheapside. Crowmer, an unpopular Sheriff of Kent, and son-in-law to Saye, was beheaded at Mile End. As Jack Cade did not wish to be publicly recognised by those who knew his origin, he caused one Bailey, who was supposed to be an old acquaintance, to be beheaded at Whitechapel.

Attention to the rules of order and honesty at length tired the leader, and Stow relates that 'he went into the house of Philip Malpas, draper and alderman, and robbed and spoiled his house, taking from thence great substance, and returned unto Southwark. On the next morrow he again entered the city, and dined that day in the parish of Saint Margaret Pattens, at one Ghersti's house, and when he had dined, like an uncourteous guest he robbed him, as the day before he had Malpas. For which two robberies, although the poor people drew to him and were partners in the spoil, yet the honest and wealthy Commoners cast in their minds the sequel of this matter, and fear lest they should be dealt with in like manner.'

On Sunday, the 5th of July, Cade and his followers remained in Southwark all day, and in the evening the Mayor and citizens, with a force under the command of Matthew Gough, occupied London Bridge to prevent the Kentish men from entering the city. Desperate fighting on the bridge continued all through the night, from nine o'clock till nine on the following morning. 'Sometime the citizens had the better and sometimes the other, but ever they kept them upon the bridge, so that the citizens never passed much the bulwark at the bridge foot, nor the Kentishmen no farther than the drawbridge. Thus continued the cruel fight to the destruction of much people on both sides.'[50] Matthew Gough, John Sutton, alderman, and Roger Hoysand, citizen, were among the killed.

When the rebels got the worst of the encounter a truce was made. A conference was arranged, and Waynflete, Bishop of Winchester, and some others, met Cade in St. Margaret's Church, Southwark. The bishop produced two general pardons sent by the Chancellor—Cardinal Kemp, Archbishop of York; one for the Captain himself and the other for his followers. These were eagerly accepted, as the insurgents were disgusted with their leader, and they were only too glad to return to their homes.

It seems to have been generally believed that Cade was entitled to the name of Mortimer, but after this conference the truth got abroad, and his pardon was necessarily invalidated in consequence of this discovery. On the 12th of July, therefore, a proclamation of the King was issued for the apprehension of Cade, and the offer of a reward of one thousand marks to anyone who should take him alive or dead. Cade escaped in disguise towards the woody country round Lewes. He was pursued by Alexander Iden, and captured and mortally wounded by him at Heathfield, Sussex, on the 13th inst. The place is known as Cade Street, and a stone with an inscription stands on the site of the capture. Cade's body was taken to London; his head was placed on London Bridge, and his four quarters were sent to different parts of Kent. Thus ended this dangerous rebellion.

The whole history of the origin of the rising is most complicated. Not only, as already mentioned, were the gentry of Kent on the side of the rebels, but most of the important persons in Southwark supported them. There were Richard Dartmouth, abbot of Battle; John Danyel, prior of Lewes, and Robert Poynings, uncle of the Countess of Northumberland and husband of Margaret Paston. 'When the pardon time came, a goodly list of names was recorded, with which it was thought wise to deal leniently.'[51]

The Second Part of King Henry VI., which Shakespeare slightly altered from *The First Part of the Contention betwixt the two famous houses of Yorke and Lancaster*, is chiefly concerned with Cade's Rebellion; but it is sad that such a perversion of history should in any way be connected with the honoured name of our greatest poet. The libel against Suffolk,

'There let his head and lifeless body lie,
Until the queen his mistress bury it,'

is apparently devoid of the slightest foundation. The representation of Cade is also a ridiculous travesty. His proclamation, which has come down to us, will be seen to be a very clear and ingenious piece of composition Moreover, Latin is quoted in it, and therefore the writer is not likely to have considered it a crime to speak Latin.

Cade's description of Lord Saye: 'Thou hast most traitorously corrupted the youth of the realm in erecting a grammar school; and whereas before our forefathers had no other books but the score and the tally, thou hast caused printing to be used; and contrary to the King, his crown and dignity, thou hast built a papermill,' has no foundation whatever in history. In spite of the anachronism of the allusion to the printing press, Gibbon was deceived by the description, and, in claiming Lord Saye as an ancestor, styled him a martyr to learning.

Dr. Gairdner discovered in Gregory's Chronicle a very remarkable statement, which, if true, would throw great light upon the origin of the outbreak.

'Ande aftyr that [the Battle of Sevenoaks], uppon the fyrste day of Juylle, the same Captayne come agayne, as the Kenttysche men sayde, but hyt was anothyr that namyd himselfe the Captayne, and he come to the Blacke Hethe.'[52]

Dr. Gairdner is inclined to take this as something more than a mere rumour, but he waits for some corroboration from another source before entirely accepting it. He adds in a note: 'The story of Jack Cade, however, is attended with difficulties from any point of view, and it is remarkable that when Cade's body was brought to London it was taken to the White Hart at Southwark, where he had lodged before his entry into the city, and identified by the woman who kept the house. We hear nothing of its being identified by any one who had seen the leader before the Battle of Sevenoaks.'[53]

CHAUCER'S PILGRIMS ISSUING FROM THE TABARD.

CHAPTER III

Round the Town with Chaucer and the Poets of his Time

HAVING considered some of the chief conditions of life in a walled town, and the manners of the inhabitants, we can now proceed to look at old London through the eyes of the great English poets of the later mediæval period, to whom we are so much indebted for the insight they give us into the habits of a long-dead past.

That wonderful book, *Piers Plowman*, not only brings before us in the most vivid fashion the life of the fourteenth century, but opens out to us the thoughts and hopes of the leaders of men. One of the most striking passages contains a description of the interior of a beerhouse in the reign of Edward III., with the company assembled therein.[54] This is a scene common to the whole country, but London places are also frequently mentioned in *Piers Plowman*.

The author, William Langland, called 'Long Will,' probably from his tallness, was an inhabitant of London, but he has little to say in its favour. He wrote: 'I have lived long in London, but have never found charity; all whom I have seen are covetous.'[55]

Prof. Skeat says: 'One great merit of the poem is, that it chiefly exhibits London life and London opinions, which are surely of more interest to us than those of Worcestershire. He does but mention Malvern three times, and those three passages may be found within the compass of the first eight passus of Text A. But how numerous are his allusions to London! He not only speaks of it several times, but he frequently mentions the Law Courts of Westminster; he was familiar with Cornhill, East Cheap, Cock Lane in Smithfield,[56] Shoreditch, Garlickhithe, Stratford, Tyburn and Southwark, all of which he mentions in an offhand manner. He mentions no river but the Thames, which is with him simply synonymous with river; for in one passage he speaks of two men thrown into the Thames, and in another he says that rich men are wont to give presents to the rich, which is as superfluous as if one should fill a tun with water from a fresh river and then pour it into the Thames to render it wetter. To remember the London origin of a large portion of the poem is the true key to the right understanding of it.'[57]

M. Jusserand, in his interesting study of *Piers Plowman*, says of Langland: 'He tells us what he has seen and nothing else; his sole guide is the light that shines over the town where Truth is imprisoned.' He continues: 'It clears the darkness of the London lanes, where, under the pent-roof of their shops, the merchants make Gyle, disguised as an apprentice, sell their adulterated wares; it brightens the hovel in Cornhill where the poet lodges his emaciated body; it throws its rays on the scared faces of sinners for whom the hour of punishment has rung. We have here a whole gallery of portraits which stand out in an extraordinary manner.'

M. Jusserand takes a somewhat unfavourable view of Langland's character. He says that the poet 'blames those who go to London and sing for souls, yet he confesses that he does the same. He blames people of a wandering habit, yet he is a wanderer; he heaps scorn on the men who seek for invitations at the houses of the great, yet he does so; he condemns "tho that feynen here folis" (Bk. x. 38), and he assumes the appearance of a "fole"; he hates lazy people, "lorels," "lolleres," yet he lives himself as a lorel, a loller, a "spille-tyme";

' "and lovede wel fare,
And no dede to do bote drynke and to slepe." ' (C. vi. 8).

The satirist and the censor cannot always be consistent, and without deciding upon the character of Langland, gratitude to him causes us to forgive his inconsistencies, and makes us more inclined to agree with the high estimate of Professor Skeat, rather than with the condemnation of Mons. Jusserand.[58]

Langland was taken by the leaders of the Peasants' Rising as the great prophet of their movement, but he himself stood outside the political circle. He complained of the evils that were everywhere rampant, but he did not wish to set himself against the Government; as Dr. Skeat says: 'His Richard the Redeles is a tender and touching remonstrance to the King, Richard II.'

Thomas Hoccleve and John Gower were Londoners,—the former a clerk in the Privy Seal Office and the latter probably a city merchant.

Hoccleve is supposed to have taken his name from the village of Hockliffe, Bedfordshire, on the Roman Road, 4½ miles south of Woburn, and 3½ east of Leighton Buzzard. He intended at first to become a priest, but instead he entered the Privy Seal Office in 1308, when he was nineteen or twenty years of age. He complained of the drudgery of copying, and seems to have been always ready to shirk his work. Dr. Furnivall's side-notes to the autobiographical portion of the *Regement of Princes* show what the complaints are like: 'A copier must always work mind, eye and hand together. He can't talk to other folk, or sing, but must give all his wits to his work. Workmen talk, sing, and lark. We labour in silence, stoop and stare on the sheepskin. Our copying hurts our stomachs, our backs and our eyes. Anyone who has copied for twenty years like I have suffers for it in every bit of his body. It's nearly done for me. Had I always lived in poverty, I shouldn't feel it so much now, but the change is strange. God keep me from poverty. I'd sooner die than live miserably.'

As there were many copyists employed in London, we must hope that they were not all so weary of their work as the poet was.

He lived at Chester Inn, which stood on part of the site of the present Somerset House.

'At Chestre ynne, right fast be the Stronde.'

His daily occupation took him to Westminster, where the Privy Seal Office was situated, and as the Strand was but a poor road we may suppose that he went from home to office in a boat. He went frequently to Paul's Head Tavern, in St. Paul's Churchyard, where he made love to the waitresses and others. He also belonged to a dining club, called the Temple Club, 'the court of good company.' Often after dinner, instead of going back to the office, he took his pleasure on the Thames, being flattered by the watermen, who fought amongst themselves for his patronage, and called him master, because he paid them well.

He was a good Churchman, and denounced the Lollard Rising in St. Giles's Fields in January 1414 in good set terms.

Hoccleve was not a very lively poet, and he always seems to have been in want of money. He enjoyed the early part of his life, but when he married and the pinch of poverty came upon him he was very dejected. In spite of his faults we cannot but esteem him, and feel that he has a claim on our gratitude because he was devoted to Chaucer, and was the cause of our possessing the best portrait there is of the poet. Hoccleve was near Chaucer in his last days. He could easily pass from Westminster Palace to the garden of the Chapel of St. Mary. Dr. Furnivall suggests that he was with Chaucer when the great poet died there.[59]

Dr. G. C. Macaulay, in the Introduction to his valuable and exhaustive edition of Gower's *Complete Works*, says that the poet speaks with special respect of the estate of merchants, which seems to suggest that it was as a merchant he made the money which he spent in buying his land, and this inference is supported by the manner in which he speaks of 'our city,' and by the fact that it is with members of the merchant class that he seems to be most in personal communication. Dr. Macaulay supposes Gower to have been a dealer in wool, with the natural dislike of the Londoner for foreigners. The jealousy of the Lombards which he expresses has every appearance of being a prejudice connected with rivalry in commerce. 'I see Lombards come,' he says, 'in poor attire as servants, and before a year has passed they have gained so much by deceit and conspiracy that they dress more nobly than the burgesses of our city.'[60]

John Gower at one time lived at Southwark, and in St. Saviour's Church his tomb still stands. One day, in the year 1390, when he had taken boat on the Thames, he accidentally met the King (Richard II.) in his tapestried barge. The river was the silent highway for all Londoners, also the royal road from Westminster to the Tower, and from thence to Greenwich. Brilliant scenes were to be seen on the river, which joined all parts of the town in one. Here all classes were brought together—the gentry and the working-classes—and Court pageants were constantly being enacted.

When Richard saw Gower he commanded him to come into the royal barge, and then charged him to write some new thing which he might read. The poet obeyed the command, and produced the *Confessio Amantis*, with a Prologue, in which occur these lines:—

'In our engglish, I thenke make
A bok for King Richardes sake,
To whom belongeth my ligeance
With al myn hertes obeissance
In al that evere a liege man
Unto his King may doon or can,
So perforth I me recomande
To him which al me may comande,
Preyende unto the hihe regne
Which causeth every king to regne
That his corone longe stoude.
I thenke and have it understoude,
As it bifel upon a tyde,
As thing which scholde tho betyde,—
Under the toun of newe Troye,
Which tok of Brut his ferst joye,
In Temse whan it was flowende
As I be bote cam rowende,
So as fortune hir tyme sette,

My liege lord par chaunce I mette;
And so befel, as I cam nyh,
Out of my bot, whan he me syh,
He bad me come in to his barge.
And whan I was with him at large,
Amonges othre thinges seid
He hath this charge upon me leid,
And bad me doo my besynesse
That to his hihe worthinesse
Som newe thing I scholde boke,
That he himself it mihte loke
After the forme of my writynge.
And thus upon his comandynge
Myn herte is wel the more glad
To write so as he me bad;
And eek my fere as wel the lasse
That non envye schal compasse
Without a resonable wite
To pyne and blame that I write.'

As time went on Gower lost faith in Richard. The personal reference to the King was suppressed, and instead of

'A bok for King Richardes sake,'

he wrote

'A bok for Engelondes sake.'

The original picture is of all the more interest, because Gower's verse is not usually allusive to the characteristics of London life.

John Lydgate was a countryman and monk of Bury, born at Lydgate, near Newmarket, about 1370, as he himself tells us in the *Tale of Princes*. He was not in sympathy with the doings of the city, but his *London Lickpenny* is an invaluable record of London life in his day; in which are related the adventures of a poor Kentishman who comes to London in search of justice, but cannot find it for lack of money.

First he went to Westminster Hall, and visited successively the different courts of law—the King's Bench and the Common Pleas, and then to the Rolls, 'before the clerks of the Chancerie.'

'Within this Hall, neither rich nor yet poor
Would do for me aught, although I should die.
Which seeing, I got me out of the door,
Where Flemings began on me for to cry,
"Master, what will you copen or buy?
Fine felt hats, or spectacles to read?
Lay down your silver and here you may speed." '

At Westminster Gate:—

'Cooke's to me they took good intent,
And proffered me bread with ale and wine,
Ribs of beef, both fat and full fine,
A faire cloth they gan for to sprede,
But wanting money I might not then speed.'

No doubt the countryman had sufficient cause for many of his complaints, but we cannot but ask, Why should he expect to obtain things without paying for them?

He proceeds to London and hears the various cries of the streets—'Hot peascodes,' 'Strawberry ripe,' 'Cherries in the rise' (*i.e.*, on the bough). Some of the tradesmen offered spice, pepper and saffron. In Cheapside he saw velvet, silk and lawn, and 'Paris thread, the fin'st in the land.' He goes by London Stone through Cannon Street, where drapers offered him much cloth. Others cried 'Hot sheep's feet,' 'Mackerel,' 'Rushes green.' In East Cheap there were ribs of beef, many a pie, and pewter pots in a heap. A taverner in Cornhill took him by the sleeve:—

'Sir,' saith he, 'will you our wine assay?'

He was now tired of his excursion, and walked to Billingsgate, where he prayed a bargeman to take him in his boat for nothing. All this is a groundless complaint; but he was also robbed at Westminster of his hood, in Cannon Street he was asked to buy a new one, and in Cornhill, among much stolen property, he saw his own hood hanging up for sale. This reminds one of the oft-repeated story of the man who, walking through Petticoat Lane, was robbed as he entered and found the object stolen from him ticketed for sale as he turned out of it. The countryman soon has enough of London and its ways, and conveys himself back into Kent, ending his account of adventures with these words:—

'Save London, and send true lawyers their meed.
For whoso wants money with them shall not speed.'

The words of the poets already referred to are of the greatest value to us, and we are grateful for the vivid pictures of mediæval life they have left us, but we have in Chaucer an ideal Londoner, far beyond the others in the charm of his writing, one who loved the city in which he lived and died.

Langland was too much occupied in denouncing the evils of his time to be able to see the good. Lydgate, Hoccleve and Gower also took partial views of the life around them. It is the great genius and large-heartedness of Chaucer that enables us to see the mixed good and evil.

Thanks to the labours of many scholars[61] we seem to know Chaucer, who died five centuries ago, better than many great men who have lived nearer our own days, and, strange to say, although we take him as a representative of the Middle Ages—and he was that—he was so imbued with the modern spirit that we cannot but feel that he is at one with us in his views of the life around him. He was associated with all parts of London, so that in a walk through the town with him we can illustrate our journey from the facts known of his life and with extracts from his works.

The facts of Chaucer's life, as written in official documents which have been found by enthusiastic searchers, are largely illustrative of London history, and it is only with these special facts that we are here concerned.

Geoffrey Chaucer was the son of a citizen and vintner of the city of London, and probably born at his father's house in Thames Street, in the Vintry, at or near the foot of Dowgate Hill. The house came into Geoffrey's possession after his father's death, when he sold it. There has been much discussion as to the date of his birth. It must have been after 1328, because we know that in that year his father was a bachelor. There is much to be said in favour of the supposition that he was born about 1340.

His family must have stood well in public esteem, with good connections, as the young man was early attached to the Court, and during his lifetime he filled several offices of distinction. His grandfather, Robert le Chaucer, was one of the collectors at the Port of London of the new customs upon wine, granted by the merchants of Aquitaine.

We have no information as to Geoffrey's schooling, but doubtless the position of his father was such that he would find a place at one of the schools that were attached to the chief religious houses of London. Fitz-Stephen tells us that the three chief schools were connected with St. Paul's, St. Martin's-le-Grand, and Holy Trinity, Aldgate. Neither of these schools is far from the Vintry, and Chaucer might have gone to either of them. St. Paul's is, of course, the nearest, but if he went to this school there ought to be some tradition of the fact still existing. There is no claim, however, to

Chaucer set up by the historians of the successor of the old school—the new foundation of Dean Colet.

Chaucer's early life was spent at Court and in diplomatic missions. In June 1374 he was appointed Comptroller of the Customs and Subsidy of wool skins and tanned hides in the Port of London. Attached to his office was the obligation to keep the records with his own hand and to be continuously present. In the previous May, looking out for a convenient residence, he rented Aldgate from the city authorities.

In *The Hous of Fame* (Bk. ii.) we have a picture of the poet at Aldgate after a hard day's work, writing of love (with his head aching) in his study at night:—

'That ther no tyding cometh to thee,
But of thy verray neyghèbores
That dwellen almost at thy dores,
Thou herest neither that ne this;
For when thy labour doon al is,
And hast y-maad thy rekenynges,
In stede of reste and newé thynges,
Thou gost hoom to thy hous anoon,
And also domb as any stoon,
Thou sittest at another boke,
Til fully daswèd is thy looke,
And lyvest thus as an herémyte,
Although theyn abstinence is lyte.'

Here, at Aldgate, Professor Hales tells us he wrote most of the works of his middle period.

'It was in the old Tower of Aldgate that he made himself a supreme master of the poetic craft, and turned his mastery to immortal account in the production of so exquisite a piece as *Troilus and Cressida*, and in the designing of a work that should give yet ampler expression to his manifold gifts and graces, to his maturest thought and his highest inspiration.'[62]

In 1382 he obtained an additional comptrollership, that of the Petty Customs of the Port of London, with leave to nominate a substitute on the understanding that he was responsible for him. In February 1385 the same privilege was allowed him in regard to his old comptrollership, and soon afterwards he left the gate house of Aldgate. In October 1386 he was elected Knight of the Shire for Kent, and then political troubles caused him to lose both his comptrollerships.

Professor Hales finds that the premises were granted in October 1386 to Richard Foster, possibly identical with Richard Forrester, who was one of Chaucer's proxies when he went abroad for a time in May 1378.[63]

The date of *The Legend of Good Women* is given as probably in the spring or summer of 1386, and as the house in which he was then living had a garden and an arbour, it could not have been the dwelling-house of Aldgate. Professor Hales believes that when the poet left the latter place he went to live at Greenwich.

'When that the sun out of the south gon weste,
And that this flower gon close and go to reste
For darkness of the night, for which she dredde,
Home to mine house full swiftly I me spedde,
To go to rest and early for to rise,
To see this flower spread, as I devise;
And in a little arbour that I have
That benched was on turves fresh ygrave,
I bad men shoulde me my couche make,
For dainty of the newe summer's sake,
I bad them strawen flowers on my bed.'[64]

The year 1387 has been fixed as the date of the framework of the Pilgrimage to Canterbury, starting from the Tabard, fast by the Ball in Southwark. Some of the Tales had certainly been written before this, but then it was that they were gathered together.

A very interesting note by Professor Hales, on the date of the *Canterbury Tales*, is printed in the *Athenæum* (April 8, 1893), in which some excellent reasons are given in support of this date: 'It has been and is by some still placed as late as 1393. But the evidence for placing it so late is extremely slight, if, indeed, there is any at all that bears investigation; whereas assuredly many things point to the year 1387 or thereabouts as the year of the pilgrimage and of Chaucer's immortal description of it.'[65]

In 1389 Chaucer was Clerk of the King's Works at the Palace of Westminster, the Tower of London and various royal manors. In 1390 he was employed to repair St. George's Chapel, Windsor, and to erect scaffolds at Smithfield for Richard II. and his Queen, Anne of Bohemia, for them to view a great tournament.

He was also appointed one of the Commission for the repair of the roadways on the banks of the river between Greenwich and Woolwich. About this time a great misfortune overtook the poet. In the pursuit of his duties, with the King's money in his purse to pay the workmen, he was robbed by highwaymen twice on the same day. The first time at Westminster of £10, and the second at Hatcham, near the 'foul oak,' of £9, 3s. 8d. This was a serious loss, and he was forgiven the amount by writ dated 6th January 1391.

In this same year Chaucer lost his lucrative clerkships, and we hear no more of him from the records till 1399, when he took a lease for fifty-three years of a tenement in the garden of St. Mary's Chapel, Westminster (on the site of Henry VII.'s Chapel). Here he died ten months after, on the 25th of October 1400. Thus ended the full and busy life of the many-sided poet, who was also man of science, soldier, esquire of the King's household, envoy on several foreign missions, Comptroller of Customs and Member of Parliament.

From this catalogue of Chaucer's offices and official movements we can see that a better guide to the London of his day could not be found. We may take it for granted that he walked over the greater part of the city continually.

As a boy he was an inhabitant of the Vintry, and from here he would walk to school either in a north-easterly direction to Holy Trinity, Aldgate, or in a westerly direction to St. Paul's or St. Martin's-le-Grand. Then at about seventeen years of age he was attached to the Court, and for some years he was a frequent attendant at the palace of Westminster.

When he settled to his duties at the Custom House he went backwards and forwards to Aldgate. Sometimes he would walk up Spurriers' Lane (now Water Lane), cross Tower Street, along Fenchurch Street, up Mark (then Mart) Lane to the gate. At other times he would probably find his way to Great Tower Hill, and pass through the Tower Postern to Little Tower Hill. From here he would walk northward among the trees between the wall and town ditch on the one side, and the Nunnery of the Minoresses on the other.

In 1381, at the time of the Peasants' Revolt, Chaucer was, we may suppose, in London, but he does not allude at all fully to the reign of terror which for four days overshadowed the city. The men of Essex were outside Aldgate waiting to be let in, and when the Bridgegate was opened to the men of Kent the eastern gate was also thrown open. One would wish to have known what Chaucer was doing then. Did he look out of the window of his house and watch the threatening crowd, or had he gone to the support of the King in the Tower.

He only makes a passing allusion to the murder of the Flemings in the *Nun's Priest's Tale*:—

'Certes he Jakke Straw and his meyné,
Ne maden schoutes never half so scrille,
Whan that they wolden eny Fleming kille,
As thilke day was maad upon the fox.' (ll. 574-577.)

Chaucer must often have wandered outside Aldgate, and after a hard day's work he would naturally stroll along the wide and pleasant Eastern Road. He introduces the Benedictine Nunnery of Stratford atte Bowe in his description of the prioress (Madam Eglentyne):—

'And Frenssh she spak ful faire and fetisly—
After the scole of Stratford atté Bowe,
For Frenssh of Parys was to hire unknowe.'

And certainly he must have passed over the bridge built by Queen Matilda in the twelfth century—which gave its name to the village.

In 1389, after he had left Aldgate, and when he was probably settled at Westminster, of which palace he was clerk of the works, he was often called to the Tower (close by his old office at the Custom House), to see to the necessary repairs. Like others, Chaucer probably used the river as often as possible, for many of the streets were not very pleasant to walk along, but in carrying out his many official duties he was obliged to visit all parts of the city, and he must therefore have left few streets within the walls untraversed.

We have chiefly noted the places on the east side of London, and we can therefore now pass to the west.

The controversy that raged over the question of the respective claims of the families of Scrope and Grosvenor to a certain coat-of-arms is of high interest to the herald, but in the voluminous evidence the lover of Chaucer, and of London, scarcely expects to find a statement by the poet himself as to his being in Friday Street on a certain day, and what he saw there. The whole account of the poet's examination is of the greatest interest.

'Geffray Chaucere, Esquier, of the age of forty years and more, armed twenty-seven years, for the side of Sir Richard Lescrop, sworn and examined, being asked if the arms, azure a bend or, belong or ought to pertain to the said Sir Richard by right and heritage, said, Yes; for he saw him so armed in Fraunce [1359], before the town of Retters [qy. Réthel], and Sir Henry Lescrop armed in the same arms with a white label, and with banner; and the said Sir Richard armed in the entire arms, azure a bend or, and so during the whole expedition, until the said Geffray was taken. Being asked how he knew that the said arms belonged to the said Sir Richard, said that he had heard old knights and esquires say that they had had continual possession of the said arms; and that he had seen them displayed on banners, glass painting and vestments, and commonly called the arms of Scrope. Being asked whether he had ever heard of any interruption or challenge made by Sir

OLD ST. PAUL'S.
(*From a drawing by Walter H. Godfrey, reconstructed from information obtained from leading authorities.*)

Robert Grosvenor, or his ancestors, said, No: but that he was once in Friday Street, London, and walking up the street he observed a new sign hanging out, with these arms thereon, and inquired what inn that was that had hung out these arms of Scrope? And one answered, saying: "They are not hung out, Sir, for the arms of Scrope, nor painted there for those arms; but they are painted and put there by a knight of the county of Chester, called Sir Robert Grosvenor," and that was the first time he ever heard speak of Sir Robert Grosvenor, or his ancestors, or of anyone bearing the name of Grosvenor.'[66]

Friday Street was close by old St. Paul's, the glory of the city, which was magnificent within and without. When Chaucer knew it, the fine tomb of Sir John Beauchamp (d. 1358), constable of Dover Castle, in the middle aisle of the nave, was new. This monument was the chief object in the nave, and came to be called incorrectly Duke Humphry's Tomb, and the nave from it was styled Duke Humphry's Walk. The stately tomb of John of Gaunt (d. 1399), which was later on the most prominent object in the choir, was probably not erected in Chaucer's lifetime.

The old Cathedral was full of chantries, as were the other churches of London. The number of chantry priests gave great offence, as appears in *Piers Plowman*, and the works of the other poets. The Poor Parson is described in the Prologue of the *Canterbury Tales* as attending to his own flock, and not performing the services of the dead at other shrines:—

'He sette not his benefice to hire,
And lette his sheep accombred in the mire,
And ran unto London, into Seint Paules,
To seken him a chaunterie for soules.'

Outside Newgate, Chaucer went up Cow Lane (now King Street) to Smithfield, the open space appropriated to tournaments, markets and shows, to prepare for the jousts to be held before the King and his Queen in 1390.

Passing from London to Westminster we come to the Mews (the site of the present National Gallery), which Chaucer had for a time under his charge. He settled in the precincts of Westminster Abbey, and there passed away. It has been erroneously stated, on the authority of Stow, that Chaucer was first buried in the cloisters. This is refuted by Caxton's distinct statement that the body was first buried in front of the Chapel of St. Benedict. In 1555 or 1556 it was removed to its present position in the tomb prepared for it by Nicholas Brigham, where it has become the central object of the world-renowned Poets' Corner.[67] The last place to be mentioned, and the one which he has chiefly immortalised, is the High Street, Southwark, called also Long Southwark. Here was the Tabard,[68] where gathered the Canterbury Pilgrims, who set out on their pilgrimage under the leadership of Harry Bailly. Bailly was a real personage, and at one time Member of Parliament for Southwark.

Of all the pictures drawn by Chaucer, the portraits of the pilgrims in the Prologue to the *Canterbury Tales* are the most valuable for our present purpose, as showing us the men and women who were to be seen daily in the streets of London.

It is a difficult matter to appraise the relative positions of our great authors, but probably the true test of immortality is the creation of living characters. It is largely the dramatic power displayed in the Prologue to the *Canterbury Tales* which places Chaucer by the side of Shakespeare.

CHAPTER IV

The River and the Bridge

THE river has made London, and London has acknowledged its obligations to the Thames. It was the Silent Highway along which the chief traffic of the city passed during the Middle Ages, and, probably, the roads of London would have been better if the water carriage had not been so good. The river continued to be the Silent Highway until the nineteenth century, when it lost its high position. With the construction of the Thames Embankment the river again took its proper place as the centre of London, but it did not again become its main artery.

We have seen in the previous chapter how the poet Gower met King Richard II. near Westminster and was summoned to the royal barge.

Fitz-Stephen gives a vivid description of the sports on the Thames: 'In the Easter holidays they play at a game resembling a naval engagement. A target is firmly fastened to the trunk of a tree which is fixed in the middle of the river, and in the prow of a boat, driven along by oars and the current, a young man, who is to strike the target with his lance; if in hitting it he break his lance, and keep his position unmoved, he gains his point, and attains his desire; but if his lance be not shivered by the blow he is tumbled into the river, and his boat passes by, driven along by its own motion. Two boats, however, are placed there, one on each side of the target, and in them a number of young men to take up the striker when he first emerges from the

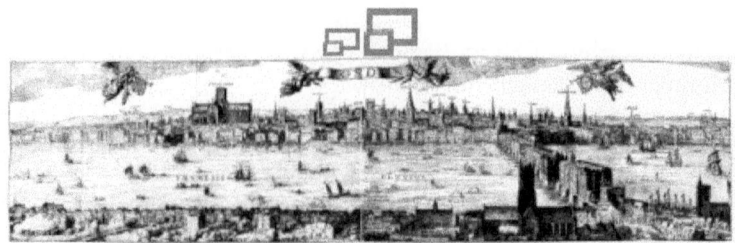

VISSCHER'S VIEW OF LONDON, A.D. 1616.
Section (reduced) from the Re-production by the Topographical Society of London.

stream.... On the bridge, and in balconies on the banks of the river, stand the spectators.' Four centuries after this Stow describes a somewhat similar scene: 'I have also in the summer season seen some upon the river of Thames rowed in wherries, with staves in their bands, flat at the fore end, running one against another, and for the most part, one or both overthrown, and well ducked.'

One of the most remarkable incidents in the life of the Middle Ages is connected with the history of that highly-placed lady, the unfortunate Eleanor Cobham, Duchess of Gloucester, whose enemies succeeded in condemning her to do penance in London in three open spaces on three several days. She was brought by water from Westminster, and on the 13th of November 1441 was put on shore at the Temple Bridge; on the 15th at the Old Swan; and again, on the 17th, at Queenhithe, and from these landing-places she walked to the place of penance. The Old Swan, which stood near London Bridge, just where its successor now stands, can be traced further back than the reign of Henry VI., for a tavern with the sign of the Swan is mentioned in a deed of Edward II.'s time.

The old Chronicles are full of references to what took place on the river. Thus Edward Halle has a vivid picture of how the Archbishop of York, after leaving the widow of Edward IV. in the Sanctuary at Westminster, returned home to York Place at dawn of day, 'and when he opened his windows and looked on the Thames he might see the river full of boats of the Duke of Gloucester [Richard III.], his servants, watching that no person should go to sanctuary, nor none should pass unsearched.'

Cavendish, in his *Life of Wolsey*, shows us two prelates talking confidentially in the cardinal's barge: 'Thus this court passed from session to session, and day to day, in so much that a certain day the King sent for my lord the breaking up one day of the court to come to him into Bridewall. And to accomplish his commandment he went unto him, and being there with him in communication in his grace's privy chamber from eleven until twelve of the clock and past at noon, my lord came out and departed from the King, and took his barge at the Black Friars, and so went to his house at Westminster. The Bishop of Carlisle, being with him in his barge, said unto him (wiping the sweat from his face), "Sir," quoth he, "it is a very hot day." "Yea," quoth my lord cardinal, "if ye had been as well chafed as I have been within this hour, ye would say it were very hot." '

The river swarmed with watermen, and these men had their songs and choruses. A favourite song was in honour of Sir John Norman (Mayor in 1454), who first broke the rule of riding to Westminster on Mayor's day, and 'rowed thither by water,' a practice which continued for many years, and might now be revived with advantage.

'Row the boat, Norman, row to thy leman.'

We can see from this how much, both of the business and pleasure of London, took place on the Thames. It reminds us vividly of the busy life on the canals of Venice.

The river was the highway of business as well of pleasure, and the intimate relations between England and Normandy after the Conquest naturally encouraged commerce between the Continent and England, and London rapidly became the centre of this trade. Ships came here from Flanders, Germany, Gascony, Italy, and also from Norway. Wharves lined the sides of the Thames, and each class of goods was landed at a wharf set apart for a special nationality.

In Henry II.'s reign London and Bristol became the chief commercial ports of the kingdom, the former trading with Germany and the central ports of the Continent, and the latter with the Scandinavian countries and with Ireland.

The Normans had special privileges, and Mr. Horace Round points out that the charter of Henry Duke of the Normans (afterwards Henry II. of England) to the citizens of Rouen, 1150-1151, confers to them their port at Dowgate, as they had held it from the days of Edward the Confessor. Mr. Round adds that this is a fact unknown to English historians.[69]

The early history of Queenhithe, for many years the chief rival to Billingsgate, is somewhat difficult to follow. In the Saxon period it appears to have belonged to one Edred, who gave the wharf his name, by which it continued to be called for some years after the Conquest. It was granted to Holy Trinity within Aldgate by William de Ypre, who received it from King Stephen. After some time it again came into the possession of the King, and John is said to have given it to his mother Eleanor, Queen of Henry II., after whom it received its name of Queenhithe. By some means not recorded the *Ripa Regina* came into the possession of Richard Earl of Cornwall, who in 1246 granted it to John Gisors, then Mayor, and the Commons of London to farm at an annual rent of £50. Henry III. confirmed this grant, and the custody of the hithe was thereupon committed to the Sheriffs, and half a year's rent had been allowed, as the place appears to have fallen into decay, owing probably to the death of John de Storteford during his shrievalty. According to Stow, 'Edward II. in the first year of his reign gave to Margaret, wife to Piers de Gavestone, forty-three pounds twelve shillings and ninepence halfpenny farthing out of the rent of London to be received of the Queen's hithe.'

Queenhithe was the usual landing-place for wine, wool, hides, corn, firewood, fish, and all kinds of commodities. It was probably to Queenhithe that the wine fleet which brought to London the produce of the vineyards of the banks of the Moselle was bound. In the *Liber Custumarum* there is a full account of the yearly visit of this fleet, and the regulations as to its arrival at the New Wear, in the vicinity of Yanlade (the present Yantlet Creek), at the mouth of the Medway, which was the limit of the civic jurisdiction of the Thames. Here it was the duty of the fleet of adventurous hulks and keels 'to arrange themselves in due order and raise their ensign; the crews being at liberty, if so inclined, to sing their kiriele or song of praise and thanksgiving, 'according to the old law,' until London Bridge was reached. Arrived here, and the drawbridge duly raised, they were for a certain time to lie moored off the wharf.... Here they were to remain at their moorings two ebbs and a flood; during which period the merchants were to sell no part of their cargo, it being the duty of one of the Sheriffs and the King's Chamberlain to board each vessel in the meantime.... The two ebbs and a flood expired, and the officials having duly made their purchases or declined to do so, the wine-ship was allowed to lie alongside the wharf, the tuns of wine being disposed of under certain regulations, apparently meant as a precaution against picking and choosing, to such merchants as might present themselves as customers, those of London having the priority, and those of Winchester coming next.'[70] The boats were bound to leave London by the end of forty days.

Mr. Riley refers to the fondness of the merchants in the Middle Ages for music on board ship, and quotes from M. Michel (*Recherches sur les Etoffes*, etc., tome ii. p. 63) the following:—

'En mer sempaignent, et drescerent lor voilles;
Li jugleor leanz les esbanoient.'

'They put to sea, and set their sails;
The jongleurs on board amused them.'

Another passage from the *Roman de Tristan*, tome ii. p. 64, 1375-1378, quoted by Riley, is also very much to the point:—

'A sun batel en va amunt,
Dreit a Lundres, desuz le punt;
Sa marchandise iloc descovre,
Ses dras de seie pleie e ovre.'

'On board his bark he goes straight to London, beneath the bridge; his merchandise he there shows, his cloths of silk smooths and opens out.'

Mr Riley gives an interesting account of the localities adjoining the northern banks of the Thames in the fourteenth century:—

'The banks of the Thames from the Postern of Petit Wales [near the Tower], so far probably as the Friars Preachers, or Black Friars, near the entrance of the Fleet River, seem to have been intersected in these times by numberless small lanes, which, themselves public property, ran from Thames Street, by the side of a private residence or other edifice, and led to the owner's wharf in front of his dwelling-house; these wharfs again, in some instances, being separated by water-gates, through which apparently the public had a right to claim, as an easement, right of passage. From many of the wharfs there also projected bridges or jetties into the river, for the same purposes as the stairs of modern times.'[71]

Many of the wharves on the Thames were known as gates besides Billingsgate, as Ebbgate, identical with the present Old Swan Lane and Wharf, Upper Thames Street, and Oystergate, on the site of the north end of the present London Bridge. The latter was the principal place for the sale of shell-fish, which was only to be sold 'from the way of London Bridge towards the west, unto the corner of the wall of the Church of St. Mary Magdalene.'[72] Oystergate was also a place of great resort for the sellers of rushes, who paid a small rent for their standing.

We learn from Fitz-Stephen that 'London formerly had walls and towers in like manner in the south, but that most excellent river the Thames, which abounds with fish, and in which the tide ebbs and flows, runs on that side, and has in a long space of time washed down, undermined and subverted the walls in that part.' Whether there were gates or not along the river front of London, there can be little doubt that there were not structures at all the places named gates, many of these were doubtless merely ways. This use of the word gate is common enough in the South, as in Ramsgate, Margate, Sandgate, etc.

There appear to have been constant attempts made by the landowners on the Thames to close the lanes leading to the river, thus preventing the free access of the public. Special complaint was made before the Mayor and Sheriffs in 1360 against the Prior of St. John of Jerusalem for closing the right-of-way through the Temple. This place having come into the possession of the Knights Hospitallers of St. John after the suppression of the Order of Knights Templars. The evidence of John de Hydyngham and eleven others was taken—'Who say upon their oath, that time out of mind the commonalty of the city aforesaid have been wont to have free ingress and egress with horses and carts from sunrise to sunset, for carrying and carting all manner of victuals and wares therefrom to the water of Thames, and from the said water of Thames to the city aforesaid through the great gate of the Templars, situate within Temple Bar, in the ward aforesaid, in the suburb of London; that the possessors of the Temple were wont, and by right ought to maintain a bridge at the water aforesaid' [a pier or jetty for landing called Tempelbrigge]. 'They say also, that the Prior of St. John of Jerusalem in England, who is the possessor of the Temple aforesaid, molests the citizens of the said city, so that they cannot have their free ingress and egress through the gate aforesaid, as of old they were wont to have.'[73]

  The prior did not like this interference with his doings on the part of the city, and in 1374 he obtained from Edward III. a royal order to stay proceedings. The order, addressed to the Mayor, Recorder and Aldermen of London, after recapitulating the terms of complaint, proceeds: 'We, deeming it not to be consonant with reason that this matter, seeing that it concerns you and the commonalty aforesaid, should be discussed before you, inasmuch as a party ought not to be judge in his own cause, and taking into consideration that if the bridge aforesaid, which has been intended for the advantage and easement of the nobles and others coming to our Parliaments and Councils, and wishing to reach their barges and boats, these should be broken by the laying of stone and timber thereon, it would be greatly to the prejudice of such persons; and desiring for the reasons aforesaid, that this matter shall be discussed and determined before our Council, where justice therein unto you as well as to the prior aforesaid may speedily be done; do command you, that you appear before our said Council at Westminster, on that day month after Easter Day next to come.'[74] This question of the exclusion of the common people from certain wharves and stairs continued for many years to be a burning one. In 1417 an Ordinance of the Mayor and Aldermen was issued forbidding this exclusion, which commences as follows: 'Whereas heretofore, and now also from day to day, many persons dwelling in the city and the suburbs of London, more consulting and attending to their private profit and advantage than to the common good and convenience, do hold certain wharves and stairs on the bank of the Thames, which are held by encroachment upon, and are situate on, the common soil and the course of the water, without having any licence or paying anything to the community for the same; and then, the same being by favour obtained and colourably appropriated, have mixed up their own and separate soil and land therewith; and what is even worse, from day to day these persons do make new customs and imposts upon the poor common people, who time out of mind have there fetched and taken up their water, and washed their clothes, and done other things for their own needs, maliciously interfering with them in their said franchise, and demanding and taking from such as resort thereto, from some one halfpenny, and from others one penny, two or more, by the quarter, to the great injury of all the commonalty, and expressly against the good usages and ancient customs of all the city.' After this preamble, the Mayor and Aldermen, with the assent of the Commons, 'ordained and established, for all time to come, that no person who dwells on the bank of the Thames, or other person whatsoever, having or holding any wharf or stair, situate or encroaching upon the common soil, to which there has been, or been accustomed to be, common resort of the people heretofore for such needs as aforesaid, shall from henceforth disturb, hinder, or molest, any one in fetching, drawing and taking water, or in beating and washing their clothes, or in doing or executing other reasonable things and needs there; or shall demand or take privily or openly, from any person any manner of sum or piece of money, or other thing whatsoever for custom.'[75]

Many of these alleys and lanes were left in a very objectionable condition, but the consideration of their state must be postponed for chapter 7 on the Health and Sanitation of London. In spite of all the recorded impurities of the streets the water of the river was pure, as may be proved from the fact that fishing was general. In 1343 an Inquisition was held before the Mayor and Aldermen as to the use of unlawful nets, or those whose meshes were less than 2 inches wide, when it was found that four nets were good and were to be given back to the owners, and four were false and to be burnt. The custom of the city was that the meshes of the nets should be two inches wide at least, so that small fish could pass through.[76]

In the next year certain fishmongers were appointed inspectors 'to make scrutiny as to false nets placed in the water of Thames, from the place called "Yenlete" [Yantlet] on the east, as far as the bridge of Stanes on the west, for taking the small fish, to the destruction of the fish of such water; and to bring such nets to the Guildhall when found.'[77]

In another document, also of the year 1344, three nets are mentioned by name, all of which were found to be false, and were burnt near the Stone Cross by the north door of St. Paul's, in the high street of Chepe—these were a draynet belonging to the Abbot of Stratford, a second net called a codnet, belonging to Robert Pesok of Plumstede, and third net called a kidel, claimed by no one.[78]

A codnet was a net with a cod or pouch containing a stone for sinking the net (also called a pursnet), and a kidel was a net used in kidels or weirs. There were several different classes of fishermen, as 'trinkermen,' who used trinks or nets attached to posts or anchors for taking fish, and petermen, who used a broom in fishing, 'beating the bush.'[79] There are many other references to the burning of false nets in the City Archives. From certain regulations of the year 1388, we learn that 'no man shall fish in the Thames with any nets but those of the Assize ordained at the

Guildhall; and that only at the proper seasons. And that no one shall fish near to the wharves in London, between the Temple Bridge and the Tower, within a distance of twenty fathoms.'[80]

The Bridge.—It is supposed that during the early years of the Roman occupation there was a ferry across from London to Southwark, but that a bridge was built when Roman London had become a place of importance. We have already seen that a wooden bridge existed during the Saxon period. This must have been constantly rebuilt, and the last wooden bridge continued for many years after the Norman Conquest. The first stone bridge was commenced in the year 1176, under the superintendence of Peter de Colechurch, chaplain of St. Mary Colechurch, a building which stood in the Old Jewry until the time of the Great Fire, when it was destroyed. Peter died in 1205, and was buried in the crypt of the chapel built over the centre pier of the bridge and dedicated to St. Thomas of Canterbury. Here the chaplain's bones were found in 1832, when the old bridge was cleared away after the opening of the new bridge. So little public interest was taken in relics of the past at this time that the bones were sacrilegiously, flung into a barge along with the accumulated rubbish and destroyed by careless workmen.

The building of the stone bridge was a long operation, and in 1201 King John entrusted its completion to a Frenchman named Isembert. The King seems to have made a careful choice, for the Frenchman had already shown his skill by the erection of fine bridges in the French cities of Saintes and La Rochelle. M. Jusserand, in his *English Wayfaring Life in the Middle Ages*, quotes from the Original Patent, published by Hearne in his edition of the *Liber Niger Scaccarii* (1771, vol. i. p. 470). Jusserand also quotes from Hearne as to a series of Letters Patent relating to the maintenance of the bridge. John ordered certain taxes to be devoted to this purpose, and a patent of Henry III. was addressed 'to the brothers and chaplains of the Chapel of St. Thomas on London Bridge, and to other persons living on the same bridge,' to inform them that the officers of St. Katharine's Hospital by the Tower would receive the revenues and take charge of the repairs of the bridge for five years.

After the Battle of Evesham in 1265, when the city was at the King's mercy, Henry III. granted his Queen the custody of the bridge: 'Alianore, by the grace of God, Queen of England, Lady of Ireland, Duchess of Aquitaine, and by our lord the King Henry, Warden of the Bridge House.' The Queen continued to enjoy the rents and lands belonging to the bridge for nearly six years, during which time the repair of the bridge was neglected. Realising at length how matters stood, she restored it to the citizens, who, on 1st September 1271, elected again their own wardens.[81]

Early in the reign of Edward I. (1281) a patent was issued ordering a general collection throughout the kingdom on account of the bad condition of the bridge. A tariff of tolls was also issued, and pontage was exacted from all vessels for the passage of which the drawbridge was raised. One William Cross, a fishmonger, was 'sworn to well and faithfully receive all issues of rents of London Bridge, and also all other money accruing to the said bridge from whatever cause ... and to expend the same well and faithfully for the use and benefit of the aforesaid bridge.'[82]

In the 26 of Edward I. the rents of a house called 'Le Hales' were appropriated for the support of London Bridge, and this is recorded in the *Liber Custumarum*.[83] It is not known where this house was situated. Riley conjectures that it was a great house in Stocks Market, but Dr. Sharpe suggests that it is just as likely to have been one of a large number of houses which Henry le Galeys (or Waleys) erected by licence of the King (Anno 10 Edw. I.) near Old Change and St. Paul's, the profits of which were also devoted to the support of the bridge.[84] A stone was fixed before each of these tenements in token of the duty of the tenants to repair the bridge, but these appear to have been removed in the same reign by Walter Hervy, appruator of the city, a title which Riley translated as improver.[85]

The bridge was built on piles, and must have been solidly constructed, for although it needed from the first a great deal of cobbling, and underwent much alteration, it survived almost to our own day. It consisted of twenty arches, nineteen of stone, and one of wood—the drawbridge. By this drawbridge was the tower or storehouse, upon which the heads of traitors were set up. This became decayed, and was taken down in April 1577. The heads were removed and set on the gate at the Bridge-foot towards Southwark. On the 28th August Sir John Langley, Lord Mayor, laid the first stone of a foundation for a new tower, in the same place, which tower was finished in September 1579.[86] The great wonder of the bridge was the beautiful wooden structure, called Nonesuch House, which stood on the seventh and eighth arches from the Southwark side, and gave its name to the Nonesuch lock.

The great weight of the buildings caused occasional sinkings and a general insecurity. In 1481 it is recorded that a block of buildings toppled over into the river. In 1633 a fire swept from one end of the bridge to the other, and many of the houses were destroyed, which were not rebuilt. In 1757-1758 all the remaining houses were cleared away in order to make the structure more secure.

The bridge was one of the chief sights of London, and a great deal of history has grown up about it, but it would require a volume to do justice to these circumstances. One of the most curious of these was the duel between Sir David Lindsay, Earl of Crawfurd, and John Lord Welles (fifth Baron), Ambassador at the Scottish Court in 1390. Lord Crawfurd chose the place, and, furnished with a safe conduct from Richard II., came from Scotland to London for this special purpose. The duel took place in this apparently inappropriate locality in the presence of a great concourse of sightseers.

Most of the travellers in England who have written on the subject speak of the bridge with high praise. Frederick Duke of Wirtemberg, who visited this country in 1592, was pleased with what he saw, and his secretary wrote: 'Over the river at London there is a beautiful long bridge, with quite splendid, handsome and well-built houses, which are occupied by merchants of consequence. Upon one of the towers, nearly in the middle of the bridge, are stuck up about thirty-four heads of persons of distinction, who had in former times been condemned and beheaded for creating riots and from other causes.' It will be seen from this passage that when the new tower was built the heads which had been removed during the rebuilding to the Bridge-foot were taken back to the new tower. Six years later Hentzner wrote of London Bridge as 'a bridge of stone, 800 feet in length, of wonderful work; it is supported upon 20 piers of square stone, 60 feet high and 30 broad, joined by arches of about 20 feet diameter. The whole is covered on each side with houses, so disposed as to have the appearance of a continued street, not at all of a bridge.' Correr, the Venetian Ambassador in 1610, states that the bridge was so narrow that it was very difficult for two coaches meeting to pass each other without danger.[87]

Englishmen were not behindhand in singing the praises of the bridge; thus Lyly wrote in *Euphues and his England*: 'Among all the straunge and beautiful showes, mee thinketh there is none so notable as the bridge which crosseth the Theames, which is in manner of a continuall streete, well replenyshed with large and stately houses on both sides, and situate upon twentie arches, whereof each one is made of excellent free stone squared, everie one of them being three score foote in height, and full twentie in distaunce one from another.'

The chapel on the bridge had an endowment for two priests or chaplains, four clerks and other brethren, with certain chantries annexed. A dwelling-house was afterwards attached to the chapel, which, at the close of the thirteenth century, was known as the Bridge House. In the year 1298 John de Leuesham [Lewisham], brother of the London 'Bridge House,' was made bailiff of the manor of Lewisham, 'the proceeds of which were then, as they still are, devoted to the maintenance and repair of the bridge.'[88]

In the folklore of bridges the frequent practice in the Middle Ages of building a chapel forms a special feature of the subject. There are several instances still remaining, one of which is the chapel of the old bridge at Bradford-on-Avon.

The waterway of the Thames was obstructed by the bridge, which formed a sort of lock to keep the waters in the upper portion of the river. The widest of the arches was 36 feet, and some were too narrow for the passage of boats of any kind. The resistance caused to so large a body of water on the rise and fall of the tide by the contraction of its channel produced a fall or rapid under the bridge. 'With the flood-tide it was impossible, and with the ebb-tide dangerous to pass through or shoot the arches of the bridge.' In the latter case prudent passengers landed above bridge, generally at the Old Swan Stairs, and walked to some wharf, generally Billingsgate.

In 1428, according to Stow, the Duke of Norfolk was like to be drowned passing from Saint Mary Overy Stairs through London Bridge. His barge was overset and thirty persons drowned. In *A Chronicle of London* (edited by Nicolas) we read 'as God wolde, the duke hymself and too or iij othere gentylmen seeynge that myschief, leped upon the pyles and so were saved through helpe of them that weren above the brigge, with castyng down of ropes.' Many such accidents were constantly occurring, so that there was probably truth in one of Ray's Proverbs: 'London Bridge was made for wise men to go over and fools to go under.' That boats were frequently overturned is proved by Norden's View of London Bridge, in which boats, bottom upwards, fill the foreground.

THE TOWER OF LONDON.

CHAPTER V

The King's Palace—The Tower

THE Tower of London has existed for over eight centuries, and long before the Conquest the site was occupied by a Roman fortification. It is the most time-honoured building in Great Britain, and probably the foremost building (not a ruin) in the world.

With so much in London that is new, it is a source of the deepest pride to every Londoner that there is a relic of the past of unequalled interest, on whose walls are written the chief incidents of the history of England. The name has long been a puzzle, but Mr. Horace Round has explained it, and thus thrown a fresh light upon the study of Norman military architecture.

There were two different kinds of fortified places during the mediæval period, viz., (1) the Roman 'castrum,' or 'castellum,' which survived in the fortified enclosure, and (2) the mediæval 'motte,' or 'tour,' which survived in the central keep. When the 'tour' coalesced with the 'castellum,' a name was required for the entire fortress. Sometimes the keep was added to the castle, and sometimes the castle to the keep. It was then a question which word should prevail,—'tour' (turris), or chastel (castellum). Generally, the word castle has prevailed, but the respective strongholds in the capitals of Normandy and England were the 'Tour de Rouen,' and the 'Tower of London.'[89]

Gray alludes to the 'towers of Julius,' and Shakespeare's reference to the place is equally erroneous:—

'*Prince Edward.* I do not like the Tower of any place,
Did Julius Cæsar build that place, my lord?
Buckingham. He did, my gracious lord, begin that place,
Which since succeeding ages have re-edified.
Prince Edward. Is it upon record, or else reported
Successively from age to age, he built it?
Buckingham. Upon record, my gracious lord.'
(*Richard III.*, act iii. sc. i.)

Of course, Julius Cæsar had nothing to do with the Tower, but the Roman remains that have been discovered on the site prove that this grand strategical position had been utilised from the early period of London's history.

Mr. George T. Clark writes: 'When, having crossed the Thames, the Conqueror marched in person to complete the investment of London, he found that ancient city resting upon the left bank of its river, protected on its landward side by a strong wall, a Roman work, with mural towers and an exterior ditch.'[90]

In 1777 some Roman coins were discovered, and a double wedge of silver, inscribed 'Ex officina Honorii,' which makes the conjecture probable, that at this early period, as in later times, the buildings on the site of the Tower were used as a mint.

William the Conqueror was crowned in 1066, and Mr. Clark says that 'it was from Barking, immediately after the ceremony, that he directed the actual commencement of the works, which were no doubt at first a deep ditch and strong palisade; for the keep, probably the earliest work in masonry, appears not to have been begun till twelve or fourteen years later.'[91]

The keep (known later as the White Tower) was built by Gundulf, a monk of Bec, who in 1077, soon after his arrival in England, was consecrated Bishop of Rochester. We learn from the *Textus Roffensis*, written about the year 1143, that Gundulf, while employed upon the Tower, lodged at the house of Eadmer Anhoende, a burgess of London, but he is not supposed to have commenced the building until 1078.

A great work such as the construction of the Tower of London took many years to complete. It is supposed that although the Conqueror, to a great extent, planned the fortress, he did not build more than the inner ward. The existing 'curtain' of the inner ward (9 to 12 feet thick, and from 39 to 40 feet high) is thought by Clark to be the work of William Rufus.

In November 1091 there was a violent storm which did immense damage in London. Stow says in his Chronicle that 'the Tower of London was also broken,' and in the *Survey* he further writes that the Tower was sore shaken by the tempest of wind, but was repaired by William Rufus and Henry I. Clark doubts this, but adds that the outworks, both wall and towers, if in course of construction, with scaffolding about them, probably suffered severely. He further writes: 'The Tower, therefore, of the close of the reign of Rufus, and of those of Henry I., and Stephen, was probably composed of the White Tower, with a palace ward upon its south-east side, and a wall, probably that we now see, and certainly along its general course, including what is known as the inner ward. No doubt there was a ditch, but probably not a very formidable one.'[92]

Fitz-Stephen is not very full in his description of the Tower. He merely says: 'On the east stands the Palatine Tower, a fortress of great size and strength, the court and walls of which are erected upon a very deep foundation, the mortar used in the building being tempered with the blood of beasts.'

The Tower is believed to owe much to Henry III., who made extensive alterations and additions. The new works were unpopular among the citizens, and as some of them were unfortunate, a legend came into existence to account for the misfortune. St. Thomas's Tower and the 'Traitor's Gate' beneath it were in course of construction in 1240, when on St. George's night the gateway and wall fell down. They were at once re-erected, but in the following year they again fell down. The story, as told by Matthew Paris, is that on the night of the second fall a certain grave and reverend priest saw a robed archbishop, cross in hand, who gazed sternly upon the walls, with which the King was then girdling the Tower, and striking them sharply, asked: 'Why build ye there?' on which the newly-built work fell, as though shattered by an earthquake. The priest, too alarmed to accost the prelate, addressed himself to the shade of an attendant clerk: 'Who, then, is the archbishop?' 'St. Thomas the Martyr,' was the answer, 'by birth a citizen, who resents these works, undertaken in scorn, and to the prejudice of the citizens, and destroys them beyond the power of restoration!' On which the priest remarked: 'What outlay and labour of the hands he has destroyed!' 'Had it been,' said the clerk, 'simply that the starving and needy artificers thence promised themselves food, it had been tolerable; but seeing that the works were undertaken, not for the defence of the realm, but to the hurt of the citizens, even had not St. Thomas destroyed them, they had been swept away utterly by St. Edmund, his successor.' This was Edmund of Abingdon, who died in 1240. The works were resumed, and in spite of the powerful opposition of St. Thomas, they were completely successful, and the rebuilding was strong and satisfactory.

The outer ward is supposed to have been completed by Henry III. It is a strip of from 20 feet to 110 feet in breadth, which completely surrounds the inner ward, and is itself contained within the ditch, of which its wall forms the scarp.

The Tower has been (1) a fortress, and so it remains to the present day; (2) a palace, and (3) a prison. We can now consider it under these three aspects, merely mentioning in passing that it was also a mint, an armoury, and a record office.

The Tower as a Fortress.—It was regarded as impregnable in the reign of Stephen, when it was specially required by the King as a fortress, and during the whole mediæval period it was always a place of strong defence. It does not appear ever to have endured a siege of any importance, but if it had, it would doubtless have successfully resisted attack.

The Byward Tower is the great gatehouse of the outer ward, and the Middle Tower is its outwork. There was formerly a drawbridge across the ditch or moat, where now there is a stone bridge 130 feet wide. The gateway to the Bloody or Garden Tower is the main entrance to the inner ward. The inner ward is enclosed within a curtain wall having four sides, twelve mural towers, and a gatehouse. Wakefield Tower, known also as the Record Tower and as the Hall Tower, is, in its lower storey, next in antiquity to the White Tower.

Commencing with Wakefield, and passing westward, the towers are Bloody (where the Duke of Clarence is supposed to have been drowned in Malmsey, and the two sons of Edward IV. smothered), Bell (so called from an alarm bell in the little turret), Beauchamp (from Thomas de Beauchamp, Earl of Warwick, and also called Cobham Tower, after Lord Cobham), Devereux (after Robert Devereux, Earl of Essex, also called 'Robyn the Devyll's Tower,') Flint, Bowyer (so called because it was the residence and workshop of the royal maker of bows), Brick (previously Burbidge), Martin (or Jewel, at one time styled Brick Tower), Constable's, Broad Arrow, Salt (meaning saltpetre; in the sixteenth century it was known as Julius Cæsar's Tower), and Lanthorn (called in 1532 the New Tower; it was pulled down in 1788, after a fire).

The wall of the outer ward has upon it bold drum bastions at the angles of the north front; and the south or Thames front is protected by five mural towers, of which one covers the landgate and one the watergate, and two others are connected with posterns. These towers are Develin (called 'Galighmaies Tower' in 4 Ric. II.), Well, Cradle, St. Thomas's (over Traitor's Gate), and Byward.

Mr. Clark writes: 'The Tower, at the commencement of the present century, was an extraordinary jumble of ancient and later buildings, the towers and walls being almost completely encrusted by the small official dwellings by which the area was closely occupied. A great fire in 1841 removed the unsightly armoury of James II. and William III. on the north of the inner ward, but the authorities at the time were not ripe for a fire. The armoury was replaced by a painfully-durable Tudor barrack, and the repairs and additions were made with little reference to the character of the fortress. More recently, the general improvement in public taste has made its way even into the Tower.'[93]

The Tower is still a fortress. Each night the mediæval ceremony of locking the gates takes place; after which no one can enter without the password, and this after the manner at fortresses is changed daily. The password is always communicated to the Lord Mayor, who each quarter receives a list containing the password for each day in the coming three months. Residents in the Tower can enter until twelve midnight, when the wickets are locked by the yeoman on 'watch duty' and no one is allowed to enter after that hour, unless they give the password.

At a few minutes before eleven the yeoman porter takes his keys and applies to the serjeant for the 'escort for the keys.' The serjeant acquaints the officer, and the officer placing the guard under arms, furnishes a serjeant and four men. Two of the men are unarmed. Their duty is to assist in closing the gates, and to carry the ancient lantern, which contains a tallow candle. The procession is formed, and the yeoman porter with the keys places himself in the midst of the escort. He goes the round of the gates, and when he returns to the main guard, the sentry at the guard-room challenges—

'Halt! Who comes there?'

'The keys,' replies the yeoman porter.

'Whose keys?'

'King Edward's keys.'

'Advance King Edward's keys.'

The yeoman porter places himself in front of the guard. The guard present arms and the yeoman porter says, 'God preserve King Edward,' and the guard from the officer to the drummer answer, 'Amen.'

The keys are then carried by the yeoman porter to the King's House, to be delivered into the charge of the officer of the Tower in command. A similar escort is called for by the yeoman porter when the gates are opened in the morning, but no ceremony takes place at that time, nor does the guard turn out. Mediævalism is in our very midst, and here, at all events, mediæval London still exists.

The Tower as a Palace.—Most of our Kings from the Conqueror to Charles II. used the Tower as a palace; those who feared their subjects sheltered themselves there, but those who were popular preferred the comfort of Westminster and Whitehall. Mr Clark says that 'the strong monarchs employed the Tower as a prison, the weak ones as a fortress.' After the Middle Ages had closed the sovereigns kept out of the Tower as much as they could, and seldom visited it unless they were officially obliged, and these visits were almost confined to a lodging there on the day before the coronation. Charles II. was the last sovereign to carry out this convention.

William I., William II. and Henry I., all three inhabited the Tower, but it was not till the reign of Stephen that its value as a place of refuge was proved.

With the Empress Matilda at Winchester and King Stephen at London the state of public affairs, with sieges and countersieges, in which neither party gained any great success, came to a deadlock. Stephen, in 1140, sought safety in the Tower in close proximity to his trusty followers—the Londoners, but in the following year he was made a prisoner at Lincoln. The Londoners attended the synod at Winchester and requested the King's release, but without avail. Geoffrey de Mandeville, Constable of the Tower of London (whose faithless conduct in these civil wars has been fully set out by Mr. Horace Round),[94] had been made Earl of Essex by Stephen, but when the Empress came to London he had no compunction in transferring his allegiance to her, for which conduct she loaded him with honours. He was, however, short-sighted in his action, for Matilda treated the Londoners with such contumely that they rose against her and drove her from the city. They also attacked Mandeville in the Tower, but this Mr. Facing-both-ways, finding that the Empress Matilda had fled, and the Queen Matilda (Stephen's wife) taken her place in London, saw no objection to supporting the latter's cause. Stephen was soon afterwards released, and he again honoured Geoffrey de Mandeville. No amount of special favour, however, was sufficient to keep this man to his allegiance, and he planned a revolt in favour of the Empress. This came to naught, and the King captured the fortifications erected by the Earl at Farringdon and took him prisoner. Mandeville took no more part in public affairs, and ended his life as a marauding freebooter in September 1143. Thus ignominiously came to a conclusion the career of a man who held a foremost place in London. He was not wise in his conduct, because in the words of the Empress's charter to him, he made the Londoners 'his mortal foes.' As Dr. Sharpe says of these same Londoners, they 'throughout the long period of civil dissension were generally to be found on the winning side, and held, as it were, the balance between the rival powers.'[95]

In John's reign London opened its gates to the forces of the Barons, organised under Robert Fitz-Walter, Castellan of London, as 'Marshal of the army of God and Holy Church.' During the period that the Barons were at war with John, Prince Louis of France lived in the Tower prior to his renunciation of all right of sovereignty in England, and his return to France.

Henry III., in 1236, summoned the Council to meet him in the Tower, but the Barons had so little faith in their King that they refused to assemble there. The King was satisfied to be safe in the Tower in 1263, while Simon de Montfort, with the barons, pitched tents at Isleworth. The

Londoners were distinctly disloyal, and Stow tells us that 'when the Queene woulde have gone by water unto Windsore, the Londoners getting them to ye bridge in great numbers, under the which she must passe, cryed out on her, using many vile reprochfull words, threwe durte and stones at her, that shee was constrained to returne again to the Towre.'[96]

In Edward I.'s reign Raymund Lully, the alchemist, is said to have taken up his residence in the Tower at the King's desire, and to have performed in the royal presence the experiment of transmuting some crystal into a mass of diamond or adamant, of which the King is said to have made little pillars for the tabernacle of God. The biographers of Lully, however, express the belief that he never visited England.

Edward II. seldom visited the Tower, except when he sought shelter from his subjects. His Queen gave birth there to her eldest daughter, who was known as Jane of the Tower. His second son, John of Eltham, who was born on August 15, 1316, was appointed Warden of the City of London and Warden of the Tower when he was ten years of age. In 1328, a year after his father's death, John of Eltham was created Earl of Cornwall, and in 1336 he himself died.

The first years of Edward III.'s reign were spent in the Tower, and the King was forced to remain there till he had put down Mortimer and was able to assume the government himself. He made many additions to the buildings, and Clark supposes that he built the Beauchamp and Salt Towers, and perhaps the Bowyer. The King took great pride in the Tower, which he made his chief arsenal, and strongly fortified and garrisoned. Hence his anger in 1340 when he unexpectedly returned to England and found the Tower unguarded. His first act was to imprison the Constable and other officers for their negligence. The Mayor, the Clerk of the Exchequer, and many others whose duty it was to raise or receive the subsidies which had been granted were thrown into prison.[97]

The Tower stands out very prominently in the history of the reign of Richard II. We have already seen in the second chapter what crimes were perpetrated there during the Peasants' Revolt in 1381.

In 1390 a grand international tournament was arranged, when many foreigners of distinction became the guests of the King in the Tower.

On the 29th of September 1399, in the Council Room of the White Tower, occurred that sad scene when Richard in his kingly robes, sceptre in hand and crown upon his head, abdicated his throne, saying: 'I have been King of England, Duke of Aquitaine and Lord of Ireland about twenty-one years, which seigniory, royalty, sceptre, crown and heritage I clearly resign here to my cousin, Henry of Lancaster; and I desire him here in this open presence in entering the same possession to take the sceptre.' So closed the career of a King whose sun rose with so much promise, only to set in misfortune and leave behind him the recollection of one of the greatest disappointments of history.

Henry VI. had a sorry time in the Tower, but the incidents connected with the constant vicissitudes, which at one time raised the fortunes of the Yorkists and at another those of the Lancastrians, caused so many changes in the occupation of the Tower that it is impossible to note here all that took place. When the Yorkist Earls of Salisbury, Warwick and March returned to England in 1460 they marched on London, but the Common Council determined to oppose their entrance into the city. This arrangement was agreed on with Lords Scales and Hungerford who, with others, held the Tower for King Henry. The citizens, however, after a time began to doubt the wisdom of supporting the imbecile Henry, so on July 2 they admitted the Yorkist earls into the city. While London was thus on the side of the Yorkists the Tower remained true to the King, but every effort was made to obtain the surrender of the fortress. The Tower was invested by land and water, and the garrison was starved out and had to surrender.

In the following year the Earl of March became King as Edward IV., and made himself agreeable to his subjects. When in 1464 he married Elizabeth Woodville the citizens showed their respect for the Queen by riding out to meet her and escorting her to the Tower, besides presenting her with a gift of 1000 marks.

A change occurred in 1470, when Edward had to fly and Henry was restored. Henry VI., no longer a prisoner, was removed from his cell to the palace, but soon afterwards he was taken to the Bishop of London's palace at St. Paul's. In the following year, however, Edward recovered the throne, and was let into London by the Recorder and some aldermen. In May 1471, when Edward IV. was out of the city, Thomas (the natural son of William Nevill, first Lord Fauconberg, Earl of Kent), known as the Bastard Falconbridge, headed a rising of Kentish men and marched on London in support of Henry VI. He was supported by a fleet in the river. With the help of a company of shipmen and other followers he made an attempt to force Bishopsgate, Aldgate, and the Bridge. Some of his followers got through Aldgate, but the portcullis being let down those who had entered were cut off from the main body and lost their lives. A few days after this unsuccessful assault (May 21) King Henry was murdered in the Tower.

The name of Richard III. was intimately associated with the Council Chamber, and the consideration of the particulars of his violent methods helps us to obtain a vivid picture of the dark passages filled with armed men ready to do the wicked will of their employer.

The most memorable of these scenes occurred when the Council was sitting. Suddenly there is a cry of 'Treason' from the adjoining apartment. Gloucester rushes to the door and is met by a party of soldiers, who at his command arrest all the Council but the Duke of Buckingham. The astonished nobles have scarcely time to recover from their surprise before they see from the windows of their prison Lord Hastings beheaded on Tower Green.

In the following reign, when Henry VII. fixed the day for the coronation of his Queen—November 25, 1487—she came by water from Greenwich two days before, attended by the Mayor, Sheriffs and Aldermen, and many citizens, chosen some from each craft, wearing their liveries, in barges 'freshly furnished with banners and streamers of silk.' One of the barges, called the Bachelors', contained 'many gentlemanly pageants, well and curiously devised to do her highness sport and pleasure.' The King received the Queen at the Tower.

Much might be said of the doings of Henry VIII., Edward VI., Queens Mary and Elizabeth, James I. and Charles I., but there is no room in this book for a complete history of the Tower, and we must therefore hurry on in order to give some notice of a few of the celebrated prisoners.

There could never have been much accommodation in the White Tower (so called on account of the white-washing it received in the reign of Henry III.) as a suitable residence for the sovereign, so that as the centuries passed and more comfort was expected by all classes, Kings and Queens would naturally expect to be better cared for. A palace was therefore built in the inner ward, and the Lanthorn Tower formed a part of this palace, containing as it did the King's bed-chamber and his private closet. These buildings appear to have fallen into decay in the reign of Elizabeth, by whom or by James the great hall was removed. Some were destroyed by Cromwell, and others by James II., to make room for a new Ordnance office, and the remains of the Lanthorn Tower were taken down late in the eighteenth century[98] (1788).

That royalty was not always well-housed may be seen by a recorded case in the reign of Edward II. Johannes de Crombwelle, Constable of the Tower, gave great offence to the citizens by reason of certain of his high-handed actions, and in the end he was dismissed from his office, but the reason given for his dismissal was not on account of the offensive acts complained of, but for neglect of duties, by which the rooms were allowed to remain out of repair, and because the rain came in upon the Queen's bed.[99]

Some particulars are given in the *Liber Albus* respecting the legal position of the Tower. When the Exchequer was closed the Mayor was to be presented at the Tower, and the Pleas of the City with the Crown were sometimes held there; and when this was the case the city barons were to place their own 'janitors'

ST. JOHN'S CHAPEL IN THE TOWER.

outside the Tower gate, and the King's janitor was to be on the inside. They further had an 'ostiarius' outside the door of the hall when the pleas were held, to introduce the barons, and the King had an 'ostiarius' inside. Mr. Clark supposes the hall to have been the building afterwards superseded by the office of Ordnance, 'and the entrance to which is thought to have been by the modernised doorway close east of the Wakefield Tower.'[100]

St. John's Chapel is one of the most interesting ecclesiastical buildings in England. It is a singularly fine example of Early Norman architecture, and many historical events are associated with it. The triforium was used as a gallery, and it is supposed that the Queens and their maids of honour sat there at the services.

It is traditionally reported that in front of the old altar (now replaced by a new one) Brackenbury, when kneeling at prayer, was tempted by the emissaries of Richard of Gloucester to make away with the young Princes—a suggestion which he indignantly repudiated. Here also Mary I. was betrothed to Philip of Spain.

One important appanage of the palace was the menagerie of wild beasts, which was placed near the entrance at a very early date. Henry I.

kept lions and leopards, and Henry III. added to the collection. Stow tells us that in the year 1235 Frederick the Emperor sent to Henry III. three leopards in token of his regal shield of arms wherein those leopards were pictured, since the which time those lions and others have been kept in a part of this bulwark, now called the Lion Tower, and their keepers there lodged. In 1255 the sheriffs built a house 'for the King's elephant,' which was brought from France and was the first seen in England.

Edward II., in the twelfth year of his reign, 'commanded the Sheriffs of London to pay to the keeper of the King's leopard sixpence the day for the sustenance of the leopard, and three halfpence a day for diet of the said keeper.'

Edward III. appears to have taken much pride in his menagerie, and in 1364 a proclamation was issued by the King for the safe keeping of a beast called an 'oure,' which was in danger from certain persons who threatened to do grievous harm to the keepers, 'and atrociously to kill the said beast.' Mr. Riley, who prints the proclamation in his *Memorials*, supposes the animal to be either the urus, aurochs or bison, from the east of Europe, or the Ihrwy from Morocco.

The proclamation addressed to the Mayor and Sheriff runs thus: 'We, wishing to preserve the said keepers and the beast from injury and grievance, do command you that in the city aforesaid and the suburbs thereof, where you shall deem most expedient, you do cause public proclamation to be made, and it on our behalf strictly to be forbidden, that any person, native or stranger, of whatsoever condition he may be, on pain of forfeiting unto us as much as he may forfeit, shall have the audacity to do any damage, violence, misprision or grievance unto the said keepers or to the beast, which we have so taken under our protection and especial defence, or to any of them, or shall presume to intermeddle for getting a sight of the said beast, against the will of them, the keepers thereof. And if you shall know anyone to attempt the contrary hereof, then you are so to punish them that the same punishment may deter all others from attempting the like; and to answer unto us as to such forfeiture, in manner as is befitting.'[101]

In later times the collection of wild beasts must have been considerable, and Stow relates in his *Chronicle* how trials of strength between the animals were exhibited before the royal family. On the 23rd of June 1609 'the King, Queene, and Prince, the Lady Elizabeth and the Duke of Yorke, with divers great lords and manie others, came to the Tower to see a triall of the lyon's single valour, against a great fierce beare, which had kild a child, that was negligently left in the beare-house. This fierce beare was brought into the open yard, behind the lyon's den, which was the place for fight.' Two mastiffs let into the yard passed the bear and attacked the lion. Then a stallion and six dogs were introduced. The dogs worried the horse till three stout bear-wards drove them off, the bear and lion looking on. The latter was allowed to escape to his den, and other lions were brought out, but none would attack the bear. On the 5th of July this same bear was baited to death.

On the 10th April 1610 Prince Henry and attendant nobles went privately to the Tower to see a fight between the great lion and four dogs. The dogs got the better of the lion, and another lion and lioness were brought to see if they would help the first lion, but they would not, and all three were glad to escape to their dens.[102] The few animals that remained in the menagerie in the nineteenth century were removed to the Zoological Gardens in Regent's Park in 1834.

The Tower as a Prison.—It is as a State prison that the Tower is most associated in our memories. Here have been confined some of the noblest of English men and women, but besides these there were others who have richly deserved their fate. Some of the prisoners lodged here only for a time, but the majority found it to be merely the threshold of death.

The first prisoner was Ralph Flambard, Bishop of Durham, the hated Minister of William Rufus. On that King's death, Henry I., with the advice of his Council, shut the bishop up in one of the topmost chambers of the White Tower. Flambard was not very carefully guarded, and he used the liberal allowance put aside for him in providing drink for his keepers. He received a rope in a flagon from friends outside, and while his gaolers were drunk, he managed to escape by its means on the night of 4th February 1101. Although the rope proved too short, and he was injured by his fall, he reached Normandy safely.

Five years after this, the Count of Mortain, who was taken prisoner by Henry I., was imprisoned in the Tower, as we learn from the testimony of Eadmer.

The Jews in large numbers were thrown into the Tower in 1282. The Welsh next furnished victims, and then the Scots. The Battle of Dunbar in 1296 caused many prisoners, including the King, John Balliol, and a host of his nobility to fall into the hands of Edward I. In 1303 the King's treasury was robbed while Edward I. was in Scotland, and suspicion fell upon the Abbot and Monks of Westminster. The sacristan, sub-prior and others were imprisoned in the Tower. The whole affair is very difficult to understand, but it was fully investigated by order of the King, and there can be no doubt that some members of the monastery were deeply implicated. It created a great scandal, and was one of the most remarkable crimes ever committed. Mr. L. O. Pike gives a full account of the incidents in his *History of Crime in England,* 1873 (vol. i.), and says: 'It is quite evident that an enterprise which required more than four months for its accomplishment could not have been successful had there been no collusion within the abbey gates. The findings of the various juries point to a deep-laid conspiracy between some persons in the abbey and others in the neighbouring palace.'

Wallace in 1305 found a prison here before he was drawn through Cheapside and executed in Smithfield.

The Order of the Knights Templar was abolished in 1313, and all the members south of the Trent were imprisoned in the Tower, where the master died.

The earliest drawing of the Tower which has come down to us contains a curious picture of the building, and a representation of the incidents of the captivity of Charles,

DUKE OF ORLEANS IN THE TOWER. (From a copy of MS. in the British Museum.)

Duke of Orleans, who was taken prisoner at the Battle of Agincourt. This interesting picture is in one of the MSS. (Roy MS. 16 F. 2) in the British Museum. As was the custom of the early artists, a succession of incidents in the life of the prisoner are depicted in the same drawing. The duke is seen at a turret window, then writing at a desk in a large chamber. At the foot of the White Tower he is embracing the messenger who brings him his ransom. He is then seen mounting his horse, and he and a friendly messenger ride away from the Tower. Lastly, we see him in a barge with lusty rowers pulling down the stream for the boat which is to carry him home to France.

There were two places of execution, that on Tower Hill (under the authority of the governors of the city), and the other on Tower Green within the Tower walls. Edward IV. set up a scaffold and gallows upon Tower Hill, but the City of London insisted upon their ancient right of dealing with offenders within their own precincts, so the King's scaffold and gallows were taken down with many apologies, and the sheriffs maintained their ancient privileges of headings and hangings beyond the Tower walls. The city boundary existed within the Tower, and in James I.'s reign a question arose as to whether or no Sir Thomas Overbury's murder was committed within the city. As his apartment was situated on the west of the boundary, the criminals came under the jurisdiction of the city.

The place of execution on Tower Green is a spot of hallowed memories. It was marked off and railed in by command of Queen Victoria. Lord Hastings was probably beheaded here in 1483, and among the distinguished names of those who suffered on this spot are Anne Boleyn in 1536; Margaret Pole, Countess of Salisbury, daughter of the Duke of Clarence and mother of Cardinal Pole in 1541; Katherine Howard, and Jane, Viscountess Rochford, sister-in-law of Anne Boleyn, in 1542; Lady Jane Grey in 1554; and Robert Devereux, Earl of Essex, in 1601.

The Chapel of St. Peter's ad Vincula was probably first built by Henry II., although the earliest mention of it occurs in the year 1210. It was burnt in 1512, and rebuilt as we see it now about 1532. The great interest of this chapel centres round the names of the great who having suffered in life now rest in this temple of the dead. A tablet on the wall contains a list of the most distinguished of these names.

The Beauchamp Tower is one of the most interesting of the buildings, as it is full of inscriptions on the walls cut by the prisoners.

Close by is the Yeoman Gaoler's lodging, where probably Lady Jane Grey stood to see her husband taken from Beauchamp Tower to execution on Tower Hill.

Sir Walter Raleigh was three times a prisoner in the Tower, and he was very differently treated each time. In Elizabeth's reign he could converse with those outside from the walk near the Bloody Tower, which is named after him. In James's reign he had for a fellow-prisoner Henry, ninth Earl of Northumberland, known as 'the Wizard Earl.' The great philosopher Thomas Harriott was allowed to visit the two prisoners, and he travelled on the Thames between the Tower and Sion House, bringing from the latter place books out of the earl's library for the solace of Northumberland and Raleigh.

With Traitor's Gate we end this sad eventful history. Samuel Rogers wrote in his poem of 'Human Life':—

'On through that gate misnamed, through which before
Went Sidney, Russell, Raleigh, Cranmer, More.'

These are great names, but there are others. The Duke of Buckingham in 1521 was taken to Westminster in a barge furnished with a carpet and cushions. After his trial and condemnation for the crime of being too nearly related to the throne he refused the seat of honour on his return to prison, crying: 'When I came to Westminster I was Lord High Constable and Duke of Buckingham, but now—poor Edward Bohun!'

The Princess Elizabeth, in her sister Mary's reign, refused at first to land at Traitor's Gate, but agreed at last, using these words: 'Here landeth as true a subject, being a prisoner, as ever landed at these stairs, and before Thee, O God! I speak it, having none other friend but Thee.'

What misery and what cruelty a full record of the sufferings of the prisoners in the Tower would unfold to our view. Some of the prisoners reaped the natural consequences of their actions, for they were on the losing side. But others were most unnaturally treated, and among these were noble women whose only fault was that they were related to persons obnoxious to those in power.

In later times imprisonment became somewhat of a farce. Great nobles, unpopular statesmen and others who were in disgrace were sent to the Tower. It still sounded a serious punishment, but the practice gradually fell into disfavour, because people would no longer allow of the beheading of unpopular statesmen.

CHAPTER VI

Manners

OUR notices of the sports of mediæval London must commence with a reference to the curious essay of the monk Fitz-Stephen, who was the first to describe the chief features of London history.

'Moreover, to begin with the sports of the boys (for we have all been boys) annually on the day which is called Shrovetide, the boys of the respective schools bring each a fighting-cock to their master, and the whole of that forenoon is spent by the boys in seeing their cocks fight in the schoolroom. After dinner all the young men of the city go out into the fields to play at the well-known game of football.[103] The scholars belonging to the several schools have each their ball, and the city tradesmen, according to their respective crafts, have theirs. The more aged men, the fathers of the players, and the wealthy citizens come on horseback to see the contests of the young men, with whom, after their manner, they participate, their natural heat seeming to be aroused by the sight of so much agility, and by their participation in the amusements of unrestrained youth. Every Sunday in Lent, after dinner, a company of young men enter the fields mounted on warlike horses--

' "On coursers always foremost in the race,"

of which

' "Each steed's well-trained to gallop in a ring."

The lay sons of the citizens rush out of the gates in crowds equipped with lances and shields, the younger sort with pikes from which the iron head has been taken off, and there they get up sham fights and exercise themselves in military combat. When the King happens to be near the city most of the courtiers attend, and the young men who form the households of the earls and barons, and have not yet attained the honour of knighthood, resort thither for the purpose of trying their skill.'

Then Fitz-Stephen tells of the sports on the river, but these remarks have already been referred to in the fourth chapter. The description of the sports of summer and winter are then continued. We find a curious account of the Londoner's delight both in sliding and skating, and his contempt for the dangers of the sports.

'During the holydays in summer the young men exercise themselves in the sports of leaping, archery, wrestling, stone-throwing, slinging javelins beyond a mark, and also fighting with bucklers. Cytherea leads the dances of the maidens, who merrily trip along the ground beneath the uprisen moon. Almost on every holyday in winter, before dinner, foaming boars and huge-tusked hogs, intended for bacon, fight for their lives, or fat bulls or immense boars are baited with dogs. When that great marsh which washes the walls of the city on the north side is frozen over, the young men go out in crowds to divert themselves upon the ice. Some having increased their velocity by a run, placing their feet apart and turning their bodies sideways, slide a great way; others make a seat of large pieces of ice like mill-stones, and a great number of them running before, and holding each other by the hand, draw one of their companions who is seated on the ice; if at any time they slip in moving so swiftly, all fall down headlong together. Others are more expert in their sports upon the ice; for fitting to and binding under their feet the shin-bones of some animal, and taking in their hands poles shod with iron, which at times they strike against the ice, they are carried along with as great rapidity as a bird flying, or a bolt discharged from a cross-bow. Sometimes two of the skaters having placed themselves a great distance apart, by mutual agreement come together from opposite sides; they meet, raise their poles, and strike each other; either one or both of them fall, not without some bodily hurt; even after their fall they are carried along to a great distance from each other by the velocity of the motion, and whatever part of their heads comes in contact with the ice is laid bare to the very skull. Very frequently the leg or arm of the falling one, if he chance to light upon either of them, is broken. But youth is an age eager for glory and desirous of victory, and so young men engage in counterfeit battles that they may conduct themselves more valiantly in real ones. Most of the citizens amuse themselves in sporting with martins, hawks and other birds of a like kind, and also with dogs that hunt in the wood.'

It was one thing to go out into the fields to play these games, but when there was a large population within the walls it must have been very inconvenient to the inhabitants to find the streets occupied by footballers. The practice seems to have been allowed until it became a public nuisance. In the year 1406 proclamation was issued forbidding hocking in streets of London: 'Let proclamation be made that no person of this city, or within the suburbs thereof, of whatsoever estate or condition such person may be, whether man or woman, shall, in any street or lane thereof, take hold of or constrain any person, of whatsoever estate or condition he may be, within house or without, for hokkyng on the Monday or Tuesday next, called Hokkedayes, on pain of imprisonment, and of making fine at the discretion of the Mayor and Aldermen.'[104]

Hock Monday and Tuesday were the Monday and Tuesday following the second Sunday after Easter day, and Spelman describes the sport of hocking as consisting 'in the men and women binding each other, and especially the women the men.' Hone writes (*Every Day Book*): 'Tuesday was the principal day, Hock Monday was for the men and Hock Tuesday for the women. On both days the men and women alternately, with great merriment, intercepted the public roads with ropes and pulled passengers to them, from whom they exacted money to be laid out for pious uses. Monday probably having been originally kept as only the vigil or introduction to the festival of Hock-day.'

The proclamation of 1406 does not seem to have been effectual, and therefore three years afterwards another proclamation was issued against 'Hokkyng, Foteballe and Cokthresshyng.' The prohibition of hocking is expressed in the same terms as in the proclamation of 1406, and to this is added the following: 'And that no person shall levy money, or cause it to be levied, for the games called "foteballe" and "cokthreshyng" because of marriages that have recently taken place in the said city, or the suburbs thereof, on pain of imprisonment, and of making fine at the discretion of the Mayor and aldermen.'[105]

Cock-throwing and football were specially in season at Shrovetide, and at that time it was difficult for the authorities to hold the Londoners in hand, and prevent them from making the streets their playground.

The cases of punishment already referred to are connected with prohibitions, but in 1389 a curious case of a fine inflicted for stopping a procession on the festival of Corpus Christi is recorded. A citizen was brought before the Mayor, and the sheriffs, recorder, and aldermen, to answer for having prevented a procession from passing through his house, which the parishioners believed to be their right.

It is one thing for the inhabitants of a small town like Helstone, in Cornwall, to pass through houses without hindrance on Furry day, and quite another for the same right to be claimed in London, even in the Middle Ages. The case is so remarkable that it seems well to quote the whole statement:—

'Because that by the reputable men of the parish of St. Nicholas Acon, Nicholas Twyford, Knight, Mayor of the City of London, was given to understand that whereas they, time out of mind, had been wont and accustomed to have free ingress and egress with their procession, on the befitting and usual days, through the middle of a certain house belonging to John Basse, citizen and draper of London, situate in the parish of St. Mary Abbechirche, in London; the aforesaid John, together with John Creek, draper, and others of their covin, on Thursday, the Feast of Corpus Christi last past, armed with divers arms, guarded the house before mentioned by main force, and would not allow the parishioners of the Church of St. Nicholas aforesaid to enter the house with their procession, as they had been wont to do, but grievously threatened them as to life and limb; in breach of the peace of our Lord the King, and to the manifest disturbance of the tranquillity of the city aforesaid:—for the said reason the same John and John were arrested.'

'Afterwards, on the 26th day of June, in the thirteenth year, etc., they were brought before the said Mayor and the sheriffs, recorder, and aldermen, in the chamber of the Guildhall, and were there questioned as to the matter aforesaid, and were asked how they would acquit themselves thereof; whereupon they acknowledged that they were guilty of all the things above imputed to them, and put themselves upon the favour of the court as to the same; and counsel having been held hereon, according to the usage of the city in like cases, it was adjudged that the said John Basse, as being the principal and the prime mover in the contempt aforesaid, should have imprisonment for one year then next ensuing, to commence from the Friday next after the Feast of St. Botolph [17th June], namely, Friday the 18th day of June then last past; and that on his leaving prison he should pay to the Chamberlain of the Guildhall 200 marks, to the use of the commonalty, for the contempt aforesaid; unless he should meet with increased favour in the meantime. And that the aforesaid John Creek, for the contempt so by him committed, should have imprisonment for half a year after the said Friday next ensuing; and that on his leaving prison he should pay to the aforesaid Chamberlain 100 marks to the use of the commonalty, unless he should meet with increased favour in the meantime'[106]

These were truly exemplary damages, and we find that the imprisonment was remitted on the same day, and the fines were respectively reduced to £15 and 100s.[107]

Besides sports in the streets, there was a constant succession of pageants, processions and tournaments in the Middle Ages, which made the streets gay, and brought out most of the inhabitants to see the sights.

The royal processions arranged in connection with coronations were of great antiquity, but one of the earliest to be described is that of Henry III., in 1236, which was chronicled by Matthew Paris. After the marriage at Canterbury of the King with Eleanor of Provence, the royal personages came to London, and were met by the Mayor, aldermen, and principal citizens, to the number of 360, sumptuously apparelled in silken robes embroidered, riding upon stately horses.

A very interesting point is mentioned by Matthew Paris, viz., that each man carried a gold or silver cup in his hand, in token of the privilege claimed by the city, of the Mayor being Chief Butler of the kingdom at the coronation. Something further respecting this claim will be found in the eighth chapter of this book. On this occasion the streets of the city were adorned with rich silks, pageants, and a variety of pompous shows; and the citizens attending the King and Queen to Westminster had the honour of officiating at the Queen's coronation. At night the city was illuminated with an infinite number of lamps, cressets, etc.

After the death of Henry III. (1272) the country had to wait for their new King, who was then in the Holy Land. Edward I. came to London on the 2nd of August 1274, where he was received with the wildest expressions of joy. The streets were hung with rich cloths of silk, arras and tapestry; the aldermen and principal men of the city threw out of their windows handfuls of gold and silver, to signify their gladness at the King's return; and the conduits ran with wine, both white and red. The coronation took place on the 19th of August.

The happy married life of Edward I. and Eleanor of Castile came to an end in 1290, and in connection with her death was arranged the most striking and most beautiful expression of a husband's and a nation's love in our history.

The Queen died in Harby, Lincolnshire, and the funeral procession came slowly to London and Westminster. Beautiful crosses were afterwards placed on the various spots where each night the body stopped. Two of these stopping-places were in London—at Cheapside, beneath the shadow of old St. Paul's, and at Charing Cross, on the way to Westminster, where the Queen's beautiful tomb remains as one of the chief glories of our wonderful Abbey Church.

CHEAPSIDE CROSS.

Cheapside Cross was 're-edified' in 1441, and afterwards newly gilt and newly burnished. Defaced and repaired at different times, little was left of the original when the cross was cleared away in 1647, at the same time as Charing Cross.

Only three of the original Eleanor crosses remain: two in Northamptonshire—one at Geddington, and the other at Northampton, and the third at Waltham Cross. Every Englishman should be proud of these glorious records of a past age, which not only tell of the devoted love of two sovereigns, of whom we all must be proud, but also because they prove the high state of English art at this time. Until late years, when certain documents were discovered containing the names of the artists, the historians of art attempted to believe that the designs were too good for Englishmen, and must have been made by foreigners.

In order to establish peace between England and France, King Edward married Margaret of France, sister of the French King, at Canterbury in 1299, and in the following year she first came to London.

The citizens, to the number of 600, rode in one livery of red and white, with the cognisance of their mistress embroidered upon their sleeves, and received her four miles without the city, and so conveyed her to Westminster.[108]

Edward I. was buried at Westminster on October 27, 1307, and his son on coming to the throne recalled Piers Gaveston from banishment; he made him Regent of the kingdom when he crossed to France to be married to Isabella, the daughter of Philip IV. In February 1307-1308 Edward II. returned to England with his bride, and was joyfully received by the citizens. On the 24th they were crowned at Westminster. The King, we are told by Stow, offered on the altar first a pound of gold made like a King holding a ring in his hand, and then a mark of gold (8 ounces) made like a pilgrim putting forth his hand to receive the ring. The crush was very great at this coronation, and in it Sir John Blackwell was killed.

In November 1312, Queen Isabel announced to the Mayor her safe delivery of a son in the following letter: 'Isabel, by the grace of God, Queen of England, Lady of Ireland, and Duchess of Aquitaine, to our well-beloved, the Mayor and aldermen and the commonalty of London, greeting. Forasmuch as we believe that you would willingly hear good tidings of us, we do make known unto you that our Lord of His grace has delivered us of a son' [afterwards Edward III.]. The Mayor and aldermen and commonalty, on hearing the news, 'assembled in the Guildhall at time of vespers and carolled, and showed great joy thereat; and so passed through the city with great glare of torches, and with trumpets and other minstrelsies. And on the Tuesday next, early in the morning, cry was made throughout all the city to the effect that there was to be no work, labour, or business in shop on that day; but that everyone was to apparel himself in the most becoming manner that he could, and come to the Guildhall at the hour of prime, ready to go with the Mayor, together with the [other] good folks, to St. Paul's, there to make praise and offering to the honour of God, who had shown them such favour on earth, and to show respect for this child that had been born.'

At the beginning of the next week all went richly costumed to Westminster, riding on horseback, and there made offering. After dinner in the Guildhall, 'they went in carols throughout the city all the rest of the day and great part of the night.' The conduit of Chepe ran with nothing but wine, and a pavilion extended in the middle of the street near Brokencross (at the north door of St. Paul's), in which was set a tun of wine, for all passers-by to drink of. In the following February the Fishmongers Company caused a boat to be fitted out in the guise of a great ship, to be drawn to Westminster and presented to the Queen. The Fishmongers, very richly costumed, escorted the Queen through the city on the same day, on her way to Canterbury on pilgrimage.[109]

In 1330 there was an accident during the progress of a great tournament in Cheapside, which was part of an entertainment offered by the citizens to the young King (Edward III.) and Queen at the birth of their first son. The Queen Philippa displayed the same good qualities which on a later occasion she showed after the surrender of Calais, and thereby secured a lasting fame as a good woman. Stow relates the event as follows: 'There was a very solemn justing of all the stout earls, barons and nobles at London in Cheap, betwixt the great Cross and the great Conduit nigh Soper Lane, which lasted three days, where the Queen Philippa, with many ladies, fell from a stage, notwithstanding they were not hurt at all, wherefore the Queen took great care to save the carpenters from punishment, and through her prayer (which she made on her knees) she pacified the King and Council, whereby she purchased great love of the people.'

This accident was the cause of Edward III. ordering the construction in stone of a shed (seldam) on the north side of Bow Church, so that the royal party might in future be able to view the joustings and other shows with safety. Edward III. was for some years the most popular of our monarchs, for he was constantly conquering his enemies, and his people were proud of him. In 1343 a great triumph was organised in his honour, which is described in Sir William Segar's *Honour Militarie and Civil*. The King commanded that the tournament should be proclaimed in France, Henault, Flanders, Brabant and other places, 'giving passport and secure abode to all noble strangers that would resort into England.' The triumph took place in London, and continued for fifteen days.

Dr. Jessopp gives us a vivid picture of what occurred four years afterwards 'when King Edward III. entered London in triumph on the 14th of October 1347, he was the foremost man in Europe, and England had reached a height of power and glory such as she had never attained before. At the Battle of Creci, France had received a crushing blow, and by the loss of Calais, after an eleven months' siege, she had been reduced well-nigh to the lowest point of humiliation. David II., King of Scotland, was now lying a prisoner in the Tower of London. Louis of Bavaria had just been killed by a fall from his horse, the imperial throne was vacant, and the electors in eager haste proclaimed that they had chosen the King of England to succeed. To their discomfiture the King of England declined the proffered crown. He "had other views." Intoxicated by the splendour of their sovereign and his martial renown, and the success which seemed to attend him wherever he showed himself, the English people had gone mad with exultation.'[110]

Two years later (in 1349) the fearful pestilence, known of late years as the Black Death, was destroying half the population of the country.

One of the most interesting of London processions was that which took place when the chivalrous Black Prince brought his prisoners to England in 1357. Stow's account of this historic scene is so vivid that it needs must be transferred to these pages without paraphrase: 'Edward, Prince of Wales, returning into England with John, the French King, Phillip, his sonne, and many other prysoners, arrived at Plimmouth on the fifth of May, and the foure-and-twentieth of May entered London with them, where he was received with great honour of the cittizens, and so conveyed to the King's pallace at Westminster, where the King, sitting in his estate in Westminster Hall, received them, and after conveyed the French King to a lodging, where he lay a season; and after the sayd French King was lodged in the Savoy (which was then a pleasant place, belonging to the Duke of Lancaster). In the winter following were great and royal justs holden in Smithfield at London, where many knightly sights of armes were done to the great honour of the King and realme, at the which were present the Kings of Englande, France and Scotland, with many noble estates of all those kingdomes, whereof the more part of the strangers were prisoners.'

The King of France remained a prisoner for three years, but in 1360 King Edward marched upon Paris, and peace was made to the joy of the French, although the English gained a third of that kingdom by the Peace of Bretigny. When the peace was confirmed Edward III. came to England, 'and so straight to the Tower to see the French King, where he appointed his ransome to bee three millions of florences, and so delivered him of all imprisonment, and brought him with great honour to the sea, who then sayled over into France.'[111]

On the 8th of June 1376, that 'flower of chivalry,' the Black Prince, died in the Archbishop's Palace at Canterbury. His young son Richard was then created by the King Earl of Chester, Duke of Cornwall, and Prince of Wales. At Christmas the Londoners formed a torchlight procession from the city to Kennington in honour of the Prince:—

'On the Sunday before Candlemas, in the night, one hundred and thirty citizens, disguised and well horsed, in a mummery with sounds of trumpets, large trumpets, horns, shealms, and other minstrels, and innumerable torchlights of wax, rode from Newgate through Cheap over the Bridge, through Southwark, and so to Kennington, besides Lambeth, where the young Prince remained with his mother.... In the first rank did ride forty-eight, in the likeness and habit of esquires, two and two together, cloathed in red coats, and gowns of say or sandale, with comely vizors on their faces. After them came riding forty-eight knights in the same livery of colour and stuff. Then followed one richly arrayed like an Emperor, and after him at some distance one stately attired like a Pope, whom followed twenty-four Cardinals, and after them eight or ten with black vizors not amiable, as if they had been legates from some foreign princes.

'These maskers, after they had entered the manor of Kennington, alighted from their horses, and entered the hall on foot, which done, the Prince, his mother, and the Lords came out of the Chamber into the Hall, whom the said mummers did salute, shewing by a pair of dice on the table their desire to play with the Prince, which they so handled that the Prince did always win when they cast them. Then the mummers set to the Prince three jewels one after another, which were a bowl of gold, a cup of gold, and a ring of gold, which the Prince won at three casts.

'Then they set to the Prince's mother, the duke [John of Gaunt], the earls, and other lords, to every one a ring of gold, which they did also win. After which they were feasted, and the music sounded; the Prince and the lords danced on the one part with the mummers, who did also dance, which jollity being needed they were again made to drink, and then departed in order as they came.'[112]

On the 21st of June following (1377) Edward III., deserted by his mistress, Alice Perress, and his courtiers, and attended by a solitary priest, died at Shene (now Richmond). Before the breath was out of his body the citizens waited upon the young Prince Richard, and offered their allegiance, requesting him to come to London. In Walsingham's Chronicle there is an account of a pageant in honour of the young King in the following month. On the Feast of St. Swithin the Mayor and citizens assembled near the Tower, when King Richard, clad in white garments, came forth with a great multitude in his suite, also dressed in white. The streets were hung with cloth of gold and silver and silken stuff, and the conduits ran wine for three hours. At the upper end of Cheapside was erected a castle with four towers. In the towers were placed four beautiful virgins, of stature and age like to the King, apparelled in white; these damsels on the King's approach blew in his face leaves of gold and threw on him and his horse counterfeit golden florins. When he was come before the castle they took cups of gold, and filling them with wine at the spouts of the castle, presented the same to the King and his nobles. On the top of the castle, betwixt the towers, stood a golden angel, holding a crown in his hands, and so contrived that when the King came he bowed down and offered him the crown.

There was infinite variety in these pageants, and they were very frequent during the Middle Ages, and long after, but the too full description of them is likely to become monotonous. It will therefore be sufficient to refer to some of the other rejoicings in a more succinct manner.

On Friday after the Epiphany, 1382, the Mayor, aldermen and Commons rode to meet the new Queen, Anne of Bohemia, and conducted her through the city. All the crafts were charged to wear nothing but red and black.

In 1392 Richard II. wanted to borrow £1000 from the Londoners. However, they not only refused, but killed a certain Lombard who would have lent the sum. The King was very angry and deposed the Mayor, imprisoning him in Windsor Castle, and the sheriffs and various prominent citizens in other prisons. Finding that they were in a bad case, the citizens repented and offered the King £10,000. Richard, learning that the Londoners were 'in heaviness and dismayed,' said to his men, as Stow tells us: 'I will go to London and comfort the citizens, and will not that they any longer despaire of my favour.' On leaving Shene he was met on Wandsworth Common by four hundred of the citizens on horseback, clad in one livery, who in the most humble manner, craving pardon for their past offences, besought him by their recorder to take his way to his palace at Westminster through the city of London. The request having been granted, the King pursued his journey to Southwark, where at St. George's Church he was met by a procession of the Bishop of London, and all the religions of every degree, and above five hundred boys in surplices. At London Bridge a white steed and milk-white palfrey, both saddled, bridled and caparisoned in cloth of gold, were presented to the King and Queen. The citizens received them standing in their liveries on each side of the street, crying: 'King Richard, King Richard.' Handsome presents were made to the King and Queen, who proceeded to St. Paul's; after the offerings had been made there the Mayor accompanied the King to Westminster. On the following day the citizens again went to the palace with presents, and received a new confirmation of their liberties. They had, however, to present a golden tablet of the story of Edward the Confessor for the shrine of that royal saint, and were further mulcted in a heavy tax.

Seven years after this the principal actors were changed, and Henry, Duke of Lancaster, approached London with Richard as a captive. He was received in great pomp by the Mayor, aldermen and sheriffs, and all the several companies in their formalities, with the people incessantly crying: 'Long live the good Duke of Lancaster, our deliverer!'

On the 13th of October, in the same year (1399), Henry went in great pomp from the Tower to Westminster, and there was crowned.

In 1413 Henry V. passed in procession from the Tower through London to Westminster, where he was crowned. But though there was a brave show on this occasion it was as nothing to what was provided to do honour to the King's return from the glorious field of Agincourt in 1415. The Mayor and aldermen, apparelled in Orient-grained scarlet, and four hundred Commoners in murrey, well mounted, with rich collars and chains, met the King at Blackheath; and the clergy of London, in solemn procession, with rich crosses, sumptuous copes and many censers, received him at St. Thomas of Waterings, a place on the Old Kent Road, which Chaucer's pilgrims passed when they had gone about two miles from the Tabard. At the entrance of London Bridge, on the top of the tower, stood a gigantic figure, bearing in his right hand an axe, and in his left the keys of the city hanging to a staff, as if he had been the porter. By his side stood a woman of scarcely less stature, intended for his wife. Around them were a band of trumpets and other wind instruments. The towers were adorned with banners of the royal arms, and in the front of them was inscribed—CIVITAS REGIS JUSTICIE.

Henry V. made another triumphant entry into London with his bride Katharine of France, who was crowned at Westminster Abbey on the 14th of February 1421. On the 31st of August following the King died in France. On the 14th of November 1422 the infant, Henry VI., was carried through the city to the Parliament at Westminster on the lap of his mother, who sat in an open chair.

On the 6th of November 1429 the young King was crowned in Westminster Abbey. The coronation was a very imposing ceremony. At the commencement of the proceedings the Archbishop of Canterbury made proclamation at the four corners of the scaffold on which the King sat. He spoke as follows: 'Syrys, here comythe Harry, Kyng Harry the V. ys sone, humylyche to God and Hooly Chyrche, askynge the crowne of thys realme by ryght and discent of herytage. Yf ye holde you welle plesyd with alle and wylle be plesyd with hym, say you nowe, ye! and holde uppe youre hondys.' Then all the people with one voice cried, 'Yea, yea.'[113]

Henry VI. was crowned in France on the 7th of December 1431 by Cardinal Beaufort his uncle (Bishop of Winchester), and on his return to England he was met at Blackheath by the Mayor and citizens on the 21st of February 1431-1432. The Mayor and aldermen were dressed in scarlet, and the members of the gilds in white, with the cognisances of their crafts on their sleeves. The figure of a mighty giant, with a drawn sword, stood at the entrance of the bridge. When the King had passed the first gate and was arrived at the drawbridge, he found a goodly tower, hung with silk and cloth of arras, out of which suddenly appeared three ladies, clad in gold and silk, with coronets upon their head; of which the first was Dame Nature, the second Dame Grace, and the third Dame Fortune. On each side of these dames were seven virgins, all clothed in white; those on the right presented the King with the seven gifts of the Holy Ghost—sapience, intelligence, good counsel, strength, cunning, pity, and dread of God; those on the left with the seven gifts of grace—the crown of glory, the sceptre of clemency and pity, the sword of might and victory, the mantle of prudence, the shield of faith, the helmet of health, and the girdle of love and perfect peace.

On Cornhill was a tabernacle of curious work, in which stood Dame Sapience, and around her the seven liberal arts—Grammar, Logic, Rhetoric, Music, Arithmetic, Geometry, and Astronomy.

At the conduit in Cornhill was set a circular pageant, on the summit whereof was a child of wonderful beauty, apparelled like a King, upon whose right hand sat Lady Mercy, on his left Lady Truth, and over them stood Dame Clemency embracing the King's throne.

At the conduit in Cheap there were formed several wells—the Well of Mercy, the Well of Grace, and the Well of Pity, and at each a lady standing who administered the water to such as would ask it, and then the water was turned into good wine. A little further west was a tower ornamented with the arms of England and France. By its side stood two green trees, one bearing the genealogy of Saint Edward and the other that of Saint Louis.

On entering St. Paul's Churchyard Henry VI. was met by a procession of the dean and canons, the Archbishop of Canterbury, and six bishops, who conducted him to the Cathedral, where he made his oblations. He then took horse at the west door of St. Paul's, and so rode to Westminster, where he was received by the abbot and taken to St. Edward's shrine. His lords then conveyed him to his palace, and the Mayor and citizens returned joyously to London.[114]

This was probably the most elaborate and beautiful pageant ever performed in the streets of London.

The King married Margaret of Anjou in 1445, and on approaching London, on the way to her coronation, the Queen was met on Blackheath by the Mayor, aldermen and sheriffs and the principal members of the gilds, attired in 'browne blue,' with embroidered sleeves and red hoods on their heads, every craft having its cognisance, who brought her with great triumph to Westminster. There were on this occasion several pageants of a similar character to those described before.

In 1461, after the Battle of Mortimer Cross and the second Battle of St. Alban's, Edward Earl of March came to London with his forces and was chosen King in St. John's Field, Clerkenwell, on March 2. King Edward's title was set forth in a sermon at Paul's Cross by the Bishop of Exeter. After the sermon the king was conveyed in procession to Westminster Abbey, and after having offered at St. Edward's shrine he went to Westminster Hall and, sitting in the royal seat, was greeted with shouts of 'Long live the King!' He then returned to St. Paul's, and was lodged in the bishop's palace.[115] On the 26th of June the Mayor and aldermen in scarlet, and the Commons in green, brought Edward IV. from Lambeth to the Tower, and on the 28th inst. he was crowned with great solemnity at Westminster.

'And on the morrow, after the King was crowned againe in Westminster Abbey in the worship of God and S. Peter, and on the next morrow he went crowned in Paules Church in London, in the honor of God and S. Paule, and there an angell came downe and censed him, at which time was so great a multitude of people in Paules as ever was seene in any dayes.'[116]

On Whitsunday 1465 Queen Elizabeth Grey was crowned at Westminster Abbey, having on the preceding day ridden in a horse litter through the chief streets of London, preceded by the newly-created Knights of the Bath, four of whom were men of London—the Mayor and three others.

Shortly after the murder of Henry VI. in the Tower (1471) Edward was met by the Mayor, aldermen and citizens, about a mile from the city, between Islington and Shoreditch, and in the highway he knighted the Mayor, eleven aldermen and the recorder.

Edward IV. died on April 9, 1483, and his young son, Edward V., was brought from Ludlow by the Greys, his relations on the mother's side. Richard Duke of Gloucester, fearing the action of the Greys, overtook the procession, and sent Earl Rivers and Sir Richard Grey prisoners to Pontefract. Edmond Shaa, the Mayor, the sheriffs and the aldermen in scarlet, with 500 horse of the citizens in violet, met the King and the Duke at Hornsey, and, riding from thence, accompanied them into the city, which was entered on the 4th of May. The King was lodged in the bishop's palace, where a great Council was held, at which the Dukes of Gloucester and Buckingham and other great lords were sworn. Edward V. was deposed soon after this, and on the 5th of July, the day before his coronation, Richard rode from the Tower through the city, with his son, the Prince of Wales, three dukes, nine earls, twenty-two viscounts and barons, eighty knights, esquires and gentlemen 'not to be numbered,' besides the great officers of State.

After the Battle of Bosworth, Henry VII. was met at Hornsey on the 28th of August 1485 by the Mayor (Sir Thomas Hille) and the aldermen in their scarlet robes, accompanied by a great number of citizens on horseback, in violet-coloured gowns, whence they conducted him to Shoreditch, where he was received by the several companies, and then conducted to St. Paul's, where he offered three standards, one with the image of St. George, another with a red, fiery dragon, and the third with a dun cow. After the singing of the *Te Deum* he went to the bishop's palace. Less than a month afterwards Sir Thomas Hille died of the sweating sickness.

The coronation of Henry VII., in 1485, was hurried over with less ceremonial than usual and without any procession through the city, but that of the Queen (Elizabeth of York), in 1487, was attended with all the pomp customary on similar occasions. On Friday before St. Katherine's Day the Queen came from Greenwich by water. The Mayor, sheriffs and aldermen, with citizens chosen from every craft in their liveries, were waiting on the river to receive her and attend her to the Tower. On the following day she went through London to Westminster in a litter. The houses were dressed with clothes of tapestry and arras, and in Cheap with rich cloth of gold, velvet and silk. Along the streets, from the Tower to St. Paul's, stood in order all the crafts of London in their liveries, and in various places were placed singing children, some arrayed like angels, to sing sweet songs as the Queen went by.

The Battle of Bosworth we have agreed to consider as the period of the break up of the Middle Ages, but it was many years after this before the shows and amusements of the people exhibited any great change. The Tudors (especially Henry VIII.) showed a particular delight in pageantry, and the Stuarts carried on the tradition. In fact, it was in Elizabeth's reign that special attention was given to the arrangements of the Lord Mayor's pageant.

George Peele, the dramatist, is the first on the list of the city poets, although we have already seen that Lydgate was employed to write poetry in honour of King Henry VI. The pageants prepared for the triumphant passage of 'King James and Queen Anne, his wife, and Henry Frederick, the Prince,' from the Tower through the city on the 15th of March 1603-1604 were of a magnificent character. Seven beautiful arches of triumph were designed by Stephen Harrison, joiner and architect. These were erected at the expense of the livery companies and the foreign merchants. During the eighteenth and nineteenth centuries the art of pageantry was almost entirely lost. The decoration of our streets on joyful occasions has lately considerably improved, but there is still room for a more artistic treatment. With our knowledge of the past and the possession of artists who are enthusiastic for the revival of a true taste in pageantry there ought to be no difficulty in the production of pageants that would do honour to our city. It would be well if the authorities would consult with artists for the improvement of the Lord Mayor's Show.[117]

We have treated of out-of-door amusements, and must now say a few words on one of those enjoyed indoors. Music and poetry were cultivated by certain foreign merchants in England, who established in London, at the close of the thirteenth and beginning of the fourteenth century, a society or brotherhood of the 'Pui,' 'in honour of God, our Lady Saint Mary, and all Saints, both male and female; and in honour of our Lord the King, and all the Barons of the country; and for the increasing of loyal love. And to the end that the city of London may be renowned for all good things in all places; and to the end that mirthfulness, peace, honesty, joyousness, gaiety and good love, without [with?] infinity may be maintained.'[118]

The majority of the members were foreigners, but Englishmen were not excluded, for we find that John de Cheshunt was the third prince or president.

Statutes and full particulars of proceedings are given in *Liber Custumarum*, and curiously enough no other evidence of the existence of such a fraternity in England is known. From this document we learn that the society had received from the city great privileges in respect of the Chapel of St. Mary, in Guildhall, which was building towards the close of the reign of Edward I. Hence the donation in its favour for a chaplain by Sir Henry le Waleys, 1299,[119] who had been Mayor both of London and Bordeaux, and in the latter capacity would be likely to feel an additional interest in this musical society of French merchants and their English friends.

The Regulations are very full and explanatory of the various proceedings at the Festival of the Pui, as the following extracts from Mr. Riley's translation of the Latin original will show:—

As to the yearly election of a Prince.—'The Prince ought to be chosen as being good, and loyal, and sufficient, upon the oath of eleven companions, or of the twelve, to their knowledge, upon their oath, that the Pui may be promoted thereby, and maintained and upheld. And he who shall be chosen for Prince, may not refuse it, upon his oath. And when the old Prince and his companions shall leave to make a new Prince, at the great feast, the old Prince and his companions shall go through the room, from one end to the other, singing; and the old Prince shall carry the crown of the Pui upon his head, and a gilt cup in his hands, full of wine. And when they shall have gone round, the old Prince shall give to drink unto him whom they shall have chosen, and shall give him the crown, and such person shall be Prince.'

Marriage, death and burial of the Members.—'If there be any one of the companions who marries in the city of London, or who becomes a clerk-priest, he ought to let the companions know thereof, and each shall be there according to his oath, if he have not a proper excuse. And the married person ought to give them chaplets, all of one kind; and all the companions ought to go with the bridegroom to church, and to make offering, and to return from the church to the house. And if there be any of the companions of the brotherhood who departs this life and dies, all the companions ought to be there, and to carry the body to church, by leave of the kindred, and to make offering.'

Common hutch.—'There shall be a common hutch of the company of the Pui, in which the remembrances and the revised provisions of the company shall be placed in safe keeping; of which hutch, in the first place, the new Prince, each year after he is chosen, shall have one key; and two companions, by assent of the companions, for such custody chosen, each one key. And that this hutch shall stand in such safe place as the companions shall ordain within the city of London.'

Clerk and Chaplain.—'There shall be a clerk, intelligent, and residing in London, chosen by the companions, to serve the company, and that he be willing and able to be attendant upon, and obedient unto the Prince, and to the twelve companions, in all matters that concern the company.'

'That there be a chaplain, at all times singing [Mass] for the living and the dead of the company, [and] a chapel, founded in honour of God and our Lady, so soon as the improved means of the company, by the aid of God and good folks, may thereunto suffice. And if the companions of the Pui who are of sufficient means, be pressed by illness, so much as to wish to make their testaments, the Prince is to go, with two of the twelve companions with him, to visit the sick persons; and is to remind them of their faith which they have pledged unto the company, and to admonish them to devise somewhat of their property towards supplying the chapel and chaplain aforesaid, and supporting the same.'

The Grand Feast.—'Whereas the royal feast of the Pui is maintained and established principally for crowning a royal song, inasmuch as it is by song that it is honoured and enhanced, all the gentle companions of the Pui by right reason are bound to exalt royal songs to the utmost of their power, and especially the one that is crowned by assent of the companions upon the day of the great feast of the Pui. Wherefore it is here provided, as concerning such songs, that each new Prince, the day that he shall wear the crown, and shall govern the feast of the Pui, and so soon as he shall have had the blazon of his arms hung in the room where the feast of the Pui shall be held, shall forthwith cause to be set up beneath his blazon the song that was crowned on the day that he was chosen as the new Prince, plainly and correctly written, without default.'

'As to the serving up the feast, it is also ordained that all the companions shall be served amply, as well the poorest as the richest, in this form; that is to say, they shall be served with good bread, good ale, and good wine; and then they shall be served with pottage, and with one course of solid meat; and then after that with double roast in a dish, and cheese, without more.'

No ladies present.—'Although the becoming pleasance of virtuous ladies is a rightful theme and principal occasion for royal singing, and for composing and furnishing royal songs, nevertheless it is hereby provided that no lady or other woman ought to be at the great [sitting] of the Pui, for the reason that the [members] ought hereby to take example, and rightful warning, to honour, cherish and commend all ladies, at all times, in all places, as much in their absence as in their presence.'

Costume and Procession.—'The Prince ought, at his own cost, to be costumed with coat and surcoat, without sleeves, and mantle of one suit, with whatever arms he may please, at his own free will; so that at the election of a new Prince, at the great feast of the Pui, he give his mantle and his crown to the new Prince, so soon as he shall be chosen.'

'He who shall be crowned for his song upon that day may ride between the old Prince and the new one in the procession on horseback which they shall make throughout the city, after the feast, that they may have knowledge of the one Prince and of the other by the suit of the costumes.'

'Forthwith, after they have given the crown to him who shall sing the best, they shall mount their horses and make their procession through the city, and shall then escort their new Prince to his house; and there they shall all alight, and shall have a dance there, by way of hearty good-bye; and they shall then take one drink and depart, each to his own house, all on foot.'

The fraternity took its name from Le Puy en Velay, in Auvergne, the celebrated statue of the Virgin Mary in the Cathedral of which place was long a popular object of pilgrimage and devotion during the Middle Ages.

M. Aymard, Administrator of the city of Le Puy en Velay, and the historian of the Confrèries of Notre Dame du Puy, is of opinion that the document in the *Liber Custumarum* is at once more full and more ancient by far than any set of regulations of a similar French fraternity which is known to have survived to our times. Societies of the Pui flourished in Normandy and Picardy. The place of meeting of the 'companions' is not known, but Mr. Riley suggests that it was possibly in the Vintry. There is some uncertainty as to how the fraternity came to an end.[120]

Londoners were better supplied with eating-houses than their neighbours on the Continent, as we learn from the description of the street of cookshops on the Thames side by Fitz-Stephen:—

'There is also in London, on the bank of the river, amongst the wine shops, which are kept in ships and cellars, a public eating-house; there every day, according to the season, may be found viands of all kinds, roast, fried and boiled, fish large and small, coarser meat for the poor, and more delicate for the rich, such as venison, fowls and small birds. If friends, wearied with their journey, should unexpectedly come to a citizen's house, and, being hungry, should not like to wait till fresh meat be bought and cooked ... meanwhile some run to the riverside, and there every thing that they could wish for is instantly procured.

'However great the number of soldiers and strangers that enters or leaves the city at any hour of the day or night, they may turn in there if they please, and refresh themselves according to their inclination; so that the former have no occasion to fast too long, or the latter to leave the city without dining. Those who wish to indulge themselves would not desire a sturgeon, or a bird of Africa, or the godwit of Ionia, when the delicacies that are to be found there are set before them. This, indeed, is the public cookery, and is very convenient to the city, and a distinguishing mark of civilization.'

Mr. Riley points out in his Introduction to the *Liber Custumarum* that the *Coquina* of Fitz-Stephen was in reality a Cook's Row, not merely a solitary cookshop. In Fitz-Ailwyne's Second Assize (1212) the cookshops on the Thames were ordered to be whitewashed and plastered and the inner partitions to be removed, from which it would appear that lodging-rooms had been 'constructed for the harbouring of guests and travellers in contravention of the city regulations, which at all times during the thirteenth and two succeeding centuries strictly forbade cooks and pie-bakers to keep hostels for the entertainment of guests. In the fourteenth century, however, most of these cookshops had made way for genuine hostels and herbergeries,—to be kept only by freemen, and on no account by foreigners,—though we find mention made of one or two cookshops lingering on the city margin of the Thames so late as the reign of Edward the Third.'[121]

Mr. Riley adds in his glossary: 'To the celebrity which London gained at an early period for its cookshops its citizens were not improbably indebted for their nickname of 'cockney,' one which they have retained throughout England to the present day. The earliest recorded instance of its use is probably of this same period; the rhyme uttered, according to Camden, by Hugh Bigot, Earl of Norfolk, in reference to Henry II., the capital of whose English dominions was London:—

'Were I in my castle of Bungay,
Upon the river of Waveney,
I would no care for the King of Cokenay.'[122]

'Keepers of wine taverns and ale-houses and victuallers (who merely sold provisions) do not appear to have lodged their guests any more than the cooks.' 'The persons whose business it was to receive guests for profit, appear to have been divided into two classes, the "Hostelers" and the

"Herbergeours." The line of distinction between these two classes is not very evident ... but it seems not improbable that it consisted in the fact that the former lodged and fed the servants and horses of their guests, while the latter did not. At all events, hostelers are mentioned as supplying hay and corn for horses, but herbergeours never.' Hostelers were also forbidden to sell drink and victuals to any other than their guests.[123]

The established charge for a night's lodging about the time of Henry IV. was one penny per night.

'In the times of our early Kings, when they moved from place to place, it devolved upon the Marshal of the King's household to find lodgings for the royal retinue and dependents, which was done by sending a billet and seizing arbitrarily the best houses and mansions of the locality, turning out the inhabitants and marking the houses so selected with chalk; which latter duty seems to have belonged to the Serjeant-Chamberlain of the King's household. The city of London, fortunately for the comfort and independence of its inhabitants, was exempted by numerous charters from having to endure this most abominable annoyance at such times as it pleased the King to become its near neighbour by taking up his residence in the town.'[124]

By an Act (7 Edw. VI.) 1553 forty taverns and public-houses were allowed in the city and three in Westminster.

CHAPTER VII

Health, Disease and Sanitation[125]

WHEN I mentioned to a friend that I intended to devote one of the chapters of this book to the consideration of sanitation in the Middle Ages, he hinted that as there was no such thing this would partake somewhat of the character of the famous chapter on Snakes in the *History of Ireland*. In this opinion I hope to prove that he is wrong.

There are many conflicting accounts of the general sanitary condition of a walled town in the Middle Ages, but although some have painted the condition of early London in a very unfavourable light, there is sufficient evidence on the other side to induce us, in taking a general survey of so large a subject, to be careful not to use too dark colours for our picture. Probably the town was healthier in ordinary times than the country, because the regulations were stricter, but in time of pestilence it was doubtless worse, from the confined space and the want of fresh air, caused by the closeness of buildings.

We do not hear much of the health of London between the periods of pestilence, but occasional information shows how great was the mortality among infants. The vast disproportion between the births and deaths made the influx of immigrants from the country necessary to keep up the population.

As a sign that the general conditions of life were unhealthier then than now, we may note that the expectancy of life in the Middle Ages was much shorter than at present. It is said that as large a number of persons died at forty years of age as now live to seventy. Queen Elizabeth was the first of the twenty-three sovereigns of England after the Conquest who attained the age of seventy, although Edward I indeed lived to his sixty-ninth year.

Dr. Jessopp gives a vivid picture of the frightful condition of town populations. He writes: 'The sediment of the town population in the Middle Ages was a dense slough of stagnant misery, squalor, famine, loathsome disease and dull despair, such as the worst slums of London, Paris or Liverpool know nothing of.'[126]

Dr. Charles Creighton, in his monumental work on epidemics,[127] takes the view that we must receive with some scepticism the extremely unsatisfactory accounts of the condition of old London. He points out that, while Erasmus gives a most repulsive description of the state of the houses, his contemporary and friend, Sir Thomas More, takes a much more flattering view. Dr. Creighton says: 'Some part of the rather unfair opinion as to the foulness of English life in former times may be traced to a well-known letter by Erasmus to the physician of Cardinal Wolsey. There are grounds for believing that Erasmus must have judged from somewhat unfavourable instances.' Dr. Creighton further points out that William Harrison (*Description of England*) gives proof enough that the filthy floors described by Erasmus had no existence two generations later, even among the poorer classes.

Fitz-Stephen was quite satisfied with the salubrity of the city, and he becomes enthusiastic over the gardens and clear springs which abounded on all sides, and made the walks of those who took the air in the summer evenings so agreeable. In fine, he says: 'The city is delightful indeed when it has a good governor.'

Sir Thomas More at a later period saw so little amiss that he was content to consider London as a fair sample of what he would wish the capital of Utopia to be. We know, at all events, that whatever its faults it was in advance of foreign cities. It has been said that the English word 'comfort' cannot be translated, and a curious confirmation of this is found in the fact that in the old French contemporary account of Wat Tyler's Rebellion the word is introduced in a French context, as if there was no equivalent in that language.

Dr. J. W. Tripe, in 1881, took as the subject of his inaugural address on assuming the presidential chair of the Society of Medical Officers of Health: 'The Sanitary Condition and Laws of Mediæval London.' Referring to this, a writer in the *Medical Times and Gazette* says: 'His description of the streets and houses of Old London, and of the habits of our forefathers, though most graphic, was not new ... but few, we think, have any idea of the antiquity of Sanitary, Nuisance Removal and River Conservancy Acts, and Dr. Tripe has therefore done well to again set forth the accounts of them that have been exhumed from the records of the city. Rude as they may seem to modern notions, they ought to have sufficed for the prevention of the epidemics which from time to time decimated the population, if they had not, like so many more recent enactments, been in advance of the age, and consequently remained for the most part dead letters.'[128]

Before entering into particulars as to means taken for the protection of the city from disease, and as to those upon whom the duty was laid of carrying them out, it will be necessary to make a few remarks upon the healing art in the Middle Ages.

It may be presumed that at all times large numbers suffered from illnesses and required medical aid, yet little has come down to us relating to the treatment adopted by the doctors. Unfortunately the medical men of the Middle Ages do not appear to have trusted to themselves or to their own practical knowledge. Instead they put their whole trust in the little they knew of Greek practice which they learnt from the Arabs. So that, even when writing on cases that came under their own observation, they give but slight information respecting the clinical treatment they adopted, and were afraid to express an opinion without the authority of a great name.

Dr. Norman Moore says: 'The basis of medicine is the patient.'[129] This being so, as the patient always exists the medicine man must always have been required.

Those whose duty it was to combat disease among the Saxons seem to have been of little account, if we are to judge from the Rev. Oswald Cockayn's collection of *Leechdoms, Wort-cunning and Star Craft of Early England*, published in the Master of the Rolls' Series (1864); and Dr. J.F.Payne's *Fitzpatrick Lectures on the History of Medicine*, 1903.

The Saxon leech received a professional education, and was often learned although he did not advance knowledge. He seems to have placed more reliance upon charms and magic than upon any sensible treatment. He compounded recipes of the most incongruous character, and paid special attention to the use of herbs, but few instances of cures performed by him are recorded.

It is not until after the Conquest that we are able to find the first signs of the noble profession of to-day.

It is said that mediæval medicine first began to emerge from obscurity in the thirteenth and fourteenth centuries. The Jews and the clergy were among the first to practise medicine. A noted Jewish physician is recorded by William of Newburgh as practising at King's Lynn at the end of the twelfth century, but shortly afterwards the Jews were driven out of the country, and we hear no more of them except of an occasional physician who managed to escape the general outlawry of his nation. The clergy also in course of time largely gave over their noble attempts to heal their fellow-citizens, and a medical profession was gradually formed.

John of Salisbury (d. 1180), the friend and counsellor of Thomas à Becket, who is called by Bishop Stubbs 'the central figure of English learning for thirty years,' and may therefore be considered to some extent as an authority on the subject, had a very poor opinion of the medical profession of his day, and rated its members roundly for their ignorance and incompetence. He affirmed that they had two maxims which they never violated—'Never mind the poor; never refuse money from the rich.'

There was no school of anatomy or surgery throughout England in the age of Chaucer and Wyclyf, but the medical schools of Salerno, Naples and Montpellier were attended by Englishmen. St. Luke is usually considered as the patron saint of the medical profession, but in the Middle Ages he was to a great extent dispossessed by St. Cosmas and St. Damian,[130] two brothers, who practised as physicians in Cilicia, and were martyred in the early part of the fourth century. These were the patron saints of the Company of Barber Surgeons, but the Fellowship of Surgeons, whose history has been written by Mr. D'Arcy Power,[131] kept St. Luke's Day as well as that of St. Cosmas and St. Damian.

Chaucer found room for the 'Doctor of Physick' in his wonderful gallery of mediæval portraits, and a very vivid picture he gives of the studies and practice of this worthy. It is drawn with the poet's tolerant humour, but he ends by saying that the doctor loved his gold, and all accounts appear to corroborate this opinion.

'With us ther was a Doctour of Phisik,
In all this world ne was ther noon hym lik,
To speke of phisik and surgerye;
For he was grounded in astronomye.
He kepte his pacient a ful greet deel
In hourés, by his magyk natureel.
Wel koude he fortunen the ascendent
Of his ymáges for his pacient.
He knew the cause of everich maladye,
Were it of hoot or cold, or moyste or drye,
And where they engendred and of what humour;
He was a verray parfit practisour.
The cause y-knowe and of his harm the roote,
Anon he yaf the siké man his boote [remedy].
Ful redy hadde he his apothecaries
To sende him droggés and his letuaries,
For ech of hem made oother for to wynne.
Hir frendshipe was nat newè to begynne.
Wel knew he the oldé Esculapius
And Deyscorides and eek Rufus,
Olde Ypocras, Haly and Galyen,
Serapion, Razis and Avycen,
Averrois, Damascien and Constantyn,
Bernard and Gatésden and Gilbertyn.

Of his dieté mesurable was he,
For it was of no superfluitee,
But of greet norissyng and digestible.
His studie was but litel on the Bible.
In sangwyn and in pers he clad was al,
Lynéd with taffata and with sendal.
And yet he was but esy of dispence,
He kepté that he wan in pestilence.
For gold in phisik is a cordial,
Therefore he lovéde gold in special.'

Chaucer here shows great learning and knowledge of the history of medicine. He gives a full list of the Greek and Arab authorities, and also of the men living nearer to his own day. Bernard was Bernardus, Gordonius the professor of medicine at Montpellier in Chaucer's time, Gilbertyn was Gilbertus Anglicus and Gatesden was John of Gaddesden.[132]

Gilbertus Anglicus, author of a *Compendium Medicinæ* (about 1290), is said to have been the first English practical writer on medicine, but as Gilbert quotes a Master Richard, there may have been a still earlier English writer on the subject. The book contains the first description of leprosy written by a European. Little is known of the particulars of his life, but he is said to have been Chancellor at Montpellier. He travelled in the East at the time of the Crusades, probably during the Third Crusade in which Richard I. took part.

John of Gaddesden (1280-1361) was a Doctor of Physick of Oxford, graduating from Merton College, Oxford, who subsequently obtained a large practice in London. He was in priest's orders and held a stall in St. Paul's Cathedral. His famous medical treatise, entitled *Rosa Anglica*, was written about the year 1305. It treats of fevers and injuries of all parts of the body, and soon became a medical text-book throughout Europe. In this book there is an account of his special treatment of smallpox. He wrote: 'Let scarlet red be taken, and let him who is suffering smallpox be entirely wrapped in it or in some other red cloth; I did thus when the son of the illustrious King of England suffered from smallpox, I took care that everything about his couch should be red, and his cure was perfectly effected, for he was restored to health without a trace of the disease.'[133] Gaddesden was court physician to Edward II. and Edward III., and seems to have taken advantage of his position to exact high fees. He recommended his contemporaries to make arrangements about payment before undertaking a case.

The clergy were forbidden by Pope Innocent III. (1215) to undertake any operation involving the shedding of blood, and subsequently they were forbidden to practise surgery in any form. From this cause the practice of surgery largely came into the hands of the barbers.

We shall see later how the profession was divided between the military surgeon and the barber surgeon, but here we have only to deal with the physician.

We learn from Riley's *Memorials* (p. 464) that Roger Clerk, of Wandsworth, was placed in the pillory in May 1382 for pretending to be a physician. He was brought before the Mayor and aldermen, and charged with deceit and falsehood by Roger atte Hacche: 'Whereas no physician or surgeon should intermeddle with any medicines or cures within the liberty of the city aforesaid, but those who are experienced in the said arts, and approved therein, the said Roger Clerk knew nothing of either of the arts aforesaid, being neither experienced nor approved therein, nor understood anything of letters.'

He pretended to heal Roger atte Hacche's wife Johanna of her bodily infirmities by making her wear an old parchment leaf of a book rolled up in a piece of cloth of gold. This being of no avail, Clerk was adjudged to be led 'through the middle of the city with trumpets and pipes, he riding on a horse without a saddle, the said parchment and a whetstone, for his lies, being hung about his neck.'

This man evidently was an impostor, and was properly punished for obtaining money under false pretences, but many of the recipes adopted by the recognised physicians would probably be as ineffectual as the charm of Roger Clerk. John de Gaddesden made a disgusting plaster of dung, headless crickets and beetles, which was rubbed over the sick parts to cure the stone, and we are told in the *Rosa Anglica* that 'in three days the pain had disappeared.'

It was very long before the doctors gave up the making of extraordinary plasters and decoctions. Apparently they had the assistance of laymen on occasions. Dr. Furnivall has printed in his edition of Vicary's *Anatomie of the Bodie of Man* (1888) a series of ten recipes by Henry VIII., and his physicians, Dr. Augustyne, Dr. Butts and Dr. Cromer, taken at random from Sloane MS. 1047 (British Museum). Among these are 'the Kinges Majesties owne plastre,' 'a black plastre devised by the Kinges Hieghness,' 'a plastre devised by the Kinges Majestie at Grenewich, and made at Westminstre, to take awaye inflammacions, and cease payne, and heale excoriations,' 'a decoccioun devised by the Kinges Majestie,' and 'a cataplasme made ungtment-lyke of the Kinges Majesties devise, made at Westminster.'

A conjoint Faculty of Medicine and Surgery was founded in 1423. On the 15th of May 1423 the Mayor and aldermen were petitioned for this purpose. 'The petition prays that all physicians and surgeons practising in London may be considered as a single body of men, governed by a Rector of Medicine, with the assistance of two surveyors of the Faculty of Physic and two masters of the Craft of Surgery. There was to be a common place of meeting, consisting of at least three separate houses, one fitted with desks for examinations and disputations in philosophy and medicine, as well as for the delivery of lectures. The second house was for the use of the physicians, and the third for the convenience of the surgeons.'[134]

The petition was granted, and on the 28th May 1423 Master Gilbert Kymer was sworn before the Mayor and aldermen as Rector of the Faculty of Medicine. Dr. Kymer was a graduate of the University of Oxford, and physician to the household of Humphry, Duke of Gloucester, and also an ecclesiastic. Dr. John Somerset and Dr. Thomas Southwell were sworn on 27th September to act as Supervisors of Physic. The former was also a graduate of Oxford University and a physician to Duke Humphry. Of the latter's history Mr. Power could find nothing. There is no record 'of the swearing in of a Rector of Medicine after 27th September 1424, nor is there any other indication of the continued existence of a conjoint college after 1425.'[135]

Dr. Kymer went to the west of England in 1428, and became Dean of Salisbury in 1449. He continued, however, to practise medicine, 'for in June 1455 he was summoned to Windsor to attend Henry VI. in the fit of imbecility which attacked him after the first Battle of St. Albans.'[136] Little is known of the action of the physicians from 1427 until the College of Physicians was founded by Linacre in 1518.

Surgeons.—Barbers were of old humble practitioners in the art of surgery and performed minor operations such as bleeding, tooth-drawing, and cauterization. They largely assisted the clergy, in whose hands the practice of surgery and medicine was almost wholly confined. The action of the Popes, already alluded to, in forbidding the clergy to interfere in any matter connected with the shedding of blood as incompatible with the holy office caused the clergy to devote themselves specially to medicine, and the duties of the barbers were thereby largely extended.

Mr. D'Arcy Power has drawn attention to a matter which is of the greatest interest in the history of the profession, viz., that two types of surgeons flourished side by side in London during the Middle Ages—the military surgeons who formed the aristocracy of the profession, and the barber surgeons. As early as the Third Crusade (1189-1192) military surgeons 'were in attendance upon the kings and nobles, often in a purely personal capacity, but in the thirteenth century they had formal gradations of rank and were known as "the Royal Surgeon," the "Common Surgeon," etc.'[137]

In 1308 Richard le Barber, the first master of the Barbers' Guild, who dwelt opposite the Church of Allhallows the Less, in Upper Thames Street, was sworn at Guildhall, and in 1310 barbers were appointed to keep strict watch at the city gates, so that no lepers should enter the city.

John Arderne was an early surgeon of mark who is worthy of special notice as one of the first English writers on surgery. He had an extensive experience in the treatment of wounds, and it is supposed that at one time he was attached to the English forces during the French wars in the capacity of field surgeon. He was born in 1307, and practised at Newark from 1349 to 1370, when at the age of sixty-three years he settled in London.[138]

He was specially famous for his treatment of fistula, and he made his great reputation by curing Sir Adam Everyngham of this complaint after his case had been pronounced incurable by the chief doctors in France. Arderne had many distinguished patients and received very large fees. In his works he entered very fully into the history of his cases, and his mode of treatment, and when describing 'ye mannere of ye leche' he throws a remarkable light upon the professional ethics and habits of his time. He was by no means reticent as to the best means of getting over his patients and making them pay well. The surgeon is told to 'beware of scarse askings,' and as an example, Arderne says that, if he had to do with 'a worthy man and a great,' he charged 100 marks or £40 for a cure, 'with robez and feez of an hundred shillyns terme of lyfe, by year.' 'Of lesse men' he would take £40 or 40 marks without feez, but he adds 'never in alle my lyf toke I lesse than an hundred shillyns for cure of that sekeness.'

He counsels doctors to be careful in estimating the length of time of a cure, in fact to suggest double the time he expects. If the patient wonders at the rapidity of cure and asks, 'Why that he putte hym so long a tyme of curyng, sithe that he helyd hym by the halfe? Answere he, that it was for that the pacient was stony-herted and suffred wele sharpe thingis, and that he was of gode complexion, and hadde able fleshe to hale, and feyne he other causes pleasable to the pacient for pacientez of syche wordez are proude and delited.'

Arderne's instructions for the guidance of doctors are very sensible, and they help us to form a correct estimate of the manners of the public who were patients. Dr. Poore, after giving an analysis of the surgeon's work, writes: 'It is evident that John of Arderne was a consummate man of the world, and knew all the tricks of his trade. His fees seem to have been enormous, and indeed he is only one out of many examples among our early professional forerunners who made very large professional incomes.'[139]

Mr. Anderson, the biographer of Arderne, remarks that although he called himself 'Chirurgus inter Medicos,' 'there is nothing to show that he possessed a master's degree, or any formal license for the exercise of his calling.' Mr. Anderson adds, however, 'his writings prove that he was a man of clerkly attainments, with a good knowledge of Latin and French, and well read in the available literature of his profession, quoting freely from the works of the mediæval surgeons, the Arabs, and even from the Greeks.'

Mr. Anderson notes that there are no less than twenty-two manuscripts of the works of Arderne in the British Museum, both in the original Latin and in early English translations, 'some repeating or overlapping others in matter.' His book *Da curâ Oculi* is dated from London in 1377.

It was not until the next century that a surgeon of equal distinction had arisen in England.

There must have been many incompetent practitioners in London in the fourteenth century, an instance of which evil we find in Riley's *Memorials*. John le Spicer of Cornhill in 1354 attended Thomas de Shene, who suffered from a serious wound in the jaw. Certain surgeons sworn before the Mayor found that the 'enormous and horrible hurt on the right side of the jaw of Thomas de Shene' was incurable, but they held that if John le Spicer had been expert in his craft, or had called in counsel and assistance to his aid, the injury might have been cured.[140]

When the charter was granted to the Barbers' Company in the next century it is expressly stated in the preamble (1462) that through 'the ignorance, negligence and stupidity' of various barbers and other practitioners in surgery many of the King's lieges had 'gone the way of all flesh.'

Mr. D'Arcy Power states that 'a Guild of Surgeons, distinct from the Guild of Barbers, existed in London from time immemorial. The guild was always a small body, probably never more than twenty in number, and sometimes dwindling to less than a dozen. It existed and remained unincorporated at a time when many of the other guilds either vanished or were converted into companies. The earliest notice of the Surgeons' Guild occurs in 1369.'[141] This information is obtained from Letter Book G, translated from the Latin by Riley.

'On Monday next, after the Feast of the Purification of the Blessed Virgin Mary [2nd February 1369], Master John Dunheued, Master John Hyndstoke, and Nicholas Kyldesby, surgeons, were admitted in full husting, before Simon de Mordone [Mayor] and the Aldermen, and sworn, as Master Surgeons of the city of London, that they would well and faithfully serve the people, in undertaking their cures, would take reasonably from them, would faithfully follow their calling, and would present to the said Mayor and Aldermen the defaults of others undertaking cures, so often as should be necessary; and that they would be ready, at all times, when they should be warned, to attend the maimed or wounded, and other persons; and would give truthful information to the officers of the city aforesaid, as to such maimed, wounded and others, whether they be in peril of death or not. And also faithfully to do all things touching their calling.'[142]

There is a similar ordinance dated April 1390 in which Master John Hynstok, Master Geoffrey Grace, Master John Brademore, and Master Henry Suttone, surgeons, were admitted and sworn before the Mayor.[143] Mr. Power points out that this ordinance is specially interesting, because the inspecting master surgeons are sworn 'faithfully to follow their calling, and faithful scrutiny to make of others, both men and *women*, undertaking cures, or practising the art of surgery; and to present their defaults, as well in their practice as in their medicine, to the aforesaid Mayor and aldermen, so often as need shall be.'[144]

Mr. Power says: 'The officers thus put under an obligation to perform certain public duties were the masters or aldermen of the Surgeons' Guild, and it is certain that they took so wide a view of their duties as to harass the members of the Barbers' Guild who meddled with surgery. Thus in 1410 certain 'good and honest folk, barbers of the city, appeared by their counsel in the private chamber of the aldermen and sheriffs, and demanded that they should for ever peaceably enjoy their privileges, without scrutiny of any person of other craft or trade than barbers, and this neither in shaving, cupping, bleeding, nor any other thing in any way pertaining to barbery, or to such practice of surgery as is now used, or in future to be used, within the craft of the said barbers.'[145]

In 1417 there is in the city records special reference to the wardens of the faculty or craft of surgeons. Security was given by a surgeon to the Chamberlain of the city to ensure due care of his patients. John Severelle Love, surgeon, undertook to pay £20 sterling to the Chamberlain if he 'should take any man under his care, as to whom risk of maiming, or of his life might ensue, and within four days should not warn the wardens of the craft of surgery thereof.' Half of this sum was to go to the city, and the other half to the faculty of surgeons.[146]

We now arrive at the time when another great surgeon arose. This was Thomas Morestede, surgeon to Henry V. and Henry VI., and probably previously to Henry IV., who, Mr. Power says, made the first serious attempt to convert surgery into a profession. When Henry V. in the spring of 1415 entered on his campaign in France, which ended with the victory at Agincourt on the 25th October, the medical arrangements of the army were very complete. 'The agreement, dated 29th April 1415, is to the effect that Nicholas Colnet was to accompany the King for a year as physician to the forces in Guienne and France. He was to be attended by three archers as a guard, each archer receiving sixpence a day, whilst Colnet drew twelvepence for his own pay. Thomas Morstede, the surgeon, had also three archers assigned to him for protection, and he too received twelve pence a day, in addition to the usual allowance of one hundred marks a quarter—the pay, it is stated, for thirty men-at-arms, with a share of the plunder. Morestede was directed further to take with him twelve of his own craft, each subordinate surgeon to receive the pay of an archer—sixpence a day.... The scale of pay here granted is very liberal. The ordinary day's wage of a labourer at this time was one penny. Each archer and each surgeon was considered to be worth the wages of six day labourers, and the two chiefs double their assistants.... Yet in spite of these attractions the service was a perilous one, even though it only lasted a few months. Morestede engaged William Bredewardyne to act under him, but he had such difficulty in securing the services of the twelve assistants that he prayed the King 'to grant his letters of Privy Seal directed to your Chancellor of England, to cause him to deliver to your suppliant letters of commission under your great seal, by force of which he should have power to press twelve persons of his craft, such as he should choose to accompany him, and to serve your most gracious sovereign lord during your campaign.'[147] Morestede became a rich and influential London citizen, and served as sheriff in 1436. He died in 1450, and was buried in the Church of St. Olave Upwell, Old Jewry, where he had built 'a fair new aisle.'[148]

Dr. Furnivall printed in his edition of Thomas Vicary's *Anatomie of the Bodie of Man* (Early Text Society, 1888, p. 236), a paper from a manuscript in the British Museum (Royal M.S., 7 F., xiv., art. 24) containing a statement of the pay of navy surgeons in the reign of Henry VIII. *The Henry Grace de Dieu* carried two surgeons at 23s. 4d. a month; also *The Mary Rose* and *The Great Gally*, with two surgeons each at the same pay, and nineteen other vessels each with one surgeon at 10s. a month.

To return to the Fellowship of Surgeons, Mr. Power tells us that in 1435 the surgeons, then seventeen in number, became an established body, with a code of laws and regulations which still exist in a small vellum volume now preserved in Barbers' Hall. In 1462 they obtained a charter of incorporation, and in 1492 were given a grant of arms. In 1493 the guild 'was living on friendly terms with the Barbers' Company, for in this year the two guilds entered into a "composition," dated 12th May, and signed by representatives of both bodies. This composition recognised the independence of the two fellowships "of surgeons enfranchised within the city of London," and "of barber-surgeons and surgeon-barbers enfranchised in the said city." It was agreed that neither body should admit any one except a regular apprentice to practise surgery without the consent and knowledge of the other, and to ensure this being carried into effect every stranger seeking a license to practise in London was to be presented to the Mayor by the four wardens of the two guilds.'[149] The end of the Fellowship of Surgeons came in 1540, when it was united by Act of Parliament (32 Henry VIII.) with the Company of Barbers. The granting of the charter on this occasion was the cause of Holbein's famous picture being painted. This picture still decorates the Barbers' Hall in Monkwell Street.

Allusion has already been made to the Barbers' Company—to its first master in 1308, and to its incorporation by royal charter in 1462 by Edward IV. In 1376 the gild elected two masters, and at this time the members were sharply divided between the barbers proper and the barbers exercising the faculty of surgery.

In 1390 four masters were sworn in in one year, but these were really only master and wardens, as stated by Mr. Young in his most valuable and exhaustive account of the Barber Surgeons' Company.[150]

The relative positions of the city companies has frequently changed, thus at one time the Barber Surgeons were entitled to the seventeenth place, but in 1516 they only ranked as the twenty-eighth. In 1537 the Barber Surgeons formed the most numerous company in London, the number of freemen being 185. The next in order of numbers was the Skinners with 151, then the Haberdashers with 120, the Leathersellers with 113, and the Fishmongers with 109. The rest of the companies numbered less than 100, the Bowyers being the lowest with 19.[151] In 1745 the surgeons, who had long chafed under the inconveniences caused by official connection with the barbers, seceded and formed the Surgeons' Company, under the title of 'The Masters, Governors and Commonalty of the Art and Science of Surgery,' which was established by Act of Parliament. The Surgeons found a temporary home at Stationers' Hall until 1751, when the premises known as Surgeons' Hall, in the Old Bailey, were ready for occupation.

The company came to a premature end in 1796, and it was not until 1800 that the Royal College of Surgeons was established.

HOSPITALS

St. Bartholomew's Hospital.—We are justly proud of the hospitals of the twentieth century, but one of them stands out from the rest on account of its early foundation, and its enormous influence on the growth of professional feeling. In following the incidents in the history of St. Bartholomew's Hospital, we cannot doubt but that this is one of the noblest institutions in London. The hospital was founded by Rahere in 1123, and refounded in 1546. We have little history of the earlier period, but the documents relating to the refoundation evidently echo the sentiments formed during the earlier period.

Dr. Norman Moore in his paper on the Progress of Medicine at St. Bartholomew's Hospital (1888), writes: 'We are in the very middle of the sacred land of medicine, and many of the great events in the history of medicine are connected with the particular region in which our hospital is, or have occurred in our hospital itself.'

Rahere while building the hospital continued his labours by founding the priory, of which all that now remains is the Church of St. Bartholomew the Great. This consists of the choir and transept of the church of the priory, and a part of the site of the close is marked by the present Bartholomew Close. The hospital and the priory were independent but connected. The relations between the two were revised by Richard de Ely, Bishop of London in 1197; by Eustace de Fauconberg, Bishop of London in 1224: and by Simon of Sudbury, Bishop of London in 1373, and the two foundations were finally separated on the dissolution of the priory in 1537.

There is in the British Museum (Cotton MS. Vespasian, Bk. ix.), a Life of Rahere written by one who had known those who knew the founder. The manuscript is a copy of an earlier one written in the reign of Henry II., within fifty years of the foundation of the

OBVERSE OF THE COMMON SEAL OF THE CITY OF LONDON, Cir. 1225.

SEAL OF ST. BARTHOLOMEW'S HOSPITAL.

hospital. This work, which is of great value, is described by Dr. Norman Moore, and analysed in Mr. Morrant Baker's *Two Foundations of St. Bartholomew's Hospital*, A.D. 1123 *and* A.D. 1546[152]

Rahere has been described as the King's minstrel or jester, but there is no authority for this. The writer of his life says that he was a frequenter of the palace, and of noblemen's houses, and made himself so agreeable as to be highly esteemed as the leader of tumultuous pleasures. He was, however, converted to a better state of life, but probably, as is the wont of those who write about conversions, the author rather darkens the picture of the courtier's early follies. Rahere determined to go to Rome, and after visiting the shrines of St. Peter and St. Paul, he was taken ill with a grievous sickness. He feared that God was angry with him for his sins, and he vowed that if God would give him health so that he might return to his own country, 'he would make an hospital in recreation of poor men, and to them so there gathered, necessaries minister after his power.'

In the night he saw a vision which filled him with dread. He seemed to be borne up on high by a beast having four feet and two wings, and set down in a high place. From this great height he looked into a deep pit, and he feared to slide down into it. Then appeared to him a certain man of great beauty and majesty, who fastened his eye upon him and said, 'O man, what and how much service shouldest thou give to him, that in so great peril hath brought help to thee?' Rahere answered: 'Whatsoever might be of heart and of might, diligently should I give, in recompense to my deliverer.' So the kingly man spoke again: 'I am Bartholomew, the Apostle of Jesus Christ, that came to succour thee in thine anguish, and to open to thee the secret mysteries of Heaven. Know me truly, by the will and commandment of the Holy Trinity, and the common favour of the celestial Court and Council, to have chosen a place in the suburbs of London, at Smithfield, where in my name thou shalt found a church, and it shall be the house of God.... My part shall be to provide necessaries, direct, build and end this work; and this place to me accept with evident tokens and signs, protect and defend continually it under my wings; and therefore of this work know me the master, and thyself only the minister; use diligently thy service, and I shall show my lordship.'

Rahere when he got back to London made overtures to the citizens for the purpose of obtaining the land he required for building, and the authorities were favourable to his scheme, but they could not settle the matter until Henry I. had been consulted, because the place at Smithfield was within the King's market. When the petitioner applied to the King his plea was acceded to, and he was given authority to execute his purpose.

It is not quite clear where all the money came from for the carrying out so vast an undertaking, but Rahere had a winning way, and from the King downwards he appears to have obtained liberal help. Before he could build he had to drain the land, which was nothing but a marsh, and when he went there the only sign of civilisation about was a gibbet. The hospital, which from the first was a hospital for the sick, and not a mere almshouse, had a master, eight brethren and four sisters.

The first master was Alfun, an old man who had previously built the Church of St. Giles, Cripplegate, and Rahere was the first prior.

Alfun was also styled hospitaler or proctor of the poor, and the writer of the manuscript Life of Rahere tells how it was the custom of Alfun to go about begging for provisions and other necessaries for the poor men that lay in the hospital, he also looked after the welfare of those who were employed in building the church. Rahere had many troubles in his later life, and a large number of envious enemies spoke evil of him and did him injuries. There was a plot against his life, which failed on account of the confession of a penitent conspirator. He had, however, a good friend in the King, who helped him and confirmed his previous grant by a charter which gave full liberty and great privileges to the priory and hospital. When, therefore, Rahere died, after having been prior for twenty-two years and six months, he left his great establishment in a prosperous condition.

Dr. Norman Moore points out that in the Life of Rahere there is an account of the admission of the first patients of which we have any record. This was a man named Adwyne, who came up to London from Dunwich, in Suffolk, in the reign of Henry II. There are many records of people who were supposed to be healed by praying at Rahere's tomb, but this man is described as having been admitted into the hospital, and therefore a genuine patient. He was discharged cured, but although his condition is described no details of his treatment are given. Dr. Moore supposes that by long lying in bed Adwyne's muscles had become anaemic and enfeebled. He was encouraged 'to move his limbs a little, and he found that he was able to move them much more than he expected; he began to make small objects, commencing with cutting and carving, and so at last was able to work again, and to follow the craft of a carpenter.'[153]

RAHERE'S TOMB IN ST. BARTHOLOMEW'S CHURCH.

John Mirfield, a canon of St. Bartholomew's Priory, wrote a general treatise on medicine, entitled *Breviarium Bartholomei*, about the year 1380, when Richard Sutton was master of the hospital. This book is of considerable interest, both as an early medical treatise written at a time when this form of literature was not general, and for its connection with the hospital. Dr. Moore gives a full description of the contents, and adds: 'The picture is complete of the medical and surgical practice in St. Bartholomew's Hospital in the reign of Richard II.'[154]

London was doubtless well able to supply the hospital with patients, and the dismounted knights in the jousts at Smithfield must have found it convenient to have their wounds attended to at once. It is recorded that when Wat Tyler fell from his horse, half dead from his wounds, he was dragged within the hospital gate, and died in what is now the open space between the church and the outer wall of the great hall. The body was then laid in the master's chamber. Walworth, however, had the body brought out and beheaded, the head being sent to London Bridge to replace that of Archbishop Sudbury.

By a composition, dated 1373, the master of the hospital was ordered to be presented to the Prior of St. Bartholomew's Priory after election, and previous to presentation to the bishop. The last master was John Brereton, who subscribed to the King's supremacy in 1534. The last prior, Robert Fuller, surrendered the priory to the King in 1540.

About the year 1423 the famous Richard Whittington repaired the hospital at his own expense. Little more than a century after this it was refounded by Henry VIII., but with very little pecuniary help from the King.

In 1538 the Mayor, aldermen and commonalty of the City of London petitioned Henry VIII. that they might from thenceforth have the order, rule, disposition and governance of St. Mary's Spital, St. Bartholomew's Spital, and St. Thomas's Spital, and the new Abbey at Tower Hill, with the rents and revenues appertaining to the same, for the only relief of the poor, sick and needy persons. In 1544 the King confirmed by letters patent the grant and establishment of St. Bartholomew's Hospital to the master and chaplains, but in 1546 a deed of covenant between Henry VIII. and the Mayor, commonalty and citizens of London respecting the hospital was sealed, by which they came under the rule of the city. It is stated in the deed that 'his Highness of his bountiful goodness and charitable mind was moved with great pity for and towards the relief, aid, succour and help of the poor, aged, sick, low and impotent people.' Additional letters patent were issued in 1547.[155]

In 1552 was published *The Ordre of the Hospital of S. Bartholomewes in West Smythfielde, in London*, with this text on the title, 'I Epist. John, ij. chap. He that sayeth he walketh in the lyght, and hateth his brother, came never as zeal in the lyght. But he that loveth his brother, he dwelleth in the lyght.'

We have already seen how the later years of Rahere's life were darkened by the attacks of enemies, and a curious revival of similar slanders appears to have occurred when the hospital was refounded, and so virulent were the slanders that it appears to have been thought that a reply from the governing body was needed, and such a reply is found in the Preface to the *Ordre*[156]—this commences as follows: 'The wickednes of reporte at thys Daie, good reader, is growen to such ranckenes, that nothing almost is able to defend it selfe against the venyme thereof, but that, either with open slander or privie whisperyng, it shalbe so undermyned, that it shall neither have the good successe, which otherwyse it myght, ne the thankes whiche for the worthines it ought.'

Henry VIII. being dead the governing body appear to have felt it possible to tell the truth as to the little he had done in endowing the hospital. In fact, both Henry VIII. and Edward VI. have gained credit as founders, when they really did little more than give buildings for public purposes that were of no use to themselves and then leave others to find the money to support them.

The writer of the Preface says that the slanderers ought to repent and praise both the deed and the doers so as to wipe away the slander: 'But forasmuch as it is doubtful whether thei wil do as thei maie, and of conscience are bounden, and the slaundre is so wide spred, that a narowe remedy cannot amend it: It is thought good to the Lord Mayour of thys Citie of London, as chief patrone and governour of this Hospitall, in the name of the Citie, to publishe at this present the officiers and ordres by hym appoincted, and tyme to tyme practysed and used by twelve of the citizeins the moste aunciente in their courses, as at large in the processe shal appiar, partly for the staye and redresse of such slaundre, and partly for that it myght be an open witnesse and knowledge unto all men howe thynges are administered there and by whom. Wherein if any man judge more to be set forth in woorde, than in diede is folowed there be meanes to resolve him.'

The case in abstract is as follows: For the relief of the sore and sick of the City of London Henry VIII. was pleased to erect a hospital in West Smithfield for a hundred sore and diseased. He endowed it with 500 marks a year, on condition that the citizens found another 500 marks. The citizens soon discovered that the King's endowment was far under what at first they had hoped. The 500 marks rent was to come from houses in great decay, and some 'rotten ruinous,' so that to make them again worth the wonted revenue was no small charge, and after paying certain pensions, etc., there only remained towards succouring the hundred poor sufficient for the charge of three or four harlots then lying in childbed. The citizens therefore, to relieve their own poor and others coming daily out of all quarters of the realm, spent above their covenant of 500 marks yearly not much less than £1000, which enabled them to receive the number agreed upon. In spite of this, certain busy bodies more ready to espy occasion to blame others than skilful to redress things blameworthy indeed, rounded into the ears of the preachers their tender consciences. These preachers took upon them to make known these slanders, so that the good citizens for their five years' loathsome work done for Christ's sake received only open detraction and the poor a greater hindrance.

During these five years (1547-1552) 800 sick folk were healed in the hospital and 92 died. The Preface writer ends by saying that if any man spieth aught in the Ordre worthy to be reformed he will find those at the hospital glad and willing to reform it, and the city wish, if by any means it is possible, to raise the number of those receiving the benefits of the hospital from 100 to 1000.

The number of distinct paid officers is given as seven, in this order— (1) The Hospitaller, (2) the Renter Clerk, (3) the Butlers, (4) the Porter, (5) the Matron, (6) the Sisters (twelve), (7) the Beadles (eight). 'There are also as in a kynde by themselves iii. chirurgeons in the wages of the Hospitall, gevyng daily attendaunce upon the cures of the poore.'

The charges in this little book of orders are of great interest, and will well repay careful perusal. The surgeons are charged to the uttermost of their knowledge to help cure the diseases of the poor without favouring those with good friends; they are not to admit the incurables, so as to keep out those who are curable; when they dress any diseased person they are to advise him to sin no more and be thankful unto God; they are to receive no gift from anyone, and never to burden the house with any sick person, for the curing of which person they have received any money. In conclusion, they are to report any wrongdoing to the almoners.

The nurses of the present day would be surprised at the stringency of the instructions in the charge to the sisters. Mr. Morrant Baker specially refers to one command: 'And so muche as in you shall lie, ye shall avoyde and shonne the conversacion and company of all men,' and adds, 'An order which, I have no doubt, was as implicitly obeyed then as any similar command would be now.'

At the end of the charges is 'A daily service for the poore,' and 'A thankesgeving unto Almyghtie God to be said by the poore that are cured in the hospital, at ye time of their delivery from thence, upon their knies in the hall before the hospitaler, and twoo masters of this house, at the least. And this the hospitaler shal charge them to learne without the booke, before they be delivered.'

Thomas Vicary, serjeant surgeon to the King, and the foremost surgeon of his time, was first appointed Governor of St. Bartholomew's on the 29th of September 1548, and in January 1552 he was made governor for life. He was the first medical officer of the hospital. Dr. Norman Moore describes his position as 'intermediate between that of the master of older times and that of the surgeons subsequently appointed. For some years he seems to have had both medical and general charge of the hospital.'[157]

At this time he had long held a distinguished position, although not originally a trained surgeon, and at first in small practice at Maidstone. In 1525 he was junior of the three wardens of the Barber Surgeons' Company. In 1528 he was upper warden and one of the surgeons to Henry VIII. On 29th April 1530 he was granted the office of serjeant surgeon to the King 'as soon as Marcellus de la More shall die, or resign or forfeit his post,' and in the same year he became master of the Barber Surgeons' Company. La More died, or disappeared from England at some time after Easter 1535, when he received his last payment. Vicary received his first quarter's salary as serjeant surgeon on the 20th September 1535, and filled this distinguished office under Henry VIII., Edward VI., Mary and Elizabeth. The serjeant surgeons were originally military surgeons, whose first duty was to attend the King upon the battlefield. John Ranby was the last to perform this duty when he attended George II. at the Battle of Dettingen in 1743.[158]

In 1541 Vicary was appointed first master of the Amalgamated Company of Barbers and Surgeons, and in 1548 he is said to have published for the first time his *Anatomie of Man's Body*. This work was reprinted in 1577 by the four surgeons of St. Bartholomew's of that time— William Clowes, Wil. Beton, Richard Story and Edward Bayly, who dedicated it to the president and governors. The book is one of great interest, but Dr. Payne has lately proved that it is not an original work, but merely a *rechauffé* of an anatomical treatise of the fourteenth century, from which the greater portion has been transcribed word for word.[159]

The first physician of St. Bartholomew's was Dr. Roderigo Lopus, a Portuguese Jew, who was appointed about 1567.

St. Thomas's Hospital.—This hospital is almost of as great antiquity as St. Bartholomew's. The original hospital belonged to the canons of the Priory of St. Mary Overy, and was situated on the west side of the road running south from London Bridge. In 1207 the hospital was destroyed in the fire which devastated the borough of Southwark, but a temporary building was erected on the old site (now occupied by the Bridge House Hotel and the London and Westminster Bank). Peter de Rupibus, Bishop of Winchester, projected a new hospital on a more suitable site on the east side of the road, and appealed for funds for this purpose by means of a charter of indulgence, 1228: 'Behold at Southwark an ancient hospital built of old to entertain the poor, has been entirely reduced to cinders and ashes by a lamentable fire; moreover, the place wherein the old hospital has been founded was less appropriate for entertainment and habitation, both by reason of the straitness of the place and by reason of the lack of water and many other conveniences; according to the advice of us, and of wise men, it is transferred and transplanted to another more commodious site, where the air is more pure and calm, and the supply of water more plentiful.'

The new hospital was dedicated to St. Thomas (à Becket) the Martyr, and became independent of St. Mary's Priory. It was frequently referred to as Becket's Spital.

The third building was erected about 1507, and in 1535, a short time before the dissolution of the religious houses, the custos or master, the brethren and the three lay sisters, had the charge of forty beds for poor and infirm people, who were to be supplied with food and firing.

The hospital was refounded in 1553 by Edward VI., and endowed with 4000 marks a year. It was dedicated to St. Thomas the Apostle, but was often called, in honour of Edward, the King's Hospital. The parish of St. Thomas Apostle, Southwark, contained within its limits the two hospitals of St. Thomas and Guy's, and was often called the parish of St. Thomas's Hospital. Thus the old name remained, but the dedication was changed from that of the famous saint of the Middle Ages to that of the Apostle St. Thomas.

Dr. Payne, who wrote an essay 'On some old Physicians of St. Thomas's Hospital,' says that in old times the staff was exclusively surgical. Dr. Eliazer Hodson, who was appointed about 1620, was the first named that Dr. Payne could find, but he does not think that Hodson was the first physician.

The building having fallen into disrepair was entirely rebuilt in 1701-1706, and the hospital remained on the same spot from 1228 until 1862, when the property was sold to the South Eastern Railway Company, and a new hospital was opened on the Albert Embankment at the southern end of Westminster Bridge.

Lepers.—There were other mediæval hospitals in London besides those now described, which were the two chief ones. Many smaller buildings in the suburbs were devoted to the reception of lepers.

Dr. Creighton writes: 'The remarkable Ordinance of Edward III. in 1346 for the expulsion of lepers from London seems to have been the occasion of the founding of two so-called Lazar-houses, one in Kent Street, Southwark, called "the Loke," and the other at Hackney or Kingsland. These are the only two mentioned in the subsequent orders to the porters of the city gates in 1375, and as late as the reign of Henry VI.

ST. GILES' IN THE FIELDS

they are the only two besides the ancient Matilda's Hospital in St. Giles's fields.... Another of the suburban leper-spitals was founded at Highgate by a citizen of 1468, and it is not until the reign of Henry VIII. that we hear of the spitals at Mile End, Knightsbridge and Hammersmith.'[160] Dr. Creighton adds that the Lock was doubtless the house of the 'Leprosi apud Bermondsey,' who are designated in the Royal Charter of 1 Hen. IV. (1399) as recipients, along with the *Leprosi* of Westminster (St. James's), of five or six thousand pounds.

The village of St. Giles in the Fields, as shown in the accompanying plan, is of great interest, largely because the place still retains some of its old special features. Up to the middle of the nineteenth century, when the Rookery of St. Giles's was destroyed, and New Oxford Street was built on the site, the lines of its contour were little altered since the Hospital was founded at the beginning of the twelfth century.

The Ordinance of Edward III. (1346), and the swearing of the porters of the city gates that they will prevent lepers from entering the city, are printed in Riley's *Memorials* (pp. 230, 384).

Dr. Creighton states that, as far as he knows, the Ordinance of 1346 is the only one of the kind in English history, and adds: 'The statutes of the realm contain no reference to lepers or leprosy from first to last; the references in the Rolls of Parliament are to the taxing of their houses and lands. The laws which deprived lepers of marital rights and of heirship appear to have been wholly foreign; in England, leprosy as a bar to succession was made a plea in the law courts.'[161]

Doubtless there were many cases of true leprosy in the Middle Ages, but there was a great confusion of diseases under this generic term, and we are told that, 'in some instances of leper hospitals with authentic charters, the provision for the leprous was in the proportion of one to three or four of the non-leprous inmates.'[162]

It was a very terrible fate for a man or woman to be accused of being a leper, for the sufferers were driven from the haunts of men, and being in many cases uncared for, they grew worse and worse. The disease was largely caused by bad food, and this cause was quite neglected in many places.

A monstrous Ordinance of the Scottish Parliament at Scone in 1386 is recorded in the *Ancient Laws and Customs of the Burghs of Scotland*: 'Gif ony man brings to the market corrupt swine or salmond to be sauld, they sall be taken by the bailie, and incontinent, without ony question, sall be sent to the lepper folke; and gif there be na lepper folke, they sall be destroyed all uterlie.' The Rev. W. Denton, in quoting this instance of horrible cruelty, writes: 'Sir Walter Scott must have had instances of such economy in his mind when he put into the mouth of John Girder the directions—"Let the house be redd up, the broken meat set by, and if there be ony thing totally uneatable, let it be gien to the puir folk."—*Bride of Lammermuir*.'[163]

Men sometimes took advantage of a charge of leprosy to injure an enemy. In 1468, Johanna Nightyngale, of Brentwood, in Essex, was accused of leprosy. She refused to remove herself to a solitary place, and appealed to Edward IV., who issued a Chancery warrant for her examination by his physicians and certain lawyers to be associated with them. The court of inquiry reported that they found the woman to be in no way leprous, nor to have any sign of lepra. The case is recorded in Rymer's *Foedera*.[164]

There was another evil caused by the privilege of begging which was accorded to lepers, for men sometimes pretended to be lepers in order to avail themselves of this privilege.

It is worthy of mention, in passing, that the two districts of London which have given their names to the extremes of high and low life—viz., St. James's and St. Giles's—both have their origin in the leper hospitals of the Middle Ages.

The Plague.—The greatest scourge among the epidemics which have devastated the world is the Eastern bubonic plague, which entered Europe for the first time in the fourteenth century. All epidemics, when they find a new field, appear to be specially virulent, and this was the case with the first appearance of the plague, which so terrified the inhabitants of Europe that they applied to it this ominous name; but the epidemic of 1349 has of late years received the new name of the Black Death, which distinguishes it in the popular mind from the later visitations. The name, which came from Germany, will not be found in the old descriptions of the plague in

England. A writer in the *Quarterly Review* says: 'The term "Der Schwarze Tod" may have been used in Germany in the fourteenth century, but it does not seem to have been current in England before Hecker's work [on Epidemics] was translated into English in 1833.'[165]

The Black Death entered Dorsetshire in August 1348, moving on to Bristol, Gloucester and Oxford. From Oxford the infection marched to London, which city it reached at Michaelmas or November. It soon swept over the whole country. Dr. Creighton writes: 'The Black Death may be said to have extended over three seasons in the British islands—a partial season in the south of England in 1348; a great season all over England, in Ireland, and in the south of Scotland, in 1349; and a late extension in Scotland generally in 1350. The experience of all Europe was similar, the Mediterranean provinces receiving the infection as early as 1347, and the northern countries, on the Baltic and North Seas, as late as 1350.'[166]

This plague had the most momentous effect upon the history of England, on account of the fearful mortality that it caused. It paralysed industry, and permanently altered the position of the labourer. Ineffectual attempts were made to neutralise these effects by the Statute of Labourers and by enactments 'that every workman and labourer shall do his work just as he used before the pestilence'; 'that the servants of substantial people shall take no more than they used to take'; and 'that labourers and workmen who will not work shall be arrested and imprisoned.'[167]

The effects of the pestilence on the Church and on morals is seen in the writings of Wiclif and Langland. Wiclif, who was an Oxford student, in 1348 predicted in his book, *The Last Age of the Church*, the end of the world in 1400 at latest. The effects upon architecture has been dwelt upon by the antiquaries; upon the growth of the country, by political economists; and upon the general health of the country, by doctors; so that it is not necessary here to enter into further explanations.

The statistics of the writers of the Middle Ages are of little value, and the estimates of those who died are very various, but the statement that half the population of England died from the plague is probably not far from the truth.

In East Anglia, which suffered most severely, upwards of 800 parishes lost their parsons, eighty-three of them twice, and ten of them three times, in a few months. In Norfolk and Suffolk nineteen religious houses were left without abbot or prior.[168]

The details of the Black Death in London are not numerous, but Riley gives some particulars of mortality among the City Companies at this time. In the Articles of the Cutlers (1344) the names of eight wardens are given, and below it is stated that in the 23rd year of Edward III.'s reign (five years after) they were all dead, and others chosen in their place.[169] In the Articles of the Hatters (1347) six wardens are named as being chosen on Tuesday after the Feast of St. Lucy, 13th December, 21 Edw. III., and a note is added that by the Saturday after the translation of St. Thomas the Martyr, 7th July, 24 Edw. III., they had all died.[170] Four wardens of the Goldsmiths' Company are recorded to have fallen victims to the Black Death, and doubtless the other companies suffered in a like manner.

The most striking fact in respect to the mortality in London is that recorded by Stow in his Chronicle, of 50,000 persons buried in Sir Walter de Manny's burial place in Spittle Croft (now the Charterhouse). Although doubtless the number is grossly exaggerated, it is certain that it was very great. One of the victims in high places was Dr. Bradwardine, Archbishop of Canterbury, who died at Lambeth on 26th August 1349, just one week after he had landed at Dover from Avignon.

In January 1349 the meeting of Parliament was prorogued because 'a sudden visitation of deadly pestilence had broken out at Westminster and the neighbourhood.'

Dr. Creighton writes: 'For 300 years plague was the grand zymotic disease of England—the same type of plague that came from the East in 1347-1349, continuously reproduced in a succession of epidemics at one place or another.' He goes on to quote Peinlich's *Pest in Steiermark* [i.e. *Styria*], 1877-1878, to show that similar cases occurred over Europe. From 1349 to 1716 seventy years are marked in the annals of Styria as plague years.[171]

The second great pestilence occurred in 1361, when the number of deaths was about a third of those from the plague of 1349. The mortality was greater among men than women. The third pestilence, of 1368-1369, is referred to by Langland in *Piers Plowman*. The fourth was in 1375-1376, and the fifth in 1390-1391.

Dr. Creighton describes several other plagues, and writes that 'in the decade from 1430 to 1440 there were no fewer than four distinct outbreaks of plague, three of them confined to London, and one of them, that of 1439, general throughout the realm.'[172]

The constant recurrence of the plague must have taught the authorities some mode of treatment, but although certain sanitary regulations were made (which will be referred to later on), it is only incidentally that we learn what was done during the earlier visitations. Probably panic reigned generally in the time of the Black Death. Such writings as are left us give this impression, and there is little reason for surprise that it should have been so.

Dr. Creighton has entered very fully into the history of the various plagues and the different expedients which were adopted to mitigate their severity. His valuable work is so thorough in its treatment of the subject that to a great extent I have drawn the following particulars from his luminous pages.

The first plague order, of which the full text is extant, was issued in 1543. The following transcript is taken from an *An Abstract of several Orders relating to the Plague* (British Museum. Addit. MS., No. 4376):—

'35 Hen. VIII. A precept issued to the aldermen:—That they should cause their beadles to set the sign of the cross on every house which should be afflicted with the plague, and there continue for forty days: that no person who was able to live by himself, and should be afflicted with the plague, should go abroad or into any company for one month after his sickness, and that all others who could not live without their daily labour should as much as in them lay refrain from going abroad, and should for forty days after [illegible] and continually carry a white rod in their hand, two foot long. That every person whose house had been infected should, after a visitation, carry all the straw and [illegible] in the night privately in the fields and burn; they shall also carry clothes of the infected in the fields to be cured.

'That no housekeeper should put any person diseased out of his house into the street or other place unless they provided housing for them in some other house.

'That all persons having any dogs in their house, other than hounds, spaniels or mastiffs necessary for the custody or safe keeping of their houses, should forthwith convey them out of the city, or cause them to be killed and carried out of the city and buried at the common laystal.

'That such as kept hounds, spaniels or mastiffs should not suffer them to go abroad, but closely confine them.

'That the churchwardens of every parish should employ somebody to keep out all common beggars out of churches on holydays, and cause them to remain without doors.

'That all the streets, lanes, etc., within the wards should be cleansed.

'That the aldermen should cause this precept to be read in the churches.'

Dr. Creighton says that this order was a development of the measures devised by the King or his Minister before 1518, and probably in the plague of 1513. The wisps put out on the infected houses are replaced by crosses, which above are described simply as 'the sign of the cross.'[173]

On 15th November 1547 it was ordered by the Mayor, recorder and aldermen (*vicecomites*) that 'everye howseholder of their severall wardes, which sithe the feast of all seyntes last past hath bein vysyted with the plage ... shall cause to be fyxed upon the uttermost post of their strete dore a certain crosse of saynt Anthonye devysed for that purpose, there to remain xl. dayes after the setting up thereof.'[174]

The cross of St. Anthony was a crutch, such as was used by the Crutched Friars. It was painted in blue on canvas or board, and the legend under or over the cross was 'Lord have mercy upon us.'

In the plague of 1563 it was ordered, on the 3rd of July, that two hundred blue headless crosses be made with all convenient speed by the Chamberlain, and again, on the 6th of the same month, two hundred more were ordered. On the 8th of July blue crosses were delivered to the Bailiff of Finsbury to be used there.[175]

Dr. Creighton says that before the plague of 1603 the colour of the crosses had been changed to red. The white rod or wand was used in France as well as in England, as we learn from a letter of the Venetian Ambassador to France (20th November 1580): 'This city [Paris] I hear is in a very fair sanitary condition, notwithstanding that as I entered a city gate, which is close to where I reside, I met a man and a woman bearing the white plague wands in their hands, and asking alms; but some believe that this was merely an artifice on their part to gain money.'[176]

The white wand was afterwards retained as the peculiar badge of the searchers of infected houses and of the bearers of the dead. In 1603 it had become a red wand, just as the blue cross had become a red one.

The regulation about dogs is of great interest, as it incidentally shows that dogs were commonly kept in London houses for the purpose of protection. It was believed that dogs carried infection in their hair. Brasbridge, in his *Poor Man's Jewel*, 1578, relates how, 'not many years since, I knew a glover in Oxford who, with his family, to the number of ten or eleven persons, died of the plague, which was said to be brought into the house by a dogge skinne that his wife bought when the disease was in the citie.'

The plague orders contained the clause against dogs to the last, and thousands of them were killed. A proclamation during the London plague of 1563 was directed against cats as well as dogs.[177]

The early literature of the plague is very unsatisfactory, and we have to come to a time much later than the mediæval period for information as to treatment. The main points of the various regulations were isolation of the infected and special attention to sanitation. These in principle are in accord with the best opinion of to-day, but the way in which they were carried out left much to be desired. Those who were imprisoned in their houses must have felt that they were given over to death. Yet some of these patients did recover, and we naturally ask what was the treatment which caused these cures? Was the cure due to the doctor or to nature alone? The answer is not easy to find.

Dr. Payne, in his Inaugural Address as President of the Epidemiological Society in 1893, specially alludes to the literature of the plague, of which he says: 'The number of publications relating to the plague in Europe during the sixteenth, seventeenth and eighteenth centuries is very large, those in Germany being probably the most numerous, while those published in England are comparatively few. We might expect, however, that those works published at the time of great epidemics would furnish us with valuable material for epidemic history. It is very disappointing, therefore, to find how very seldom these writings, whether of continental or English origin, have any historical value. What generally happened was this. When an epidemic broke out, or was expected in any particular place, some local physician thought it his business to furnish the public with a tract on the subject, and he accordingly compiled from the best authorities a pamphlet, good or bad as the case might be. Such a physician, if he survived, would no doubt have been able to acquire some experience of the disease during its continuance, and if he had chosen to put this down in plain words when the epidemic was over he might have done some service to medical history, but unfortunately when the disease had once disappeared the physicians seemed to have lost all interest in the subject, and it is only in rare instances that the medical literature of the plague contains any account of contemporary epidemics. One exception is Guy de Chauliac's well-known account of the "Black Death" at Avignon, but we have nothing in English literature to compare at all with this till much later. The only medical work on the plague in the Elizabethan times which has much value is that of Thomas Lodge, and this cannot be called original.... It is not till after the great plague of 1665 that we have, in the well-known work of [Nathanael] Hodges [*Loimologia, sive Pestis Narratio*, 1672], some attempt at a scientific description of the epidemic.'

Dr. Furnivall has printed in his edition of Vicary some extracts from the Guildhall Repertories relating to the appointment and payment of surgeons and physicians to attend to the plague-stricken folk. William King, surgeon to the Pesthouse, petitioned for a pension in 1611. He affirms that he had shown 'great care and diligence in curinge of such persons as have been sent thither, and by reason of his attendance and imployment there, his friendes and former acquaintances do utterly refuse to use him in his profession.' On September 10 the city authorities agreed to give King a stipend of £3 a year, which does not seem very liberal pay for his onerous services.[178]

In the British Museum there is a MS. of some importance (Sloane MS., 349), entitled 'Loimographia, an account of the Great Plague of London in the year 1665, by William Boghurst, apothecary.' This was first referred to by Mr. E. W. Brayley in his edition of Defoe's *Plague Year*, and it was analysed by Dr. Creighton in his work on Epidemics. Dr. Payne printed an edition of the tract in 1894. Mr. Brayley reprinted from the *Intelligencer*, July 31, 1665, the following curious advertisement:—

'Whereas Wm. Boghurst, apothecary at the White Hart, in St. Giles' in the Fields, hath administered a long time to such as have been afflicted with the plague, to the number of 40, 50, or 60 patients a day, with wonderful success, by God's blessing upon certain excellent medicines which he hath, as a water, a lozenge, etc. Also an electuary antidote, of but 8d. the oz. price. This is to notify that the said Boghurst is willing to attend any person infected and desiring his attendance, either in city, suburbs or country, upon reasonable terms, and that the remedies above mentioned are to be had at his house or shop, at the White Hart aforesaid.'

Boghurst gives a good deal of information in his book regarding the signs of the disease, and its treatment; and he describes the spread of the disease in London as follows:—

'The winds blowing westward so long together, from before Christmas until July, about seven months, was the cause the plague began first at the west end of the city, as at St. Giles', St. Martin's, Westminster. Afterwards it gradually insinuated and crept downe Holborne and the Strand, and then into the city, and at last to the east end of the suburbs, soe that it was halfe a yeare at the west end of the city before the east end and Stepney was infected, which was about the middle of July. Southwark being the south suburb, was infected almost as soon as the west end. The disease spread not altogether by contagion at first, nor began at only one place, and spread further and further as an eating spreading soare doth all over the body, but fell upon severall places of the city and suburbs like raine, even at the first at St. Giles', St. Martin's, Chancery Lane, Southwark, and some places within the city, as at Proctor's House.'

Dr. Payne writes: 'It has always been a question whether the repeated recurrences of plague in Europe were to be attributed to re-introduction of the virus from the East, or to a fresh awakening of a virus already endemic,' and then alludes to Boghurst's local explanation of the origin of the 1665 plague. He concludes his Introduction by saying: 'It seems probable that London still contained sufficient plague virus to start a fresh epidemic, when the local and temporary conditions were favourable. The only temporary conditions of this kind that we know of are, first, the rapid growth of population in London, which caused terrible overcrowding, and must have overtasked the ordinary measures of sanitation; and, secondly, the long drought in the spring of 1665, which is referred to by Boghurst. The importance of this latter fact has been explained by Dr. Creighton, in accordance with Pettenkofer's laws, but, on the other hand, the great plague year of 1625 was remarkably wet. The question is still one for discussion, and it may be left to the judgment of the reader, guided by the valuable materials which Boghurst contributes.'

From 1348 to 1665 plague was continually occurring in London, but it has not appeared since the last date on anything but a small scale.[179] It has been supposed that in the Great Fire the seeds of the disease were destroyed, but this is not a conclusive reason, and fears were expressed as to its possible reappearance in London after the plague of Bombay in 1896-1897; and the plague of Marseilles in the summer of 1720 created a panic throughout Western Europe. Renewed attention was paid to the London plague of 1665, and in 1722 Defoe wrote his renowned *Journal of the Plague Year*.

We have no thoroughly trustworthy statistics of the earlier plagues, but Dr. Creighton gives particulars of the visitations in London in 1603, 1625 and 1665 in one table:—

Year.	Estimated Population.	Total Deaths.	Plague Deaths.	Highest Mortality in a Week.	Worst Week.
1603	250,000	42,940	33,347	3385	25 Aug.-1 Sept.
1625	320,000	63,001	41,313	5205	11-18 Aug.
1665	460,000	97,306	68,596	8297	12-19 Sept.

To these may be added that, in 1593, 11,503 persons died of the plague. The figures of 1603 and 1625 in some reports differ from the above.[180]

Some of the plagues devastated the whole country, so that there was no place for the Londoner to fly to for safety, but in others the danger was more generally confined to London. In 1665 there were many places that the Londoner could visit with considerable chance of safety, but Queen Elizabeth in her reign would have none of this moving about. Stow says that in the time of the plague of 1563 'a gallows was set up in the market-place of Windsor to hang all such as should come there from London. No wares to be brought to, or through, or by Windsor; nor any one on the river by Windsor to carry wood or other stuff to or from London, upon pain of hanging without any judgment; and such people as received any wares out of London into Windsor were turned out of their houses and their houses shut up.'

Monke, Duke of Albemarle, and Samuel Pepys were two of the most prominent public servants who remained in London during the plague of 1665. The clergy and the doctors fled with very few exceptions, and several of those who stayed in town doing the duty of others as well as their own fell victims to the disease.

Dr. Hodges, author of *Loimologia*, enumerates among those who assisted in the dangerous work of restraining the progress of the infection the learned Dr. Gibson, Regius Professor at Cambridge, Dr. Francis Glisson, Dr. Nathaniel Paget, Dr. Peter Barwick, Dr. Humphrey Brookes, etc. Of those he mentions, eight or nine fell in their work, among whom was Dr. Wm. Conyers, to whose goodness and humanity he bears the most honourable testimony. Dr. Alexander Burnett, of Fenchurch Street, one of Pepys's friends, was another of the victims.[181]

Sweating Sickness.—The sweating sickness did not appear until the end of the Middle Ages, viz., the year 1485, when the Battle of Bosworth was fought, and there were five outbreaks of the epidemic up to 1551, after which date it did not appear again in England. Dr. Creighton has taken some pains to trace the origin of the disease. He writes: 'The history of the English sweat presents to the student of epidemics much that is paradoxical although not without parallel, and much that his research can never rescue from uncertainty. Where did this hitherto unheard of disease come from? Where was it in the intervals from 1485 to 1508, from 1508 to 1517, from 1517 to 1528, and from 1528 to 1551? What became of it after 1551? Why did it fall mostly on the great houses—on the King's Court, on the luxurious establishments of prelates and nobles, on the richer citizens, on the lusty and well-fed, for the most part sparing the poor? Why did it avoid France when it overran the Continent in 1529? No theory of the sweat can be held sufficient which does not afford some kind of answer to each of these questions, and some harmonising of them all.'[182]

Those who wish to follow these inquiries must consult Dr. Creighton's book. Suffice it to say here that the author is of opinion that suspicion falls justly upon the foreign mercenaries who landed with Henry

Tudor at Milford Haven on the 6th of August 1485 as the carriers of the disease.[183]

Dr. Creighton found among the British Museum manuscripts (Addit. MSS., No. 27, 582) a treatise on the *Sudor Anglicus*, or English Sweat, dedicated to Henry VII. by the author, Thomas Forrestier, M.D., a native of Normandy, who lived for a time in London. Stow says that the sickness began in London on the 21st September, and continued till the end of October, 'of the which a wonderful number died'; but Forrestier gives the date as the 19th.

The second sweat was in 1508, when many died in the city. In August public prayers were made at St. Paul's on account of the plague of sweat. The third epidemic was in 1517, and the fourth in 1528. On the 5th of June of the latter year, Sir Brian Tuke wrote to Bishop Tunstall that he had fled to Stepney 'for fear of the infection,' a servant having died in his house. Anne Boleyn, her brother George and her father caught the infection and recovered. Her brother-in-law, William Cary, died at Hunsdon. A large number of persons caught the disease, but a very considerable proportion recovered.

The fifth and last outbreak was in 1551, and it is interesting to note that Dr. John Caius, the famous physician, wrote a treatise on it. Dr. Norman Moore[184] describes this as 'the first original treatise published in England, by which I mean the first treatise in which the modern idea of observing the disease and writing a complete account of what was actually seen was carried out.'

In Machyn's *Diary* it is said that 'there died in London many merchants, and great rich men and women, and young men and old of the new sweat'; and Sir Thomas Speke and Sir John Wallop are instanced among others. Hancocke, a minister of Poole, Dorset, refers to 'the posting sweat that posted from town to town thorow England, and was named "Stop-gallant," for it spared none. For there were some dancing in the Court at nine o'clock that were dead at eleven.'

In taking stock of diseases and epidemics in London, we may note that many of the pestilences previous to the Black Death were due to famine. Dr. Creighton says of the year 1258 that 'so great was the pinch in London from the failure of the crops and the want of money that fifteen thousand are said to have died of famine and of a grievous and widespread pestilence that broke out about the Feast of the Trinity, 19th May.' The number is that given by Matthew Paris, and Dr. Creighton adds: 'It suggests a larger population in the capital than we might have been disposed to credit. The same writer says that London was so full of people when the Parliament was sitting in the year before (1257) that the city could hardly hold them all in her ample bosom. The Annals of Tewkesbury put the whole mortality from famine and fever in London in 1258 at 20,000, but the whole population did not probably exceed 40,000.'[185]

Small-pox and measles were not known to the ancients, and the latter seems to have been first noted in the fourteenth century.

Of later diseases the name of influenza is Italian of the eighteenth century, but Dr. Creighton refers to several epidemics which may have been the same disease as those of 1173, 1427, 1510 and 1557. The 'new disease' of 1643 was either typhus or influenza.

SANITATION

Having considered the condition of medical practice at the hospitals and among private patients, and having also reviewed the particulars of some of the chief epidemics, we shall now be better able to understand the sanitary condition of mediæval London, and the means taken to keep it clean. There can be little doubt that strenuous attempts were made at different periods to improve its condition.

We may allow at once that old London was not a clean or healthy town, as we understand these words now, but there can be little doubt that it was in advance of most other towns.

Dr. Poore is rather severe in his estimate of the health of mediæval London; he considers the situation of the city fairly good from a sanitary point of view. It was not healthy, however, because of its marshy surroundings. Ague and dysentery were always present and very fatal. Scurvy was very prevalent before the introduction of the potato by Hawkins.[186]

William Clowes, the well-known Elizabethan surgeon of St. Bartholomew's, was also surgeon to Christ's Hospital, and in his day twenty or thirty children had the scurvy at a time in the latter house, a fact due to a diet largely composed of fish and other salted provisions, with a scanty allowance of vegetables.

'There can be no doubt that down to the commencement of the present century London was a veritable fever-bed, the causes of death being largely malarial fever, spotted or typhus fever, plague, small-pox, measles, scarlet fever, and whooping cough, the two latter being comparatively recent introductions.'[187]

Another source of the unhealthiness of London is supposed by Dr. Poore to be due to a soil soaked with the filth of centuries, by which means the wells were probably infected.

Dr. Creighton takes a much more favourable view of the condition of London, and he writes: 'Nuisances certainly existed in mediæval London, but it is equally certain that they were not tolerated without limit.'[188] It is also probable that the polluted condition of the soil inside and outside the houses has been greatly exaggerated.

There was overcrowding in some quarters of London, but in most parts there were gardens and plenty of fresh air. Many of the streets were used as markets, and they were mostly left in a very untidy state, but attempts were made to cleanse them.

The worst parts of the town were the lanes leading down to the river. The bad state of these places was constantly complained of, but we must always remember that complaints and legal actions are evidence to some extent that in the end the evils were abated.

Very little is recorded when affairs go straight, as all are contented to let them remain as they are, but when things go wrong we are all anxious to raise complaints, and too much weight must not be given to the supposed universality of these evils. We do not judge of the general manners and morals of the country by the cases in the law courts and the police courts.

Some of the evils, of which a description has come down to us, were doubtless the cause of remedial measures being adopted. The streets soon after the Conquest must have been in a very rotten condition, if we are to judge from some accounts that have come down to us.

Stow relates in his Chronicle that in the great tempest of November 17, 1090, when 606 houses were beaten down by the wind in London, the roof of St. Mary le Bow in Cheapside 'being raised with the beames thereof were carryed in the ayre a great while, and at the last sixe of the sayde beames were driven with their fall so fast in the ground, that there appeared of some of them the seventh, and of some the eyght part, to wit, but foure foote above the ground; which beames or rafters were seaven and twentie or eyght and twentie foote long, which was a wonderful to see them so pierce the ground [not paved then with stone], and there to stand in such order as the workmen hadde placed them on the church.' There these beams remained as obstructions until they were cut even with the ground.

Little appears to have been done in general sanitation until the reign of Henry III., but it has been said that the sanitary reforms of the reign of Edward I. were as great as the reforms effected in the law and constitution. It is satisfactory to learn that it was the example of this great King which made the use of the bath popular among his subjects. In Riley's *Memorials* there are several references to sanitary ordinances at this time. In 1281 regulations were made that no swine and no stand or timber were from henceforth to be found in the streets. The swine were to be killed and the stands and timber forfeited. Melters of tallow and lard were turned out of their warehouses in Cheapside in 1283. The watercourse of Walbrook was to be made free from dung and other nuisances in 1288. Swine still wandered about the streets, and in 1292 four men whose names are given in Letter Book C were elected and sworn 'to take and kill such swine as should be found wandering in the King's highway, to whomsoever they might belong, within the walls of the city and the suburbs thereof.' The Earl of Lincoln complained to Parliament in 1307 as to the state of the River Fleet, and the gist of his complaint is reported by Stow: 'Whereas in times past, the course of water running at London under Holborne bridge and Fleete bridge into the Thamis, had beene of such large breadth and depth, that ten or twelve ships at once with merchandises were wont to come to the foresaide bridge of Fleete and some of them to Holborne bridge; now the same course (by filth of the tanners and such other) was sore decayed. Also by raysing up of wharffes, but especially by turning of the water, which they of ye new Temple made to their milles without Baynard Castle, and divers other perturbations, the said shippes now could not enter as they were wont, and as they ought, wherefore hee desired that the Maior of London, with the Sheriffes and certaine discreete Aldermen, might be appointed to see the course of the said water, and that by oth of honest men all the foresaid hindrances might be removed, and to bee made as it was wont of old time.'[189]

In the second year of Edward II.'s reign (1309) a proclamation was issued for cleansing the streets, which were more encumbered with filth than they used to be, and penalties were enforced against those who neglected their duty in this matter.[190] Between forty and fifty years after this we have evidence that one of the main thoroughfares of the city was in a very bad state. On August 22, 1358, Isabella, the widowed Queen of Edward II., died at Hertford Castle, and in the following November she was buried in the Church of the Grey Friars. In order that the passage of the body through the city should be carried out with any decency, it was necessary to enact that Bishopsgate Street and Aldgate Street should be cleansed of ordure and other filth.[191]

Dr. Creighton criticises the public regulations, and writes: 'There are several orders of Edward III. relating to the removal of laystalls and to keeping the town ditch clean, which show, of course, that there was neglect, but at the same time disposition to correct it. It is farther obvious that the connection between nuisances and the public health was clearly apprehended. The sanitary doctrines of modern times were undreamt of; nor did the circumstances altogether call for them. The sewers of those days were banked-up watercourses, or shores, as the word was pronounced, which ran uncovered down the various declivities of the city to the town ditch and to the Thames. They would have sufficed to carry off the refuse of a population of some forty or sixty thousand; they were, at all events, freely open to the greatest of all purifying agents, the oxygen of the air; and they poisoned neither the water of the town ditch (which abounds in excellent fish within John Stow's memory), nor the waters of Thames.'[192]

This seems exactly to explain the sanitary condition of the city, and we must never forget that the streets were cleared by means of surface drainage, which carried the refuse of the city to the river, to find its way to the sea at last. The streets were evidently fairly well attended to in ordinary times, and it is not for those who have polluted the Thames and made the streams into covered sewers to point the finger of scorn at the evils allowed by their ancestors, who at all events kept the Thames pure.

The proclamations and ordinances issued for the proper cleansing of the streets of London were very numerous, but the first sanitary act that appears in the Statutes of the Realm was passed in the seventeenth year of Richard II. (1388), the preamble of which Dr. Creighton prints.[193] From this and other sources, it appears that one of the chief evils complained of was due to the blood and offal in the shambles of Newgate Street.

It is impossible to mention here all the information that has come down to us as to what was done to secure a satisfactory sanitation, but special reference may be made to the useful abstract in Riley's Introduction to the *Liber Albus*.[194]

'Kennels were pretty generally made about a century after the date of Fitz-Ailwine's Assize, on either side of the street (leaving a space for the footpath), for the purpose of carrying off the sewage and rain water. There were two kennels in Cheapside at a period even when nearly the whole of the north side was a vacant space. The kennels, too, of Cornhill are frequently mentioned. By reiterated enactments it was ordered that the highways should be kept clean from rubbish, hay, straw, sawdust, dung, and other refuse. Each householder was to clear away all dirt from his door, and to be equally careful not to place it before that of his neighbours. No one was to throw water or anything else out of the windows, but was to bring the water down and pour it into the street. An exception, however, to this last provision seems to have been made in the case of fishmongers, for we find injunctions frequently issued... that they shall on no account throw their dirty water into the streets, but shall have the same carried to the river.'

It was the duty of each alderman to cause to be elected in Wardmote four respectable men to keep the roads clean and free from obstructions.[195] The same duties were carried out at another time by a

Court of Scavagers, who apparently were originally Custom House officers. The scavagers had to see that the work was done, and the labourers who actually cleansed the streets were called 'Rakyers.' In an Ordinance of the time of Edward III. we learn that twelve carts, each with two horses, were kept at the expense of the city for the removal of sewage and refuse.[196]

CHAPTER VIII

The Governors of the City

'London claims the first place... as the greatest municipality, as the model on which, by their charters of liberties, the other large towns of the country were allowed or charged to adjust their usages, and as the most active, the most political, and the most ambitious. London has also a preeminence in municipal history owing to the strength of the conflicting elements which so much effected her constitutional progress.'—Stubbs, *Constitutional History of England*, chap. xxi. par. 486.

THE history of the early government of the city is full of pitfalls for the historian. For years an account of what occurred before the establishment of the mayoralty was generally accepted, which later research has proved to be entirely erroneous. Careful students of early documents have lately given us information of the greatest value, but we still wait for more facts.

In the following pages an attempt will now be made to place before the reader a short statement of what is known, with some indication of what we still have to learn. Fortunately, there is no lack of students who are constantly adding to our knowledge, and as in the last few years considerable discoveries have been published, there is every reason to hope that in the future other discoveries will be made equal at least in importance to those which have been made in the past.

We know remarkably little as to how the government of London was carried on before the Conquest, but probably the course of procedure was not very different from what was the practice immediately after that great event.

When William the Conqueror granted the first charter to London, he addressed the Bishop and the Portreeve.[197] The former as ecclesiastical governor, and the latter as the civil governor.

It has been a generally received opinion that there was a succession of portreeves until the first appointment of a Mayor, but Mr. Round believes that the title of portreeve disappears after the Conqueror's charter.[198] In this opinion he is opposed to the view of both Bishop Stubbs and Mr. Loftie. It is necessary to bear in mind that a reeve was an officer appointed by the King, just as the sheriffs (or shire reeves) of the various counties are still so appointed. There has been some difference of opinion as to the meaning of the title Port-reeve. It might at first sight be supposed to refer to the Port of London, but this is not the received opinion. Bishop Stubbs writes: 'The word port in port-reeve is the Latin *porta* (not *portus*), where the markets were held, and although used for the city generally, seems to refer to it specially in its character of a mart or city of merchants.'[199]

The City of London obtained from Henry I. the right of appointing their own sheriffs, which was a very great privilege, and there must have been some very strong reason to induce the King to grant this great favour. Bishop Stubbs writes of this charter of Henry I. to the citizens of London: 'The privileges of the citizens of London are not to be regarded as a fair specimen of the liberties of ordinary towns, but as a sort of type and standard of the amount of municipal independence and self-government at which the other towns of the country might be expected to aim. At a period at which the other towns were just struggling out of the condition of demesne, the Londoners were put in possession of the ferm or farm of Middlesex, with the right of appointing the sheriff; they were freed from the immediate jurisdiction of any tribunal except of their own appointment, from several universal imposts, from the obligation to accept trial by battle, from liability to misericordia or entire forfeiture, as well as from tolls and local exactions such as ordinary charters specify. They have also their separate franchises secured and their weekly courts, but they have not yet the character of a perpetual corporation or *Communa*, and thus although possessing, by virtue of their associations in guilds, of their several franchises, of their feudal courts, and of their shire organisation under the sheriff, many elements of strength, consolidation and independence, they have not a compact organisation as a municipal body. The city is an accumulation of distinct and different corporate bodies, but not yet a perfect municipality, nor although it was recognised in the reign of Stephen as a *Communio*, did it gain the legal status before the reign of Richard I.'[200] Mr. Round shows, however, that the city possessed the privilege only for a short time: 'We see then that in absolute contradiction of the received belief on the subject, the shrievalty was not in the hands of the citizens during the twelfth century (*i.e.*, from '1101'), but was held by them for a few years only, about the close of the reign of Henry I. The fact that the sheriffs of London and Middlesex were, under Henry II. and Richard I. appointed throughout by the Crown, must compel our historians to reconsider the independent position they have assigned to the city at that early period. The Crown, moreover, must have had an object in retaining this appointment in its hands. We may find it, I think, in that jealousy of exceptional privilege or exemption which characterised the *régime* of Henry II. For, as I have shown, the charters to Geoffrey remind us that the ambition of the urban communities was analogous to that of the great feudatories, in so far as they both strove for exemption from official rule. It was precisely to this ambition that Henry II. was opposed; and thus, when he granted his charter to London, he wholly omitted, as we have seen, two of his grandfather's concessions, and narrowed down those that remained, that they might not be operative outside the actual walls of the city. When the shrievalty was restored by John to the citizens (1199) the concession had lost its chief importance through the triumph of the communal principle.'[201]

Mr. Round holds that the office of Justiciar of London was created by Henry I.'s charter, and as that officer took precedence of the sheriff he must have been for a time the chief authority of the city. Mr. Round's explanation of this position is of so much importance that it is necessary to quote it here in his own words: 'The transient existence of the local *justitiarius* is a phenomenon of great importance, which has been wholly misunderstood. The Mandeville charters afford the clue to the nature of this office. It represents a middle term, a transitional stage between the essentially *local* shire-reeve and the *central* justice of the King's court.... The *justitiarius* for Essex or Herts, or London or Middlesex, was a purely local officer, and yet exercised within the limits of his bailiwick all the authority of the King's justice. So transient was this state of things that scarcely a trace of it remains.... Now, in the case of London, the office was created by the charter of Henry I. (as I contend) towards the end of his reign, and it expired with the accession of Henry II. It is, therefore, in Stephen's reign that we should expect to find it in existence, and it is precisely in that reign that we find the office *eo nomine* twice granted to the Earl of Essex and twice mentioned as held by Gervase, otherwise Gervase of Cornhill.'[202]

The question of the date of the charter of Henry I. is discussed in *Geoffrey de Mandeville* (p. 364), and reasons are given for dating it after 1130 instead of 1100 or 1101.

Bishop Stubbs specially refers to the foreign element in London at this time thus: 'Richard the son of Reiner, the son of Berengar, was very probably a Lombard by descent; the influential family of Bucquinte, Bucca-uncta, which took the lead on many occasions, can hardly have been other than Italian; Gilbert Becket was a Norman.' And further, in a note, he adds: 'Andrew of London, the leader of the Londoners at Lisbon in 1147, is not improbably the Andrew Bucquinte whose son Richard was the leader of the riotous young nobles of the city who in 1177 furnished a precedent for the Mohawks of the eighteenth century.'[203] Andrew, who was present at the transference of the Cnihtengild's land to the Priory of Holy Trinity (1125 or 1126), was one of the witnesses of the agreement between Ramsay Abbey and Holy Trinity after that date, where his name is written 'Bocunte.'[204] He was Justiciar of London in Stephen's reign.[205] The Buccarelli were another Italian family whose name is said to be preserved in Bucklersbury, and Round also mentions Osbert Octodenarii (otherwise Huitdeniers), a kinsman and employer of Becket.

The origin of the Commune of London has always been an exceedingly obscure problem, but Mr. Round has succeeded in throwing a flood of light upon the subject.

In the twelfth century there was a great municipal movement over Europe. Londoners were well informed as to what was going on abroad, and thoroughly dissatisfied with the existing organisation they waited and were constantly looking for an opportunity of obtaining the privileges of the Commune. Mr. Round points out that 'even so early as 1141, when the fortunes of the Crown hung in the balance between rival claimants, we find the citizens forming an effective *Conjuratio*, the very term applied to their "Commune" half a century later by Richard of Devizes. Moreover, earlier in the same year (April), William of Malmesbury applies to their government the term *Communio*.[206] Miss Mary Bateson has gone to the manuscript from which Mr. Round obtained the Oath of Commune (B.M. Add. MS., 14,252), and her conclusion after consideration is that 'the collection as a whole leaves the impression that "Communio quam vocant Londoniarum" (1141), as it is styled by William of Malmesbury, was not merely a unit in the eyes of the Exchequer, that the jurisdictional unity of the city organised in folkmoot and husting gave something substantial whereon the foundations of mayoralty and Commune could be laid.'[207]

Mr. Round writes: 'The assumption that the mayoralty of London dates from the accession of Richard I. (1189) is an absolute perversion of history,' and he adds that 'there is record evidence which completely confirms the remarkable words of Richard of Devizes, who declares that on no terms whatever would King Richard or his father have ever assented to the establishment of the *Communa* in London.'[208]

In October 1191 the conflict between John, the King's brother, and Longchamp, the King's representative, became acute. William of Longchamp, Bishop of Ely (1189) and Chancellor to Richard I., was once described by Henry II. as the 'son of two traitors.' When Richard called a Council in Normandy in February 1190 Longchamp hurried over to the King in advance of his enemies and returned to England as sole justiciar. The Pope also made him Legate.

Longchamp bitterly offended the Londoners who, finding that they could turn the scales to either side, named the Commune as the price of their support of John.

Bishop Stubbs, in his Introduction to the Chronicle of Roger de Hoveden, after referring to the negotiations between Longchamp and John, and describing the hastening of the two parties to London on Monday, 7th October, when Longchamp met the citizens in the Guildhall, writes: 'The magnates of the city were divided—Richard Fitz-Reiner, the head of one party, took the side of John. Henry of Cornhill was faithful to the Chancellor. These two knights had been sheriffs at Richard's coronation, and both represented the burgher aristocracy.' Longchamp betook himself to the Tower, and a meeting was held at St. Paul's on Tuesday the 8th, and the barons welcomed the Archbishop of Rouen as chief justiciar, and saluted John as Regent. 'This done, oaths were largely taken: John, the justiciar and the barons swore to maintain the *Communa* of London; the oath of fealty to Richard was then sworn, John taking it first, then the two archbishops, the bishops, the barons, and last the burghers, with the express understanding that should the King die without issue they would receive John as his successor.'[209]

Mr. Round writes: 'The excited citizens, who had poured out overnight, with lanterns and torches, to welcome John to the capital, streamed together on the morning of the eventful 8th October at the well-known sound of the great bell, swinging out from its campanile in St. Paul's Churchyard. There they heard John take the oath to the "Commune" like a French King or lord; and then London for the first time had a municipality of her own.'[210] After this the influence of Longchamp at once faded away. He stood a three days' blockade in the Tower, after which he was forced to surrender, and was deposed from all secular offices.

As to the results of this revolution Mr. Round writes: 'Of the character of the "Commune" so granted, of its ultimate fate, and of the part it played in the municipal development of London, nothing has been really known. The only fact of importance ascertained from other sources has been the appearance of a Mayor of London at or about the same time as the grant of a "Commune." It cannot, indeed, be proved that, as has been sometimes supposed, the two phenomena were synchronistic, for no mention of the Mayor of London, after long research, is known to me earlier than the spring of the year 1193. But there is, of course, the strongest presumption that the grant of a "Commune" involved a Mayor, and already, in 1194, we find a citizen accused of boasting that, "come what may, the Londoner shall have no King but their Mayor.' "[211]

Mr. Round then states very clearly the divergent views of Bishop Stubbs, Mr. Loftie and Mr. Coote on the question of the concession of the Commune. The bishop held that it was difficult to decide with certainty on the point, as no formal record of the confirmation of the Commune is now preserved. Mr. Coote believed that a charter was granted in 1191, which has been lost, and Mr. Loftie dates the mayoralty from 1189, and deemed the Commune to have been of gradual growth, and to have been practically recognised by the charter of Henry I.

In reply to Mr. Coote's view that in the case of London, which had acquired all other things, the Commune expressed for its citizens the mayoralty only, Mr. Round writes: 'We find, however, that on the Continent the word "Commune" did not of necessity imply a Mayor, for Beauvais and Compiègne, though constituted "Communes," appear to have had no Mayors during most of the twelfth century. The Chroniclers, therefore, had they only meant to speak of the privilege of electing a Mayor, would not have all employed a word which did not connote it, but would have said what they meant. Moreover, his theory rests on the assumption common till now to all historians that the citizens had continuously possessed from the beginning of the twelfth century the privileges granted in the charter of Henry I. But I have shown in my *Geoffrey de Mandeville* that these privileges were not renewed by Henry II. or Richard I., and this fact strikingly confirms the explicit words of Richard of Devizes when he states that neither the one nor the other would have allowed the Londoners to form a "Commune" even for a million of marcs.'[212]

Of Mr. Loftie's argument that Glanville's words prove that London, if not other towns as well, had already a Commune under Henry II., Mr. Round remarks that it had been disposed of by Dr. Gross in his *Gild Merchant* (i. 102).[213]

We have now to refer specially to Mr. Round's remarkable discovery among the manuscripts of the British Museum of the Oath of the Commune, which proves for the first time that 'London in 1193 possessed a fully-developed "Commune" of the continental pattern.'

This discovery not only gives us information which was unknown before, but upsets the received opinions as to the early governing position of the aldermen. From this we learn that the government of the city was at that time in the hands of a Mayor and certain échevins (skivini).

Of the existence of these skivins in England no suspicion has previously been expressed. Mr. Round, indeed, points out that Dr. Gross, in his *Gild Merchant*, considers these governing officers as a purely continental institution.

Twelve years later (1205-1206) we learn from another document, preserved in the same volume, that '*alii probi homines*' were associated with the Mayor and échevins to form a body of twenty-four (that is twelve skivini, and an equal number of councillors).

In these documents there is no mention of aldermen, and further information is required as to when the Court of Aldermen first came into existence. This point will be discussed later on in this chapter, when the position of the alderman as a governor is considered.

Mr. Round holds that the Court of Skivini and *'alii probi homines,'* of which at present we know nothing further than what is contained in the terms of the oaths, was the germ of the Common Council. He prints the oaths and compares the oath of the twenty-four with that of the freemen in the present day.[214]

The striking point in this municipal revolution is that the new privileges were entirely copied from those of continental cities, and that the names of Mayor and échevins were French, thus excluding the aldermen who represented the Saxon element. Still, as time went on, the aldermen obtained their natural position in the government of London, and the foreign name of échevin sank before them.

The intimate connection between Normandy and England made it certain that Englishmen would seek inspiration from Normandy. Mr. Round has devoted considerable attention to Monsieur Giry's valuable work, *Les Etablissemens de Rouen*, and shows that there is conclusive proof of the assertion that the Commune of London derived its origin from that of Rouen. The *vingt-quatre* of the latter city formed the administrative body annually elected to act as the Mayor's Council. Mr. Round further found that the oath of this 'twenty-four' bears a marked resemblance to the oath of the London Commune discovered by him. 'The three salient features in common are—(1) the oath to administer justice fairly; (2) the special provisions against bribery; (3) the expulsion of any member of the body convicted of receiving a bribe.[215]

Much attention has been given lately to the important question of continental influence on English municipalities, and Miss Mary Bateson has discovered that a considerable number of boroughs in England, Wales and Ireland drew their customs from the little Norman town of Breteuil.[216] These are Bideford, Burford, Chipping Sodbury, Hereford, Lichfield, Ludlow, Nether Weare, Preston, Ruyton, Shrewsbury; Llanvyllin, Rhuddlan, Welshport; Drogheda, Dungarvan, Kildare and Rathmore. Besides these there are eight suspected cases and a number of derived cases.[217]

Although the fact that the Council of twenty-four seemed to exclude the already existing aldermen from the chief government of the city was opposed to our previous views, Mr. Round has set himself to show that a Mayor's Council of twenty-four (not aldermen) was not unusual, and he draws especial attention to the case of Winchester. There the Mayor had a Council of twenty-four, who continued to exist down to the year 1835. This Council was elected by the city as a whole and not by the wards, and Mr. Round believes that this was also the case in London. He then quotes from Dean Kitchin's book on Winchester (*Historic Towns*) where it is said: 'The aldermen, in later days, the civic aristocracy, were originally officers placed over each of the wards of the city and entrusted with the administration of it.... It was not till early in the sixteenth century that they were interposed between the Mayor and the twenty-four men.' We learn from Mrs. Green (*Town Life in the Fifteenth Century*) that there was a Council of twenty-four at Colchester, Ipswich, Leicester, Northampton, Norwich, Oxford, Wells, and Yarmouth.

When the city obtained the long-coveted privilege of the Commune and the power of electing their own Mayor, one would naturally expect the electors to choose the most distinguished citizen. We cannot however say whether Henry Fitz-Ailwin was that. At all events, he seems to have retained the esteem of the city, as he was continued in office until his death in 1212.

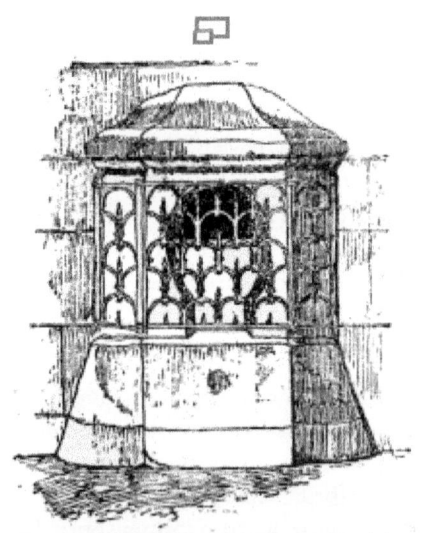

'LONDON STONE,' CANNON STREET.

Mr. Round wrote the Life of Fitz-Ailwin in the *Dictionary of National Biography*, but he was unable to discover much of the Mayor's history. He presumes that he was the grandson of an unidentified Leofstan, but he rejects the view that he was the grandson of Leofstan, Portreeve of London before the Conquest. Leofstan was a common name among the Saxons, and two or three of the same name have been confounded by historians.

Fitz-Ailwin is described as 'of London Stone,' because his dwelling— 'a very fair house'—stood on the north side of the Church of St. Swithin, and over against the London Stone, which was situated on the south side of Cannon [Candlewick] Street, but afterwards removed to the north side of the street. The advowson of the church was appropriated to the mansion. London Stone itself is one of the most valued relics of London, and its history is lost in antiquity. We know that in the Middle Ages it was esteemed to possess a special value as a representative stone monument.

The seal of Fitz-Ailwin is attached to a deed preserved among the public records. It represents a man on horseback with a hawk perched on his wrist. There is an inscription round the circumference of the seal, but it is so defaced as to be illegible.[218]

The city was given the right of electing the Mayor, but we do not know for certain who it was who first exercised this right. Bishop Stubbs says that two years after the death of Fitz-Ailwin, King John granted to the 'barones' of the City of London the right of annually electing the Mayor.[219]

**SEAL OF FITZ-AILWIN,
FIRST MAYOR OF LONDON.**

The roll of Mayors is one of considerable distinction, and those who obtained this position were mostly men of great character and authority. Some of them were on the side of popular freedom, while others were active in the support of the prerogatives of the privileged classes.

Sometimes the King degraded the Mayor and appointed a custos or warden in his place. As early as 1222, twenty years after the death of Fitz-Ailwin, in the reign of Henry III., Hubert de Burgh, chief justiciar, superseded the Mayor and appointed a custos in his place. Again, in 1266, William Fitz-Richard was appointed by the King warden of the city. In November of the same year Fitz-Richard was replaced by Alan Souche, and

John Adrian and Luke de Batincourt were elected by the citizens bailiffs of London and Middlesex. 'The bailiffs and the whole Commune (*Communa*) of the said city' are mentioned in 1267.[220] In 1268-1269 Hugh Fitz-Otho was custos, and then follow some stirring times in London.

Sir Walter Hervey, the predecessor of the famous Sir Henry Waleys in the Mayor's chair, was the popular leader against the proceedings of his successor.

Sir Henry de Waleys, Le Waleis, Le Walleis, or Le Galeys (for in all these forms does his name appear), was elected sheriff with his distinguished contemporary Gregory de Rokesley in 1270. His first mayoralty was in 1273, and in 1275 he was Mayor of Bordeaux.

He was a very active chief magistrate and a good administrator; he was also high in the royal favour. He proceeded against bakers, butchers and fishmongers, and ordered them to remove their stalls from West Cheap. He also came in conflict with the Barons of the Cinque Ports. The King sent a mandate to the justices in Eyre at the Tower commanding them not to molest Waleys for his reforms.

In the year 1285 the city again lost its franchise. Gregory de Rokesley was deposed from the mayoralty by Edward I. for refusing to render any account of how the peace of the city was maintained, thus omitting to show proper respect to the King's justices at the Tower. For the next thirteen years London was governed by a warden appointed by the King, in the person of Sir Ralph de Sandwich or John le Breton.[221]

Sir Ralph de Sandwich is described in Letter Book A as warden of the city, as well as warden of Cordwainer Street.

In 1297, a few months before the King restored the mayoralty to the citizens, John le Breton who had for many years acted as the King's warden of the city in place of the Mayor, is recorded as having summoned the aldermen and six representatives of each ward and in their presence to have declared, *inter alia*, that the weighing machines for weighing corn at the mills should be abolished, and that bakers convicted of fraud should no longer be drawn on the hurdle, but suffer instead the punishment of the pillory.

As soon as the citizens recovered their liberties and Le Breton ceased to be warden, Le Waleys was again elected to the chair. The charter of restitution of the city's liberties bears date 12th April, 26 Edw. I. [1299], and it is preserved at the Guildhall.[222] The particulars of the various stages of these proceedings are set out fully in the city's records. The writ was sent to the late warden on the 5th April, and the notification to the citizens took place on the 9th. Le Waleys was elected and admitted by the King at Fulham on the 16th.[223]

The King issued a writ to the Barons of the Exchequer from York, notifying the restitution of the city's liberties, on 28th May, and a proclamation followed. The day after the Mayor was sworn he was compelled by business of his own to proceed at once to Lincoln, and during his absence his official duties were committed to William de Betoyne and Geoffrey de Nortone.

It is very important to bear in mind that the Mayors of London, besides holding a very onerous office, were men of great distinction. They held rank outside the city, and naturally took their place among the rulers of the country. They were mostly representatives of the landed interest, as well as merchant princes, but sometimes, as already stated, the Mayor sided with the populace in opposition to the views of his own compeers. Bishop Stubbs describes the struggles between the magnates and the Commons, and shows how Thomas Fitz-Thomas favoured the latter.

'In 1249, when the Mayor and aldermen met the judges at the Temple for a conference on rights claimed by the Abbot of Westminster, the populace interfered, declaring that they would not permit them to treat without the participation of the whole "Communa."... In 1262 Thomas Fitz-Thomas, the Mayor, encouraged the populace to claim the title of "Communa civitatis," and to deprive the aldermen and magnates of their rightful influence; by these means he obtained a re-election by the popular vote in 1263, the voices of the aldermen being excluded: in 1264-1265 he obtained a reappointment, but his power came to an end after the Battle of Evesham.'[224]

To pass on to the fourteenth century, we learn that in 1326 Queen Isabel sent a letter to the citizens permitting them to elect a Mayor, as in the days before the Iter of 1321. They elected Richard de Betoyne, whom the barons had that day appointed warden of the Tower conjointly with John de Gisors.[225]

Sometimes the sovereign, when he went abroad, endowed the Mayor with considerable powers for the preservation of peace. This was the case in 1340 when Andrew Aubrey, the Mayor, acted on the authority of Edward III. A conflict had taken place in the streets of the city between the skinners and the fishmongers, which the Mayor attempted to stop. John Hansard, a fishmonger, brandishing a drawn sword, seized Aubrey by the throat and offered to strike him, while John le Brewere wounded one of the city serjeants. The delinquents were at once seized, carried to Guildhall, arraigned, found guilty, condemned to death, and beheaded in Cheap. When the King heard of this bold proceeding he immediately wrote to the Mayor, warmly approving of his conduct, congratulating him on his spirit, and adopting and ratifying the deed—'*Si vous en savons très bon gree et votre fait acceptoms et le ratifioms.*'[226]

Sir William Walworth, the most famous of Mayors, died in 1385, after a full and strenuous life. He is said to have suppressed usury in the city, and we have seen how important a figure he was during Wat Tyler's insurrection. He was a prominent member of the Fishmongers' Company, and improved the old Church of St. Michael's, Crooked Lane (in which parish he lived), adding the Fishmongers' aisle.[227]

The end of the fourteenth century was, perhaps, the most stirring period in the history of the London municipality. There was a deadly feud between the leaders, who were men of strong character, endued with courage to carry out their views to the extreme. These feuds were no matters of merely local interest, but the incidents were followed with the greatest attention by the Court and the whole country.

The feuds arose from the increased power of the livery companies and the antagonism between the victualling and clothing trades. This division existed in most of the towns of the land, but the battle was fought out with deadly effect in the City of London. Walworth, a fishmonger, was the chief of the victualling party, but the two prominent leaders of the two parties were Nicholas Brembre and John of Northampton.

Doubtless the victualling companies had obtained a preponderating influence, and it is recorded that at one time sixteen of the aldermen belonged to the Grocers' Company, of which Brembre was a member.[228]

When John of Northampton, a draper, was elected Mayor in 1381, in succession to Walworth, he set himself to crush the victualling party. The Act of Edward II. having been evaded, another was passed in 1382 (6 Richard II. cap. 9), by which it was ordained that 'no victualler shall execute a judicial place in a city or town corporate.'[229] (*See* p. 305.)

He forced Sir John Philipot, a public-spirited man and ex-Mayor, but a friend of Walworth's and of the King's, to resign his aldermanry. On 7th November 1382, John Filiol, a fishmonger, was brought before the Mayor and aldermen on a charge of having 'said that John Norhamptone, the Mayor, had falsely and maliciously deprived the fishmongers of their bread.' For this offence Filiol was adjudged to be 'imprisoned at Newgate, in a place then called "Bocardo," for one year then next ensuing, unless he should deserve more extended favour in the meantime.'

On the 6th December John Filiol 'was liberated at the instance of his friends, on the surety of William Naufretone and others.' When the charge was made against Filiol, Richard Fiffyde was one of those questioned on the subject, and he 'said that he and all the other fishmongers of London were bound to put their hands beneath the very feet of Nicholas Extone, for his good deeds and words in behalf of the trade aforesaid.'[230]

John of Northampton was Mayor for two years, and had held the office of sheriff in 1377 (M.P. for the city, 1378). He was head of John of Gaunt's supporters and a prominent follower of Wyclif in London. He was leader of the party which sought to gain the favour of the populace, and he encouraged the citizens to set at naught the jurisdiction of their bishop.

He would probably have been returned again in October 1383 as the champion of cheap food if the King had not carried the election of Brembre by force.

Brembre was the chief supporter of Richard II. in the city, and he was the King's financial agent in 1381. He was first elected Mayor in 1377, and at the Parliament of Gloucester in 1378 Thomas of Woodstock, the King's uncle, demanded his impeachment as Mayor.

From 1379 to 1386 Brembre was one of the two collectors of customs for the Port of London, with Chaucer for his controller. He was M.P. for London in 1383.

When he succeeded Northampton, in 1383, he set himself to undo the evil caused by the action of his predecessor. Northampton was arrested in 1384, when returning from a riotous demonstration at Whitefriars. He was tried at Reading, before the Council over which the King presided. After a brief imprisonment, the condemned man was brought up for a fresh trial, before Chief-Justice Tresilian, in the Tower of London, and was imprisoned in Tintagel Castle, Cornwall.

Brembre was also opposed to Nicholas Twyford, who would probably have been elected Mayor but for the high-handed proceedings of Brembre. Twyford's party was confident of victory, and shouted at the election 'Twyford, Twyford!'; but when the voting commenced the soldiers placed by Brembre behind the arras in the Guildhall rushed out and drove Twyford's followers from the building. Brembre's party were allowed to remain, and they carried the election for their candidate.

It is worthy of note that during Brembre's mayoralty, in 1378, Nicholas Twyford, one of the sheriffs, was brought up for contumacy towards the Mayor, and punished for the same. There had been a conflict in Cheapside between the goldsmiths and the pepperers (grocers), and John Worsele, one of the sheriff's suite, was brought before the Mayor as a principal mover in the strife. Twyford refused to do the Mayor's behests as to the imprisonment of his follower after arrest.[231]

With the fall of the King, Brembre also fell, and there was a revolution in the government of the city as well as in that of the country. Northampton was released from Tintagel Castle, and restored to his property; and Brembre was tried for his life, condemned to death, and executed in the Tower in February 1388. The companies who petitioned for Brembre's punishment were Mercers, Cordwainers, and eight others, all opposed to the victualling trades.

In 1387 a proclamation was made in the city, by the King's command, forbidding, on pain of death and forfeiture of goods, all true lieges of London to speak evil of the King and Queen. The issuing of this proclamation in the city formed one of the charges of high treason against Brembre and his followers.

In this same year, 1387, a book of civic regulations called *Jubile*, promulgated by John de Northampton and his party, was ordered to be burnt. Mr. Riley refers to the petitions in Parliament for 1386-1387,[232] where we learn from the petition of the Cordwainers against Nicholas Brembre and his adherents that in this book of *Le Jubile* 'were comprised all the good articles pertaining to the good governance of the said city, and that Nicholas Extone, the Mayor, and all the aldermen and good Commons of the city had sworn for ever to maintain them, to the honour of God and the profit of the common people; but that the said Nicholas Extone and his accomplices have burnt it without consent of the good Commons of the city, to the annihilation of many good liberties, franchises and customs of the city.'[233]

The feuds of those days continued to agitate the city for some years, but at last the differences between the various trades cooled down somewhat. In 1391, however, a proclamation was issued that 'no person shall speak or give his opinion as to either Nicholas Brembre or John Norhamptone' on pain of imprisonment for a year and a day. The preamble is as follows: 'Whereas many dissensions, quarrels and false reports have prevailed in the City of London as between trade and trade, person and person, because of divers controversies lately moved between Nicholas Brembre, knight, and John Norhamptone, of late Mayors of the same city, who were men of great power and estate, and had many friendships and friends within the same; to the great peril of the same city, and maybe of all the realm.'[234]

The names of many other Mayors who have conferred distinction on their office might be mentioned here, but the space at our disposal will not allow of any statement of the claims to honour of these men who have made their mark in the history of London.

It is a curious fact that we have no authority whatever for fixing a date for the first use of the title 'Lord Mayor,' and there can be little doubt that it was originally assumed without any positive right. Dr. Sharpe thinks that possibly the expression 'domino maiore,' strictly 'Sir Mayor,' may account for the origin of the Lord Mayor's title.[235] A claim has been set up for Thomas Legge, Mayor the second time in 1354, that he was the first Lord Mayor, but there is positively no authority whatever for this claim, although it is boldly stated that he was created Lord Mayor by Edward III. in this year.

One point is worthy of special attention, although it does not throw any actual light on the matter. Bishop Stubbs says that the Mayor of York was known as Lord Mayor in 1389 [1389]. Richard II. had in that year presented his own sword to the Mayor, who was thence-forward known as the Lord Mayor; and in 1393 he had given the Lord Mayor a mace.[236]

If this were so, we can scarcely believe that the Londoners, who had always been very tenacious of their pre-eminent position, would be content to allow their chief magistrate to continue without a title possessed by the Mayor of York. Still, there is not the slightest evidence that the title of Lord Mayor was used in London at this early period, and it is possible that Bishop Stubbs's statement is too definite. There is no doubt that the title 'Lord Mayor' was used at an early date in York, but the prefix 'Lord' was not always applied, and as late as 1565 there is reference in the Chamberlain's account book 'to Mr. John Bean, Mayor.'[237]

A correspondence of some interest was printed in *The Times* in November and December 1901 on this point; but although Legge's claim was disproved, few if any positive facts were brought forward. The most satisfactory letter was one from Mr. W. H. St. John Hope, of the Society of Antiquaries, who, as the result of a search in the city books, gave some definite information as to the use of the title. 'Down to about 1540 the chief magistrate was invariably styled Mayor.... There are, however, instances as early as 1519 where he is referred to as "my lorde mayr," but seemingly in the same way as we speak of "my lord bishop" or "my lord the King," for the same entry that refers to him as "my lorde mayr" nowe beyng, continues "as well as all other mayres his successours." After 1540 the use of the term "Lord Mayor" becomes general—*e.g.*, 1542, "every lorde mayer's house"; 1545, "the lorde mayers of the same cytie"; 1546, "the lorde mayor," &c.'

We have seen how important was the office of Mayor in mediæval times, and how like a king the holder's dignity was upheld.

The Mayor has certain very remarkable privileges, which prove the high esteem in which he was held by the sovereign. These privileges are of considerable antiquity, and have not yet been traced to their source. The four principal are:—

I. The closing of Temple Bar to the sovereign.

II. The Mayor's position in the city, where he is second only to the King.

III. His summons to the Privy Council on the accession of a new sovereign.

IV. His position of Butler at the Coronation banquets.

I.—The closing of Temple Bar to the Sovereign.

The gates of Temple Bar were invariably closed by the city authorities whenever the sovereign had occasion to enter the city. A herald sounded a trumpet before the gate—another herald knocked—a parley ensued—the gates were then thrown open and the Mayor for the time being presented the sword of the city to the sovereign, who graciously returned it to the Mayor. The earliest record of this custom is connected with Queen Elizabeth's visit to St. Paul's to return thanks for the defeat of the Spanish Armada, but evidently the custom must be one of great antiquity, and probably in the case of the early kings it was carried out at one of the city gates long before the bars of the liberties were thought of, although no records have come down to us.

Stow's account of the proceedings in his *Annales* is as follows: 'Over the gate of the Temple bar were placed the waites of the cittie, and at the same barre the Lord Maior and his brethren the aldermen in scarlet received and welcomed her Majestie to her cittie and chamber, delivering to her hands the scepter, which after certaine speeches had, her Highnesse redelivered to the Maior, and hee againe taking his horse, bare the same before her. The companies of the cittie in their liveries stoode in their rayles of tymber, covered with blew cloth, all of them saluting her highnesse, as shee proceeded along to Paules Church.'

II.—The Mayor's position in the City.

None of the privileges connected with the Mayor's office has been so jealously guarded as the one upon which is founded the claim to the Mayor's supremacy in the City of London, where the sovereign only takes precedence of him. In Riley's *Memorials* there is an extract from Letter Book I (1415) which refers to Henry V.'s speech on the contemplated invasion of France and the seat of honour accorded to the Mayor, in presence of the Archbishop of Canterbury and the King's brothers. When these notabilities met together diligent council was held as to the order in which they ought to sit, and 'the Lords agreed together among themselves to the effect that the Mayor, in consideration of the reverence and honour due to our most excellent Lord the King, of whom he is the representative in the city, should have his place, when sitting, in the middle, and that the said Lords of Canterbury and Winchester should be seated on his right hand, and John, Humphrey and Edward on the left, upon seats arranged for them; these to make declaration on behalf of our said Lord the King.'[238]

The actual right to pre-eminence was seldom challenged in the city, but there were certain places which were supposed to be outside the Mayor's jurisdiction, such as the Inns of Court, where misunderstandings were frequently taking place. A very interesting instance is given in Gregory's Chronicle, and it is well worth quoting here for the striking light it throws upon the dignity of the office:—

'Thys yere [1465], abute mydsomyr, a[t] the ryalle feste of the Sargentys of the Coyfe, the Mayre of London [Mathew Phylyppe] was desyride to be at that feste. And at denyr time he come to the feste with his offecers, agreyng and acordyng unto hys degre. For withyn London he ys next unto the kyng in all maner thynge. And in tyme of waschynge the Erle of Worseter was take before the mayre and sette downe in the myddis of the hy tabelle. And the mayre seynge that hys place was occupyd hylde hym contente, and went home agayne with-owt mete or drynke or any thonke, but rewarde hym he dyd as hys dygnyte requyred of the cytte. And toke with hym the substance of hys bretheryn the aldyrmen to his place, and were sette and servyd also sone as any man couthe devyse, bothe of sygnet and of othyr delycatys i-nowe, that alle the howse mervelyd howe welle alle tynge was done in soo schorte a tyme, and prayde alle men to be mery and gladde hit shulde be a-mendyd a-nothyr tyme.

'Thenn the offesers of the feste, fulle evylle a-schamyd, informyd the maysters of the feste of thys mysse-happe that ys be-falle. And they consyderynge the grete dygnyte and costys and change that longgyd unto the cytte, and anon sende unto the mayre a present of mete, brede, wyne, and many dyvers sotelteys. But whenn they that come with the presentys say [saw] alle the gyftys, and the sarvyse that was at the borde, he was fulle sore a-schamyd that shulde doo the massage, for the present was not better thenn the servyse of metys was byfore the mayre, and thoroughe-owte the hyghe tabylle. But hys demenynge was soo that he hadde love and thonke for hys massage, and a grette rewarde with-alle. And thys the worschippe of the cytte was kepte, and not loste for hym. I truste that nevyr hyt shalle, by the grace of God.'[239]

Another and a later difficulty with the lawyers is recorded by Pepys on March 3, 1668-1669. In order to understand the cause of contention it is necessary to bear in mind that within the city the Mayor's sword was held up before him, but outside it was held down.

'Meeting Mr. Bellwood, did hear how my Lord Mayor [Sir William Turner] being invited this day to dinner at the Reader's at the Temple, and endeavouring to carry his sword up the students did pull it down, and forced him to go and stay all the day in a private councillor's chamber, until the Reader himself could get the young gentlemen to dinner; and then my Lord Mayor did retreat out of the Temple by stealth, with his sword up. This do make great heat among the students; and my Lord Mayor did send to the King.'

On Sir William Turner's complaint, the King agreed to have the case argued before him in council, but after hearing the evidence his Majesty thought it best to suspend the declaration of his pleasure until the right and privilege should be determined at law, and apparently the question remains unsettled to the present day.

A note may here be made of the Mayor's position in the city as the chief of the military forces within his jurisdiction, with the right of forbidding the entry of troops without his sanction. 'The 3rd regiment of foot, raised in 1665, known by the ancient title of the Old Buffs, have the privilege of marching thro' London with drums beating, colours flying, which the city disputes, not only with all other corps, but even with the King's Guards going on duty to the Tower.'—Major R. Donkin, *Military Collections*, New York, 1777, p. 134.

III.—The Mayor's summons to the Privy Council on the accession of a new Sovereign.

This is intimately connected with the claim of the city to a voice in the election of the King, which found practical expression even before the Conquest. There can be no doubt that in mediæval times the support of London was eagerly sought for in cases of disputed succession. During the nineteenth century it was the custom to belittle the Mayor and Corporation, and Lord Macaulay in his history ignores the considerable influence of the city in securing the succession of his hero William III. to the throne.

At the Councils held on the accession of Queen Victoria and King Edward VII. the respective Lords Mayor, although summoned, were not allowed to remain to the meeting of the Council.

Little has been written upon this very important privilege of the Lord Mayor, but its consideration opens up a very remarkable constitutional question which requires very careful investigation. There ought to be sufficient information available to settle the question.

On the accession of his present Majesty, the Lord Mayor (the late Mr. Alderman Green, afterwards Sir Frank Green, Baronet) was invited to sign the proclamation immediately after the Royal Family, the Archbishop of

Canterbury and the Lord Chancellor and his colleagues' signatures following his lordship's.

It is said that the great Duke of Wellington laid great stress upon the attendance of the Lord Mayor, and it was supposed that as the death of the sovereign cancelled the appointments of Court officials, the Lord Mayor, who continued in office, was an official of considerable importance on the occasion of the accession of a new sovereign. The continuance of Court appointments is now settled by an Act of Parliament.

IV.—*The Mayor s position at the Coronation Banquets.*

The privilege of assisting the chief butler at the coronations of the Kings of England accorded to the citizens of London appears to date back before the appointment of a Mayor. Dr. Sharpe, referring to the double coronation of Richard I., writes: 'His first coronation had taken place at Westminster (3rd Sept. 1189), soon after his accession, and the citizens of London had duly performed a service at the coronation banquet—a service which even in those days was recognised as an "ancient service"—namely, that of assisting the chief butler, for which the Mayor was customarily presented with a gold cup and ewer. The citizens of the rival city of Winchester performed on this occasion the lesser service of attending to the viands. The second coronation taking place at Winchester [17th April 1194] and not at Westminster, the burgesses of the former city put in a claim to the more honourable service over the heads of the citizens of London, and the latter only succeeded in establishing their superior claim by a judicious bribe of 200 marks.'[240]

Andrew Bokerel, Mayor in the year 1236 (21 Henry III.), claimed to serve as butler at the coronation of Eleanor, daughter of Raymond Berengar IV., Count of Provence, Queen of Henry III., but his claim was set aside on this occasion by the King's command.[241]

In the remarkable record of the Court of Claims held before the coronation of Richard II. (over which John of Gaunt presided as High Steward), *Close Roll*, I *Ric. II. mem. 45*. (Public Record Office), the claim of the Mayor and citizens is fully set forth: The King 'willed and decreed that the citizens of the said city should serve in the hall of botelry helping the chief butler, while the King himself sat at table on the day of his coronation, and when the same our lord the King, after dinner, entered his chamber and asked for wine, the said Mayor should serve our said lord the King with a bowl of gold, and afterwards should receive that bowl with the ewer appertaining to the same bowl, as a gift from the King.'[242]

At the coronation of Henry VI. (6th November 1429), William Estfield, the recently elected Mayor, received the customary gold cup and ewer used on the occasion, which he afterwards bequeathed to his grandson.[243]

The latest instance of this jealously guarded privilege occurred at the coronation of George IV., July 19, 1821.[244]

The claim to this honourable service in the cases of the coronations of William IV and Queen Victoria was not made because no banquet took place on these occasions.

In the case of the coronation of his present Majesty the claim was excluded from the consideration of the Court of Claims under the royal proclamation. The terms of the judgment on a further claim is as follows: 'The Court considers and adjudges that the Lord Mayor has by usage a right, subject to His Majesty's pleasure, to attend the Abbey during the coronation, and bear the crystal mace.'[245]

It will be seen that of these four special privileges two relate to the Mayor's position in the city and two to his position outside the city.

The pageants connected with the election of the Mayor are of great antiquity, but we have little information respecting the earlier ones. It is a tradition that when the mayoralty was granted by the King, a stipulation was made that the Mayor should be presented for approval either to the King or his justiciar, and the processions then commenced.

In 1415 the Mayor proceeded to Westminster on horseback, but in 1453 Sir John Norman, the Mayor, was infirm, and he introduced the custom of making the progress from London to Westminster by barge. This continued till the horseback procession was revived in 1657, much to the disgust of the London watermen.

Even when the water procession was the regular practice, the procession on horseback to the Guildhall and then to the waterside for embarkation took place.

No Lord Mayor in a city procession used a coach before 1712, and then only an ordinary one. The present State coach was built in 1757.

Sir John Shaa, Mayor in 1482, was the first to give the annual banquet in the Guildhall. Previously, the feast had taken place either at Grocers' Hall or some other convenient place. The practice of dining at the Guildhall did not become general until 1501, when alterations were made in the kitchen, and the requisite offices having been added the series of annual banquets was commenced there.

There was no feeling of contempt of trade in the Middle Ages, and the Merchant Princes of London were held in high esteem. The custom of ridiculing the city and its rulers did not then exist, but it seems probable that it first came into being in the reign of Elizabeth.

Richard Johnson's *Nine Worthies of London* (1592) contains the praise of the worthies, written by the author in a mock heroic style. Of the nine four were Mayors, namely, Sir William Walworth, 1374, 1380; Sir Henry Pitchard (Picard), 1356; Sir William Sevenoke, 1418; and Sir William White, 1553.

Most of the Mayors of the Middle Ages were men of birth and position, and it is difficult to understand how it was that the popular idea of a poor boy coming up to London penniless, making his way here, and eventually rising to be Mayor, first came into existence. The elaboration of this idea in the chap-book life of Sir Richard Whittington is entirely opposed to the facts of the case.

Aldermen

The consideration of the actual position of the alderman in the government of London is one of great difficulty, and Mr. Round's discovery of the Oath of the Commune in which aldermen are not mentioned has made it difficult to conjecture when it was that they took their natural place as the advisers of the Mayor.

The title 'alderman' is a survival of the Saxon period (as is also that of 'sheriff'), but the duties of the holders of the office have frequently been changed.

The word 'alderman' was a generic term as well as the distinctive title of a special officer. King Alfred appointed an alderman over all London, and the chief officer of the various guilds was originally known as an alderman.

The various wards were each presided over by an alderman from an early period, but, as already noted, we cannot fix the date when they were united as a Court of Aldermen.

Bishop Stubbs writes: 'The governing body of London in the thirteenth century was composed of the Mayor, twenty-five aldermen of the wards and two sheriffs. All these were elective officers.'[246]

The difficulty is, that although aldermen were undoubtedly elected as the heads of wards they are not referred to as the colleagues of the Mayor until the very end of this century.

In March 1298-1299 letters were sent from 'the Mayor and Commune of the City of London' to the Echevins, Jurats and Commonalty of the town of Burges' [Bruges]; 'to the Provost, Bailiffs and Commonalty of the town of Caen'; and 'to the Provost, Echevins and Commonalty of the City of Comerac' [Cambray?].[247]

Although the official form of 'The Mayor and Commune' was continued until the end of the thirteenth century, and it was not until early in the fourteenth century that the form 'Mayor, Aldermen and Common Council' came into existence, there is sufficient evidence to show that the aldermen and Common Council before that time were acting with the Mayor as governors of the city.

As already quoted from Bishop Stubbs, that authority describes the aldermen as assistants of the Mayor as early as 1249. At all events, in the record of the election of aldermen in 1293, they are specially described as elected for the government of the city.

In 1299 (27 Edw. I.) 'it was agreed by Henry le Galeys, Mayor, and the aldermen, that Strago, the sweeper of litter in the ward of Chepe, should be taken and imprisoned until, etc., because he, the said Strago, had scandalized the aldermen by saying that they take the money of the commonalty at the Guildhall under pretext of wardship of orphans and then waste such money for their own profit.' In consequence of these unfounded charges Strago was committed to the Tun.[248]

There are in Riley's *Memorials* about this date several other references to aldermen acting with the Mayor, thus, on the 14th September 1301: 'Walter Swan appeared before Sir Elias Russel, Mayor of London, and other aldermen then present';[249] and in December 1310 Roger de Eure having insulted and assaulted Richard de Gloucestre, alderman, the two parties 'appeared in the Guildhall before Sir Richer [de Refham] the Mayor, and the aldermen.'[250]

In 1311 (4 Edw. II.) the form of description of the governors was 'The Mayor, Aldermen and Common Council of the City.'[251] From this time the general form was either this or 'The Mayor, Aldermen and Commonalty.' It is necessary, however, to mention that a congregation of Mayor and aldermen is referred to in Fitz-Ailwin's Assize of 1189.[252]

The title of 'echevin,' as applied to a governor of the city, is at present only known to us as used in the Oath of the Commune, found by Mr. Round, and it may therefore have had a very short existence. It is possible that aldermen were elected on to the Mayor's Council under the title of 'echevins.' This, however, is not the opinion of Mr. Round, who is inclined to believe that the body of echevins became in course of time the Court of Common Council.

The whole question is at present one of great difficulty, and I only state the facts here without venturing to express any confident opinion until more evidence is forthcoming.

We may be allowed to think that too great an importance has been ascribed to the position of the early aldermen in connection with their wards. It is generally affirmed that the aldermen were hereditary owners of the various wards, on account of the fact that the wards were named after them, an instance of which practice remains in Farringdon, Bassishaw and Basingshall. There is no evidence of this proprietorship, and it seems improbable on the face of it. Mr. Round believes that what an alderman inherited can only have been the aldermanry of his ward, like, he suggests, an hereditary sheriff.

Mr. Baddeley writes that 'early in 1276 we find mention made of "the ward of Henry de Frowyk within the Gate" (*i.e.*, Cripplegate), and ten years later (*circ.* 1285) he figures in the earliest list of aldermen extant in the city's records as alderman of the same ward.'[253]

At the election of aldermen in 1291 (19 Edw. I.) sixteen of the wards were named after the aldermen and eight after places. The latter being the wards of Chepe, Castle Baynard, Walebroke, Douegate, Bridge, Portsoken, Vintry, and Bassieshawe.

At the election two years afterwards (1293) all the wards were named with their proper names, and not after the aldermen.

The ward of Ludgate and Neugate presented Nicholas de Farndone, it being styled in the previous list 'the ward of William de Farndone.' Many of the same names are found in the two lists, but they represent different individuals of the same family.

The preamble to the list of elections in 1293 is of considerable interest: 'Be it remembered that on Tuesday before the Feast of St. Botolph, 21 Edw. I., in the presence of Sir John le Bretun, Warden of London, the whole commonalty of the city aforesaid was assembled, viz., from each ward the wealthier and wiser men, who each by their several wards elected for themselves aldermen freely, of good will and of their full consent, and the aldermen so elected, they presented to the warden aforesaid in this form, that all and singular the things which the aforesaid aldermen of their wisdom and discretion shall do and ordain for the government of the city and the maintenance of the King's peace, in conjunction with the warden and their superiors for the time being shall be straitly observed, and shall be held ratified and confirmed before other provisions touching the commonalty without any challenge or opposition in the future; and each ward elected its aldermen, for whom it would answer as to all his acts affecting the city, the Commune (*Communam*) and its estate.'[254]

It will be seen from the above that the election of aldermen was only in the hands of a few of the 'wealthier and wiser men' of the wards, but later on the electors were freemen of the city, 'paying scot and bearing lot.'

There was much difference of practice in the election of aldermen. Various orders were issued from time to time, and some of them fell out of use.

In 1377 it was ordered that aldermen should be elected annually, as appears from the following entry in Letter Book H (f. 58):—

'51 Edw. III. Precept (*bille*) for the men of each ward to meet on Saturday, the 7th March, and elect an alderman other than the sitting alderman, and to have the name of the alderman so elected endorsed on the Bill at the Guildhall on the Feast of St. Gregory next, at eight o'clock at the latest, under penalty.'

This precept was elaborated in an Ordinance made on Friday, 6th March, 51 Edw. III., with the assent of the Mayor, aldermen and divers representations of the livery companies.

It was ordered that 'aldermen removed for good and reasonable cause shall not be open for re-election, but that those who go out of office on St. Gregory's Day and have not misconducted themselves may be re-elected after the interval of one year.'

In 1384 the rule was modified so as to allow an alderman to be re-elected for his ward at the expiration of his year of office without any interval (Letter Book H, f. 173).

In 1394 the Ordinance respecting annual elections was repealed by the King, and aldermen were henceforward elected for life.

6th March, 17 Ric. II., 'and have also ordained for the honour and greater increase of the good government of our said city, that they who should be chosen aldermen of our same city should not be removed out of their offices during their lives, unless for just, reasonable and notable cause.'

Shortly after this an order of the Mayor, aldermen and commonalty was issued which took away the right of the wards of directly electing their aldermen. A ward was only allowed to nominate two persons, of whom the Mayor and aldermen were to choose one. Five years later, that is in 1402, the number of names to be nominated was raised to four, and in 1420 this order was reaffirmed.[255]

Distinct rank was accorded to aldermen; thus the Common Seal of the Corporation bears the inscription: *Sigillum Baronum Londoniarum*, and we are told by John Carpenter in *Liber Albus*, 'it is a matter of experience that even since the year of our Lord 1350, at the sepulture of aldermen, the ancient custom of interment with baronial honours was observed; for in the church where the alderman was about to be buried a person appeared upon a caparisoned horse, arrayed in the armour of the deceased, bearing a banner in his hand, and carrying upon him his shield, helmet and the rest of his arms, along with the banner, as is still the usage at the sepulture of lords of baronial rank. But by reason of the sudden and frequent changes of the aldermen, and the repeated occurrence of pestilence, this ceremonial in London gradually died out and disappeared.'[256]

When the poll tax of 1379 was imposed the Mayor was assessed as an earl and the aldermen as barons.[257]

On August 12, 1417, a royal mandate (5 Hen. V.) was issued to the Mayor enjoining that the aldermen shall reside within the city: 'We do therefore will, and do command and charge you that you cause your letters to be addressed unto each one of the said aldermen so absent from our said city, charging them strictly thereby on our behalf that they return unto our said city and do tarry and remain there, to support you and to administer counsel and assistance in all that may touch the preservation of the said peace and good governance of our said city.'[258] This was an irksome regulation, and in the charter of Edward IV. the aldermen were released from the obligation.

'It is well-known and manifest that those of the said city which are elected aldermen have sustained great cost and pains for the time they make their abode and residence in the same city, and for that cause oftentimes do leave their possessions and places in the country that therefore they and every of them may without fear of unquietness or molestation peaceably abide and tarry in such their houses and possessions, when they shall return thither for comfort and recreations sake.'

It has sometimes been the fashion of the wits to gird at the aldermen and other city magnates, but although some of the names on the list may be of little account there are many which are written on the page of history, and a large number of noble families owe their origin to famous aldermen.

Sir Geoffrey Boleyn, Mayor in 1457, was great-grandfather to Anne Boleyn, and therefore ancestor of Queen Elizabeth; Sir Thomas Canynge, Mayor in 1456, was ancestor of George Canning, Earl Canning, and Lord

Stratford de Redcliffe; Sir William Loke, sheriff in 1548, the favourite of Henry VIII., who had a key of the King's private chamber so that he might come whenever he would, was the ancestor of John Locke, Lord Chancellor King, and the Earl of Lovelace; John Cowper, alderman in 1551, was the ancestor of Lord Chancellor Cowper and the poet William Cowper; Sir Edward Osborne was the ancestor of the Dukes of Leeds.

Among other distinguished men descended from aldermen may be mentioned Bacon, Beckford, Byron, Cromwell, Howe, Marlborough, Newcastle, Melbourne, Nelson, Palmerston, the two William Pitts, Raglan, Salisbury, and the Walpoles.

SHERIFFS.

The government of the city by reeves dates back to a very early period of our history, and these reeves were appointed by the King. When William the Conqueror demanded entrance to London the joint governors were the bishop and the portreeve. How long before the Conquest a portreeve had been appointed and how long after his office was continued we do not know. The sheriff to some extent took his place, but Henry I. gave the city the right of appointing justiciars and sheriffs, and the justiciar, according to Mr. Round, took precedence of the sheriff.

After the establishment of the Commune and the appointment of a Mayor the sheriffs naturally lost much of their importance, and they became what they are styled in *Liber Albus*, 'the Eyes of the Mayor.' They often in early times were called also bailiffs. When Middlesex was in ferm to London the two sheriffs were equally Sheriffs of London and Middlesex. There is one instance only in the city records of a Sheriff of Middlesex being mentioned as distinct from the sheriffs, and this was in 1283 when Anketin de Betteville and Walter le Blond are described as Sheriffs of London, and Gerin as Sheriff of Middlesex.[259] This anomaly has not been explained, but Dr. Sharpe remarks respecting a writ of 1308: 'The King to the Sheriff of Middlesex, greeting,' that this was 'presumably addressed to and the return made by the Sheriffs of London acting as Sheriff of Middlesex according to custom.'

It was ordained and agreed in 1383 (7 Ric. II.) 'that no person shall from henceforth be Mayor in the said city if he have not first been sheriff of the said city, to the end that he may be tried in governance and bounty before he attains such estate of the mayoralty.'[260]

Mr. Baddeley has very clearly described the changes made at various times in the election of sheriffs, and I therefore quote from his book: 'Until the commencement of the fourteenth century the sheriffs were elected by the Mayor, aldermen and commonalty of the city. In 1301 an attempt was made to restrict the number of electors to twelve representatives of each ward, but this, like other subsequent attempts, proved unsuccessful. In 1347 is met with, for the first time, a new method of procedure. In that year one of the sheriffs was elected by the Mayor and the other by the commonalty, and this prerogative of the Mayor for the time being to elect one of the sheriffs continued to be exercised with few, if any, exceptions down to 1638.'[261]

This is the mode of election which is described in the *Liber Albus*: 'In the first place, the Mayor shall choose, of his own free will, a reputable man, free of the city, to be one of the sheriffs for the ensuing year, for whom he is willing to answer as to one half of the ferm of the city due to the King, if he who is so elected by the Mayor shall prove not sufficient. But if the Mayor elect him by counsel and with the assent of the aldermen they also ought to be answerable with him. And those who are elected for the Common Council themselves, and the others summoned by the Mayor for this purpose, as before declared, shall choose another sheriff for the commonalty, for whom all the commonalty is bound to be answerable as to the other half of the ferm so due to the King, in case he shall prove not sufficient. And if any controversy arise between the Commons as to the election, the matter is to proceed and be discussed.'[262]

COMMON COUNCIL.

We do not know when the Court of Common Council was first formed, but, as already stated, Mr. Round supposes it to have grown out of the body of echevins brought into being on the granting of a Commune. It seems probable that the two courts—that of aldermen and that of the Common Council—were formed about the same time, but it is remarkable that we have at present no definite information on the subject. Now that special attention is drawn to this matter, it is to be hoped that some facts settling the question may be forthcoming. The number of members of the Common Council varied greatly at different times, but the right to determine the number was indirectly granted by the charter of Edward III., 1341, which enables the city to amend customs and usages which have become hard.

The preamble to an Act of Common Council, 8th May 1840 (3 Vict.), passed to reduce the total number of Common Council, and to apportion more equally the members to the different wards, contains the following statement of its antiquity:—

'Whereas from time whereof the memory of man runneth not to the contrary, there hath existed, and still doth exist, within the City of London, a Common Council, consisting of the Mayor and aldermen of the said city, and certain citizens, being freemen of the said city, annually elected to be of the same Council, and called the Commons of the said city; and whereas, under and by virtue of the ancient charters, ordinances, statutes and customs of the said city, the power of appointing and regulating the number of citizens to be from time to time elected of the same Common Council hath, from time whereof the memory of man runneth not to the contrary, belonged, and still of right doth belong, to the Mayor, aldermen and Commons of the said city.'[263]

The Common Council were chosen by the wards until 1351 (25 Edw. III.), when certain Companies appointed the Common Council.[264]

In 1376 (50 Edw. III.) an Ordinance was made by the Mayor and aldermen, with the assent of the whole Commons, to the effect that the companies should select men with whom they were content, and none other should come to the elections of Mayors and sheriffs; that the greater companies should not elect more than six, the lesser four, and the least two.[265] Forty-seven companies nominated 156 members.

In 1383 the right of election reverted to the wards, but was obtained again by the companies in 1467.

ARMS OF LONDON.

The arms of the City of London are simple and of great interest, consisting as they do of the Cross of St. George with the Sword of St. Paul in the dexter quarter, but unfortunately an absurd popular blunder has been prevalent that the sword was really the dagger with which Sir William Walworth killed Wat Tyler.

The history of these arms is fully set forth in Jewitt and Hope's *Corporation Plate*, and there illustrated with figures of the old common seal of London, and the first and second mayoralty seals. The facts as there set forth are shortly stated here.

The old common seal is a fine example of the early part of the thirteenth century. Stow in his *Survey* dates it in 1224, and Gregory in his *Chronicle* in 1227-1228. Mr. Hope says that the seal may well be of a date *circa* 1225, and that it certainly was in use in 1246. The obverse of the seal represents a figure of St. Paul, with a sword in his outstretched right hand, and a banner of England in his left hand. 'The saint is represented as standing in the middle of the city over which he keeps guard; the spire of the cathedral church rises in front of him, and other steeples on each side.... In front of all is the city wall with its ditch, with lofty central gateway and two lesser flanking towers or bastions.' The legend is: SIGILLUM BARONUM LONDONIARUM.

The first mayoralty seal bears the seated figures of St. Thomas of Canterbury and St. Paul with his sword. The legend is *Sigillum Maioratus London.* and the date *circa* 1280.

The second mayoralty seal, which was produced a century after the first one, is of very special interest. It bears seated figures of St. Thomas and St. Paul, and in base a shield of the city supported by two lions. The legend is *Sigil: Maioratus: Civitatis: London.* The record of the making of this seal in 1381 is found in Letter Book K, f. cxxxijb., and Mr. Hope's remarks on the value of this piece of evidence must be quoted entire: 'This seal is of special interest, not only from its being a dated example, but because it proves beyond doubt the absurdity of the silly notion that the object in the dexter chief of the city arms is the sword or dagger wherewith Sir William Walworth slew Wat Tyler, instead of being, as it undoubtedly is, the sword of St. Paul. Wat Tyler was killed on June 15, 1381, whereas the new seal of the mayoralty had been formally adopted on April 17, two months before. This seal is also one of the earliest authorities for the city arms. Its silver matrix is still preserved at the Mansion House, but in so worn a condition that little else than the deepest parts can be traced. It is only now used for mercantile documents going abroad.'[266]

To return to the common seal, it may be noticed here that the original reverse had 'in base a view of the city somewhat resembling that on the obverse, surmounted by a segmental arch. On the top of the arch, seated on a throne or chair of state, is a figure of St. Thomas of Canterbury with cross and pall.'

In accordance with the famous proclamation of Henry VIII. (Nov. 16, 1538) which enacted 'that Thomas Becket' should no longer 'be esteemed, named, reputed nor called a sayncte, but Bysshop Becket, and that his ymages and pictures through the hole realme shalle be putte downe,' etc., it was enacted in 1539 that this reverse of the common seal should be destroyed.

'The beautiful reverse of the common seal, after doing duty for over three centuries, was therefore broken up, and presumably its silver used to make a new matrix. This is of the same size as its predecessor, but, in accordance with the resolution, it bears for device simply the city arms, *argent a cross gules and in the dexter quarter the sword of St. Paul*, with helm, mantling and crest, *a dragon's wing expanded argent charged with a cross gules*. The legend is: *Londini. Defende. Tuos. Deus. Optime. Cives.*'[267]

In connection with the arms it may be noticed that the supporters which are usually described as griffins are really dragons, in allusion to St. George.

CHAPTER IX

Officials of the City

THE chief of the officials of the City of London was for many years after the Conquest the Castellan and Bannerer. When William the Conqueror obtained possession of London he built a castle on the river at each end of the city, to intimidate the Londoners. The Tower was at the east end, and at the west end was what according to Dugdale was called at first *The Castle*. This was placed under the charge of Baynard, one of the Conqueror's followers, after whom it came to be known as Baynard's Castle. The hereditary office of Castellan was held by the family of Fitz-Walter, by virtue of their possession of Baynard's Castle, the key of the city. The duties attached to this office are among the most important and interesting in the story of mediæval London, and it is to be presumed that Baynard held the various privileges afterwards possessed by the family of Fitz-Walter, but no notice of this is recorded.

Robert Fitz-Richard was the first baron by tenure. He is said to have been the younger son of Richard Fitz-Gilbert, ancestor of the Earls of Clare. He was steward to Henry I., from whom he obtained the barony of Dunmow, and the honour of the soke of Baynard's Castle, both which had been forfeited to the Crown in 1111 by reason of the felony of William, Baron of Dunmow, son of Ralph Baynard, the Norman associate of William the Conqueror, after whom the castle was named.

In connection with this soke Robert held the hereditary office of Standard-Bearer of the city, the duties of which will be stated further on. He died in 1134, and was succeeded by his son, Walter Fitz-Robert. The latter's son was Robert Fitz-Walter, the most famous member of the family, and the one who transmitted to his descendants the permanent surname of Fitz-Walter.

This Fitz-Walter was styled 'Marshal of the Army of God and Holy Church.' He was one of the twenty-five barons appointed to enforce the observance of Magna Charta obtained from King John.

An 'agreement [dated 15-25 June 1215] between King John, of the one part, and Robert Fitz-Walter, Marshal of the Army of God and of Holy Church in England, six earls and six barons named, and other earls, barons and freemen, of the other part,' is preserved in the Public Record Office, and the following description of the document is given in the *Catalogue of*

MSS., &c., in the Museum of the P.R.O. (1902): 'The earls, barons and others shall hold the City of London, saving the royal revenues, and the Archbishop of Canterbury shall hold the Tower of London, saving the liberties of the city, until the Feast of the Assumption in the seventeenth year of the reign. In the meanwhile, oaths shall be taken throughout England to twenty-five barons, as is contained in the charter for the liberties and security of the realm, and all things shall be done according to the said charter; otherwise the city and the Tower shall be held as above, until all the said things shall be done.' It is said in a note to this document that 'none of the thirteen persons who are thus entered into an agreement with the King are mentioned among those upon whose advice he granted the great charter.'

The third baron was himself in trade, and he owned wine ships. He received special privileges from John, and the story of that King's treatment of his daughter Matilda is supposed to be an unfounded tale.

In the year 1215 the insurgent barons entered the city at Aldgate, largely owing to the assistance of Robert Fitz-Walter, whose position was of a commanding character. He died in 1235.

Walter Fitz-Walter succeeded his father Robert, and died in 1257. He was succeeded by his son Robert Fitz-Walter, the fifth baron.

It is of the latter's duties and privileges that we possess an account, written by Robert Glover, Somerset Herald in the reign of Elizabeth, extracts from which are given by Dugdale in his *Baronage of England*, 1675, i. 200:—

'In time of war [he] should serve the city in manner following, viz.: To ride upon a light horse, with twenty men-at-arms on horseback, their horses covered with cloth or harness, unto the great dore of St. Paul's Church, with the banner of his arms carried before him; and being come in that manner thither, the Mayor of London, together with the sheriffs and aldermen, to issue armed out of the church unto the same dore on foot, with a banner in his hand, having the figure of St. Paul depicted with gold thereon, but the feet, hands and head of silver, holding a silver sword in his hand.

'And as soon as he shall see the Mayor, sheriffs and aldermen come on foot out of the church, carrying such a banner, he is to alight from his horse, and salute him as his companion, saying, *Sir Mayor, I am obliged to come hither to do my service, which I owe to this city.* To whom the Mayor, sheriffs and aldermen are to answer, *We give to you, as our banner-bearer for this city, this banner by inheritance of the city, to bear and carry, to the honour and profit thereof to your power.*

'Whereupon the said Robert and his heirs shall receive it into their hands, and the Mayor and sheriffs shall follow him to the dore, and bring him an horse worth twenty pounds. Which horse shall be saddled with a saddle of his arms, and covered with silk, depicted likewise with the same arms; and they shall take twenty pounds sterling, and deliver it to the chamberlain of the said Robert, for his expenses that day,' etc.[268]

There was a vacant ground opposite the great west door of St. Paul's where this interesting ceremony took place. The folkmoots were held in the churchyard at the east end of the cathedral.

In 1275 (3 Edw. I.) Robert Fitz-Walter obtained licence from the Crown to convey Baynard Castle and the Tower of Montfichet to the Archbishop of Canterbury for the purpose of the foundation of the House and Church of the Friars Preachers or Blackfriars.[269] In the following year Edward I. confirmed the grant of two lanes adjacent to 'Castle Baynard and the Tower of Montfytchet for the purpose of enlarging the aforesaid place on condition that the said archbishop should provide the citizens with a more convenient way as he had now done.'[270] In 1277-1278 an alteration was made in the wall of the friary.[271]

When Sir Robert Fitz-Walter conveyed Baynard Castle to the Archbishop he specially reserved all his rights and privileges in the following terms: 'Provided that by reason of this grant nothing should be extinguished to him and his heirs which did belong to his barony, but that whatsoever relating thereto as wel in rents, landing of vessels and other liberties and priviledges in the City of London or elsewhere without diminution, which to him the said Robert or to that barony had antiently appertained, should be thenceforth reserved.'[272]

We know very little of this Tower of Montfichet, but it must have been closely connected with Baynard Castle. There is a reference to it and its owner in the *Chronique de la guerre entre les Anglois et les Ecossois en 1173 et 1174 par Jordan Fantosme* (Howlett's *Chronicles of Stephen, Henry II. and Richard I.*, iii. 339. Rolls Series):

"Gilbert de Munfichet has fortified his castle,
And says that the Clares are leagued with him."

As Mr. Round points out to me this reference to the Clares must relate to the proprietors of Baynard's Castle, who, as previously noted, were of the same family as the Clares. Walter Fitz-Robert is also referred to in this metrical chronicle.

The Barons Fitz-Walter possessed many privileges in time of peace, which are set out by Dugdale, among which was the right of punishing by drowning at Woodwharf persons guilty of treason, but it was as constable of Barnard Castle that they enjoyed these privileges as well as the office of bannerer to the City of London. A beautiful seal inscribed 'Sigillum Roberti Filii Walteri' was found at Stamford, Lincolnshire, in the reign of Charles II., and is the subject of a paper by John Charles Brooke of the Heralds' College in *Archæologia* (vol. v. pp. 211-215): 'In this seal we see [Fitz-Walter's] horse elegantly engraved and covered with trappings of his arms, so exquisitely represented, that they evidently appear to be of a much finer texture than those commonly used, the muscles of the animal being seen under them, and as much as engraving can represent drapery, appear to be silk, as described by Glover; and what is remarkable his arms are carved on the rest behind his saddle, which is a rare instance, and evidently alludes to that which the Mayor was to present to him.'

On the seal are represented the arms of Fitz-Walter's second wife Eleanor, daughter of Robert de Ferrers, Earl of Ferrers and Derby. She was married in 1298 and died in 1304, therefore the date of the seal is fixed within six years. Mr. Brooke refers to another seal of Baron Fitz-Walter which he used, 28 Edw. I. (Anno 1300), and in which the dragon occurring in the former seal beneath the horse is used as a supporter. Robert Fitz-Walter died in 1325, and in 1328 the wardship of his son John was granted by the Mayor and aldermen to his widow Johanna.[273]

SEAL OF ROBERT FITZ-WALTER.

In 1347 Sir John Fitz-Walter still claimed to have franchise in the ward of Castle Baynard, but the city entirely repudiated the claim as 'altogether repugnant to the liberties of the city.' He caused stocks to be set up in the ward of Castle Baynard, and claimed to make deliverance of men there imprisoned. In consequence of this action, a conference was held by the Mayor, aldermen and commonalty, at which 'it was agreed that the said Sir John Fitz-Walter has no franchise within the liberty of the city aforesaid, nor is he in future to intermeddle with any plea in the Guildhall of London, or with any matters touching the liberties of the city.'[274]

The Recorder, the chief official of the city, is appointed for life. He was formerly appointed by the city, but since the Local Government Act of 1888 he is nominated by the city and approved by the Lord Chancellor. His duties and his oath are recorded in the *Liber Albus*. In 1329 Gregory de Nortone, the then holder of the office, obtained an increase of salary—100 shillings yearly, as also his robe of the same pattern as the aldermen's robes.[275]

The Common Serjeant was formerly appointed by the city, but since 1888 by the Lord Chancellor. He is the recorder's principal assistant.

The next great official is the Town Clerk, who is appointed by the Common Council and re-elected annually. John de Batequell, clerk of the city, is referred to in Letter Book A,[276] and this is the first recorded mention of the office afterwards known as the common clerk, and later as town clerk. Next to the recorder the town clerk was the chief officer in the local courts of law called the Hustings and the Mayor's Court.

Among the distinguished men who have held the office two names stand out, viz., John Carpenter and William Dunthorn.

Carpenter, town clerk in the reigns of Henry V. and Henry VI., was elected in 1417. He was called also secretary of the city, a title not applied to any other town clerk. He is best known as the compiler of the *Liber Albus*, and as founder of the City of London school.

Dunthorn's (1462) name is associated with the *Liber Dunthorn*, which contains transcripts from the *Liber Albus*, *Liber Custumarum*, Letter Books, etc.

The Chamberlain or Comptroller of the King's Chamber is appointed by the livery. He was originally a King's officer, and the office was probably instituted soon after the Conquest. It is mentioned in documents of the twelfth century. On June 28, 1232, the office of 'King's chamberlain of London' was granted for life to Peter de Rivallis. His duties and privileges as stated in the grant are very extensive and important. 'He shall have for life the custody of the King's houses at Southampton, and the King's prise of wine there,' 'custody of the King's Jewry, of the mint of England,' and 'all other things pertaining to the office of Chamberlain of London.' By another grant of the same year the said Peter, Treasurer of Poitiers for life, was given the custody of the ports and coasts of England, saving the port of Dover.[277] When the office is mentioned in 1275 it was combined with the offices of Mayor and coroner.

The functions of coroner were often exercised by the chamberlain and sheriffs, and when the chamberlain was called away from the city by the King he appointed a deputy coroner. The office was sometimes held by the King's butler, to whom appertained the office of coroner.

William Trente, a wine merchant of Bergerac, was appointed King's butler on the 25th November 1301 (30 Edw. I.)[278] He became also the King's chamberlain of the city and coroner of London.[279]

Andrew Horn, a fishmonger by trade, who kept a shop in Bridge Street, held the office of chamberlain for several years. He was the compiler of *Liber Horn*, which contains charters, statutes, grants, etc. To him also has been attributed the authorship of the law treatise of mediæval times entitled the 'Mirror of Justice.'[280] He died in 1328.

Many attempts were made by the citizens to get the coronership into their own hands, and at last Edward IV. sold the right to appoint a coroner of their own, independent of the King's butler, for £7000.[281]

The Remembrancer or State Amanuensis is appointed by the Common Council. The office was held from 1571 to 1584 by a distinguished man, Thomas Norton, M.P., who was joint author with Thomas Sackville, Earl of Dorset, of the tragedy of *Gorbaduc*. He left a manuscript on the ancient duties of the Lord Mayor and Corporation, an account of which was published by J. Payne Collier in *Archæologia* (vol. xxxvi. p. 97).

The Common Hunt was an official mentioned in the *Liber Albus*, where we learn that John Courtenay was appointed to the office in 1417.[282] The office was abolished in the year 1807.

Of officers in immediate attendance on the Mayor may be mentioned the sword-bearer and the sergeant-at-mace.

The first notice of the office of sword-bearer occurs in the *Liber Albus* (1419), and the first record in the minute books of the appointment of a sword-bearer is in 4 Hen. VI., 1426. Mr. Hope remarks that 'the absence of earlier notices is most probably due to the

THE CRYPT OF THE GUILDHALL.

fact that the sword-bearer was appointed, according to the entry in the *Liber Allus... as propres costages du Mair*, and not at the cost of the city.'

The sword-bearer is remarkable on account of the distinctive head-covering or 'cap of maintenance' which is appropriated to his office.[283]

It is not known when the City of London first possessed a mace or maces, but Mr. Hope refers to the *Liber Custumarum* to prove that as early as 1252 there were sergeants who carried staves of some kind as emblems of authority. 'We know this from the claim put forth on the occasion of the *Iter* of the pleas of the Crown held at the Tower in 1321, that the Mayor and citizens of London should have their own porter and usher, and their own sergeants with their staves. As it was shown that the same claim had been successfully made in 1276-1277, and in 1252 it was allowed' Mr. Hope quotes from Letter Book F a record of the appointment of Robert Flambard as mace-bearer in 1338, and from this it is clear that the office was not then a newly created one.'[284]

For the due carrying on of the business of the Corporation several new offices have at various times been established, but the foregoing are the officials who carried on the work of the city during the Middle Ages. Much of interest might have been added of these men, but it is only necessary here to refer to them generally as those to whom so much of the history of London was due.

The chief business of the city has been carried on for many centuries in the Guildhall, which is of unknown antiquity. It is almost certain that the building was in existence on the same spot as early as the twelfth century. It was rebuilt in 1411, and has been greatly altered at different times since then. The most interesting portion of the old building will be found in the extensive Gothic crypt which is shown in the illustration on page 273. The open timber roof of the Hall was not added until the alterations of 1866-1870 by the late Sir Horace Jones.

CHAPTER X

Commerce and Trade

THE earliest trade recorded as carried on in the British Isles consisted of the exchange of tin with the Gauls, and, perhaps, also with Phœnician traders.

Under Roman rule the agricultural and mineral resources of Britain were more fully developed. Julius Cæsar praised the Southdown mutton, and Rome was supplied with oysters which came from Whitstable and Reculvers (*Regulbium*), and were carried through the River Stour (forming the western boundary of the Island of Thanet), and were exported from Richborough (*Rutupiæ*). Corn was exported in large quantities, and Londinium, the principal port for trading with Gaul, was the centre of commerce.

There is no notice of commerce during the early Anglo-Saxon period, but Bede, at the beginning of the eighth century, speaks of London as a great market which traders frequented by land or sea. The letter of protection for English pilgrims given to Offa of Mercia by Charlemagne (A.D. 796), which refers to trade carried on by them, has been called 'the first English commercial treaty.' One remarkable fact is that this commerce was mainly in the hands of foreigners. London in the early times was mainly a city of foreigners. Hence the jealousy of the natives, which grew in strength as time went on.

Commerce greatly increased during the reign of Edgar, so that Ethelred his son deemed it time to draw up a code of laws to regulate the Customs to be paid by the merchants of France and Flanders, as well as by the Emperor's men, but the promulgation of the laws of Athelstane (A.D. 925-929), which ordained that a merchant who had made three sea voyages should be of right a Thane, is a proof of the small number as well as of the importance of such native traders.

We learn from the Colloquies of the Abbot Ælfric (eleventh century) that most of the commodities imported into England were articles of luxury.

The port of Dowgate was granted to the City of Rouen as early as Edward the Confessor's reign, and the right was afterwards confirmed.[285]

The Confessor also gave a portion of Waremanni-Acra within London, 'with the wharf belonging to it, and with its market rights and places for merchandise, its stalls and shops, its rents and dues and rights, its toll and wharfage' to St. Peter's at Ghent, which grant was confirmed by William I. 1081.[286]

After the Conquest, communication with Normandy naturally increased greatly. Rouen was particularly favoured, and was granted a monopoly of trade with Ireland and freedom of commerce in London. In the twelfth century silver was imported in exchange for meat, fish and wool, which were all sent to the manufacturing districts of the Low Countries. Corn was sometimes exported, but not without a licence.

The House or Gild of the Merchants of Almaines otherwise called the House of the Teutonics, was formed about the year 1169, though the Germans, under the name of Easterlings, are known to have traded here, during the Saxon period. The gild flourished in London as the Merchants of the Steelyard till the time of Elizabeth, when their special privileges were abolished by royal decree.

Hallam tells us that from the middle of the twelfth to the thirteenth century the traders of England became more and more prosperous. The towns on the southern coast exported tin and other metals in exchange for the wines of France. Those on the eastern coast sent corn to Norway, and the Cinque Ports bartered wool against the stuffs of Flanders.

The export, of wool and the import of cloth were prohibited in 1261, and the prohibition was repeated in 1271. The cause of this prohibition may be illustrated by reference to a particular import—woad, which seems to show that a native woollen manufacture existed, although all the finer cloth came from Flanders. The restrictions originally imposed upon the woad merchants would not allow them a settlement in the city nor permit them to store their woad, which they had to sell as best they could on the wharf where it was landed. In 1237, however, the merchants of Amiens, Corby and Nesle were allowed, by special arrangement, greater freedom in the disposal of their woad and other wares. In the end the woad merchants settled in Cannon Street (Candelwykstrete), the very centre of the cloth trade in London, as Lydgate tells us in his *London Lyckpenny*:—

'Then went I forth by London Stone,
Throughout all Canwyke Street;
Drapers mutch cloth me offered anone.'[287]

London was the seat of trade in Eastern luxuries, which became known largely through the influence of the Crusades. Silks, fruits, spices and Greek wines were brought here by the Italian fleets which, after 1317, regularly visited England.

In the thirteenth and fourteenth centuries the importance of our commerce is shown by the appearance of regulations for its promotion in the Statute Book. The Statute of Merchants is dated 1283-1285, and the *Carta Mercatoria* 1303.

The trade with Bordeaux was very active, and largely carried on by English ships from London, Bristol, Dover and Hull. Wool, herrings, lead, copper and tin were taken out in these ships, also pilgrims as passengers. The ships returned to England laden with wine, and corn when the home production was short. In 1350 141 ships carried 13,429 tuns of wine from Bordeaux to England. English merchants travelled largely, and made their appearance at the great continental fairs.

As commerce increased the enemies of commerce also increased, and we find therefore that the Thames and the open sea were infested by bands of pirates. Soon after pirates had made a successful descent upon Scarborough, John Philipot, a prominent Londoner, set himself to break up the conspiracy. He fitted out a fleet at his own expense, and, putting to sea, succeeded in capturing the ringleader, a feat which rendered him so popular as to excite the jealousy of the Duke of Lancaster and other nobles. His fellow-citizens showed their appreciation of his character by electing him to succeed Brembre in the mayoralty in October 1378.[288]

How serious this danger really was may be seen from the fact that not even the King was safe. When Henry IV., in order to escape the pestilence raging in London, crossed from Queensborough, in Sheppey, to Leigh, in Essex, on his way to Plashey—though convoyed by Lord Camoys with certain ships of war—narrowly escaped capture by pirates. A vessel containing part of his baggage and retinue, together with his Vice-Chamberlain, fell into the hands of the enemy. This scandal naturally created a great stir, and Lord Camoys was tried on a charge of correspondence with the enemy. He was acquitted, but his innocence appears to have been considered doubtful.

Pirates lurked in the Thames or blockaded the mouth of the river, and to prevent them from landing within the area of the city the streets leading to the river were defended by chains. Still further to defend London from privateers, John Philipot offered to build at his own cost a stone tower 60 king's feet in height, near Ratcliff, provided the Corporation of London would levy sixpence in the pound on the rental of the city and build a corresponding tower on the opposite side of the river, so that an iron chain might be stretched from one tower to the other to protect the shipping of the river from night attack. The danger was so imminent that the Common Council agreed to the proposal, but, as the alarm died away, this scheme of defence was laid aside.[289]

In 1370 'the Mayor, aldermen and commonalty were given to understand that certain galleys, with a multitude of armed men therein, were lying off the foreland of Tanet' [Thanet], and it was therefore ordered that 'every night watch shall be kept between the Tower of London and Billingsgate, with 40 men-at-arms and 60 archers,' which watch the men of the trades underwritten 'agreed to keep in succession each night, in form as follows: On Tuesday, the drapers and the tailors; on Wednesday, the mercers and the apothecaries; on Thursday, the fishmongers and the butchers; on Friday, the pewterers and the vintners; on Saturday, the goldsmiths and the saddlers; on Sunday, the ironmongers, the armourers and the cutlers; on Monday, the tawers [curriers], the spurriers, the bowyers and the girdlers.'[290]

These pirates gave a great deal of trouble up to a much later date, and the wardenship of the Cinque Ports (then held by Cecil) was a busy post when, as in May 1616, pirate vessels were captured between Broadstairs and Margate.[291]

In connection with the trade and commerce of London, fairs and markets held a very important position, but here it will only be possible to make a passing allusion to them.

Bartholomew Fair, Smithfield, granted to the Prior of St. Bartholomew's by Henry II., 1133, was for several centuries the great cloth fair of England. Its memory is kept alive by the street which is still known as Cloth Fair. After the dissolution of the monasteries the fair was annually opened by the Mayor, attended by the aldermen. It long outlived its use and reputation, and was not finally abolished until the nineteenth century had run its course for some years.

In the City Letter Books there are references to other less important fairs; thus a fair then only recently established in Soper Lane (now Queen Street, Cheapside), and known as Nane (or Noon) Fair, was abolished about 1307 owing to its being the resort of thieves and cutpurses.[292]

There was also a fair called *la novele feyre* which was held in the parish of St. Nicholas Acons.[293]

CLOTH FAIR.

Many fairs were held at different times in Southwark, Westminster, and other places in the neighbourhood of London. How important the great fairs of the Middle Ages were may be seen in one instance among others by the fact that the citizens of London resorted in such numbers to St. Botolph's Fair, annually held at Boston, county Lincoln, on St. Botolph's Day (17th June), that all business in the Court of Husting ceased, and the Court was closed for a week.[294]

In the fourth book of the *Liber Albus* there is a list of letters and other documents relating to markets and fairs, several of which relate to St. Botolph's Fair.[295]

In Saxon times buying and selling could only be lawfully carried out before the *reeve* of Folkmote, a practice which necessitated a gathering in towns at fixed times, from which custom grew up the practice of each town having a market day. As a rule this was on a Sunday, and the market-place was often situated in the churchyard, close beneath the sheltering walls of the parish church.

By the Statute Wynton (13 Edw. I.) fairs and markets were forbidden to be held in churchyards; and the Statute 27 Henry VI., cap. 5, was the first enactment intended to enforce a due observance of Sunday. To avoid the scandal of holding fairs and markets on Sundays and upon high feast days it was decreed that 'Fairs and markets shall not be holden on Sundays or on festivals,' with the exception of four Sundays in harvest. There is no public right of holding fairs or markets, and the privilege emanates from the prerogative of the Crown.

From the earliest times the streets of London were occupied by the various trades who obtained the privilege of using them as market-places. The market of West Cheap or Cheapside was the chief of these public places, but almost all the trades had their appointed stations in the different streets, and in many cases the trades were not allowed to sell their wares in other places than those assigned to them. In the time of Edward I. it was ordered 'that all manner of victuals that are sold by persons in Chepe, upon Cornhulle, and elsewhere in the city, such as bread, cheese, poultry, fruit, hides, and skins, onions and garlic, and all other small victuals, for sale as well by denizens as by strangers, shall stand midway between the kennels of the streets as to be a nuisance to no one, under pain of forfeiture of the article.'[296]

'The pavement in Chepe' was a recognised market-place for corn, probably situated near the Church of St. Michael le Quern, at the west end of Cheapside. Stocks Market, which stood on the site of the present Mansion House, was founded in 1283, and the rents were appropriated to the maintenance of London Bridge. In 1324 the wardens of the bridge made complaint that certain fishmongers and butchers had of late abandoned the market-house, had erected sheds in the King's highway and other adjoining places, and sold their flesh and fish there, 'whereby the rents aforesaid, which formed the greater part of the maintenance of the said bridge, had become immensely reduced to the great peril and damage of the bridge and of the city, and of all passing over such bridge.'

Staples were markets where only certain goods called staple goods were allowed to be sold. The Company of Merchants of the Staple had a monopoly of exporting the staple commodities of England, and certain staple towns (which were constantly changed) were appointed as centres of the trade. The chief export was wool, 'the sovereign treasure' of England, wherewith she was said to keep the whole world warm. In 1328, and again in 1334, all staples were abolished and trade was free according to the great charter. Free trade did not last long, and the staple was fixed at Bruges in 1344.

By the Ordinance of Staple 27 Edw. III. (1353) ten staple towns were appointed in England, Wales and Ireland, Westminster and London together being considered as one of the ten. The staple of Bruges was removed from Bruges to Westminster by this Act.

In 1360 part of this Act was repealed. Calais[297] remained a staple till it was temporarily suppressed in 1369 (Statute 43 Edw. III., cap. 1). By this Act the staple of wool was in future to be confined to the following English ports: Newcastle, Hull, Boston, Yarmouth, Queenborough, Westminster, Chichester, Winchester, Exeter, and Bristol.

The staple towns continued to be changed, and there were great complaints made by the English in Tudor times that the staple was fixed abroad. We read that 'the caryage out of wolle to the stapule ys a grete hurte to the pepul of England, though hyt be profitabul both to the prince and to the merchant also.'[298] The changes in the wool trade in England during the fourteenth, fifteenth and sixteenth centuries caused an industrial revolution, the effects of which are well marked in our literature. The raw material was no longer exported, but in its place the cloth made here was sent to countries which had formerly supplied us with cloth in exchange for our wool. In consequence the number of wealthy merchants increased. With this prosperity the country became proud, and the lawgivers did all they could to foster the manufactures of the country.[299] A Statute passed in 1463 (3 Edw. IV. cap. 4) prohibited by enumeration the import of almost all wrought goods in order that 'the English artificers may have employment.' A similar Act was passed in the reign of Henry VIII., by which foreign books could only be introduced in sheets, so that work should be provided for the English bookbinders. The famous poem written by Adam de Molyneux, Moleyns or Molins, Bishop of Chichester, and Keeper of the Privy Seal (died 1450), which was entitled 'The Libel of English Policy' (1437), contains a full account of commodities exchanged between the countries of Western Europe. The full title of this important *Libellum* shows its object—'Here beginneth the prologe of the processe of the Libelle of Englyshe Polycye exhorting alle Englande to kepe the see enviroun, and namelye the narowe see, shewynge whate profete commeth thereof, and also worshype and salvacioun to Englande and to alle Englyshe menne.'

The leading idea of the little book, as may be seen from the title, is that which agitates the public mind at the present time, and shows how important it is that England should keep the seas and protect the food and clothing coming to this country.[300]

In connection with the commerce and trade of the country the official weighing of goods was a matter of great importance. As far back as the Saxon period standard weights and measures were preserved in the City of London, and with these the weights and measures throughout the kingdom had to conform. The King's great Beam or Tron was used for weighing coarse goods by the hundredweight, and the small beam or balance for silks, spiceries and goods sold by the pound weight.

The King's weigh-house in Fish Street Hill, London, and the Tron Church in Edinburgh remind us of the old weighing machines of the country.

It was formerly the custom to allow a margin to buyers at the Tron. According to the *Liber de Antiquis*, in 1305 the weigher allowed the buyer a draft of four pounds in every hundredweight.

At the present day there is a survival of this custom in the tea trade and some others, for the importer gives a precisely similar 'draft' to the dealer, viz., one pound in every chest of tea of twenty-eight pounds.[301]

Foreigners and strangers were not permitted, as a rule, to take up their residence within the walls of London for a longer period than forty days, and were subject to several restrictions as to trade. Exceptions were, however, made from time to time with various foreign towns. Natives of Denmark enjoyed the privilege of sojourning in London all the year through: in addition to which they had a right to all the benefits of 'the law of the City of London,' that is, they were entitled to the right of resorting to fair or to market in any place throughout England. Norwegians had the same right of sojourning in London all the year, but did not enjoy 'the law of the city,' as they were prohibited from leaving it for the purposes of traffic.[302]

In February 1303 the King, by the *Carta Mercatoria*, granted exceptional privileges to foreign merchants, and these concessions caused great indignation among his subjects at home. A tax was exacted from these foreigners, and in 1309 the Friscobaldi were appointed by the King to receive the 'new custom,' and two years later he ordered their arrest for failing to render an account of the money received under that head. Their detention, however, was of short duration.[303]

The Act was repealed in 1311, and again enacted in 1322, but with the accession of Edward III. it was again repealed.

Foreign commerce is said to have been better governed than inland trade, for the King had an arbitrary authority in the regulation of trading.

In dealing with the trade of London it is necessary to say something about the origin of Gilds; but this is a most difficult question, respecting which very different opinions are held by writers on the subject.

It will be impossible to discuss these points at all fully in this chapter, and therefore a few dates will be found sufficient for the present purpose.

Mediæval gilds were voluntary associations established for mutual assistance. It is quite easy to show the likeness between them and the Roman Collegia, but to do this is futile, because few now believe in any connection between the two institutions. Similar circumstances often cause similar institutions to arise.

In the Middle Ages few men and women could stand alone, and combination was a positive necessity for existence, and the people soon found that union is strength.

The great authority on this subject is Mr. Toulmin Smith's work, entitled *English Gilds*, which was edited by his daughter, Miss Toulmin Smith, and published by the Early English Text Society in 1880.

Prefixed to this great work is Dr. Brentano's valuable Essay on the History of Gilds, in which he writes: 'I write to declare here most emphatically that I consider England the birthplace of gilds.'

Some writers have fixed upon the second half of the ninth century as the date of the origin of gilds, but Miss Toulmin Smith points out that among the laws of Ina (A.D. 688-725) are two touching the liability of the brethren of a gild in the case of slaying a thief. Alfred (A.D. 871-879) still further recognised the brotherly gild spirit in his laws as to manslaughter by a kinless man, and again where a man who has no relatives is slain.[304]

Dr. Brentano writes: 'An already far-advanced development of the gilds is shown by the *Judicia Civitatis Lundoniæ*, the Statutes of the London gilds, which were reduced to writing in the time of King Athelstan. From them the gilds in and about London appear to have united into *one* gild, and to have framed common regulations for the better maintenance of peace, for the suppression of violence—especially of theft and the aggressions of the powerful families—as well as for carrying out rigidly the ordinances enacted by the King for that purpose.'[305]

A large division of the old gilds were purely social, and there is no trace of Merchant gilds before the Norman Conquest, while craft gilds did not come into existence until early in the twelfth century.

Dr. Brentano writes: 'Though the merchant gilds consisted chiefly of merchants, yet from the first craftsmen, as such, were not excluded from them on principle, if only such craftsmen possessed the full citizenship of the town, which citizenship—with its further development—depended upon the possession of estates of a certain value situated within the territory of the town. The strict separation which existed between the merchants and the crafts probably arose only by degrees. Originally the craftsmen, no doubt, traded in the raw materials which they worked with.'[306]

Mr. Ashley is of opinion that Dr. Brentano exaggerated both the independence and the economic importance of the trade gilds.[307]

He further writes: 'We do not know whether there had ever been a Gild Merchant in London; however, in 1191, by the recognition of its Commune, the citizens obtained complete municipal self-government, and, consequently, the recognition of the same rights over trade and industry as a Gild merchant would have exercised.'[308]

Dr. Gross, in his work on the Gild Merchant, says that he can find no evidence of the existence of a merchant gild in London. Still there were trade gilds which were aristocratic in origin, and governed by the great merchants, who were the chief landowners of London.

Mr. C. G. Crump, however, has quite lately found direct mention of the Gild Merchant of London in 1252 in a charter of that date (Charter Roll, 37 Hen. III. m. 20). While pointing out that this was apparently unknown to Dr. Gross, as he decides against the existence of any such institution, he adds: 'This charter, while it suggests a doubt on the point, is not conclusive, because it is a very exceptional document. There is no other charter of its kind during the whole reign of Henry III., and a Chancery clerk endeavouring to draft a charter to convert a Florentine merchant into a citizen of London might well have thought fit to mention a gild merchant as a matter of common form even if none actually existed.[309]

The year 1180 is an important one in the history of gilds, for then these bodies were required to pay their fines or licences, in token and recognition of their allegiance to the Crown. There were eighteen of these, which were amerced as 'Adulterine' gilds—the Goldsmiths, the Pepperers and the Butchers being among them. The document containing this list is translated by Herbert in his work on the Companies,[310] where it is suggested that the fining of these proves that the gilds must have been numerous, because some of them only could have subjected themselves to the penalty.

The Mercers claim an existence at a still earlier date (1172), and when the Saddlers are mentioned immediately after the Conquest they are said to possess 'ancient statutes.'

Gradually the influence of the craftsmen made itself felt, and the craft gilds came into existence, but the aristocratic traders would not recognise them.

The craftsmen found an enthusiastic patron in Thomas Fitz-Thomas, the popular Mayor (1261-1265). His conduct disgusted Arnold Fitz-Thedmar, the city alderman and chronicler, who complains that 'this Mayor, during the time of his mayoralty, had so pampered the city populace, that styling themselves the "Commons of the city," they had obtained the first voice in the city. For the Mayor, in doing all that he had to do, acted and determined through them, and would say to them: "Is it your will that so it shall be?" and then if they answered "Ya, ya," so it was done. And on the other hand, the aldermen or chief citizens were little or not at all consulted on such matter, but were in fact just as though they had not existed.'[311]

After the Battle of Evesham the city was taken into the King's hands (1265-1270), and a very despotic and wicked action was perpetrated. Fitz-Thomas and some other prominent citizens were summoned to Windsor, and there were kept prisoners. Some of these regained their liberty, but nothing more was heard of Fitz-Thomas, as Dr. Reginald Sharpe writes: 'From the time that he entered Windsor Castle he disappears from public view. That he was alive in May 1266, at least in the belief of his fellow-citizens, is shown by their cry for the release of him and his companions, "who are at Windleshores." '[312]

The craftsmen lost a valiant friend, but another was raised up in his place. Walter Hervi, who was hated by the aldermen for his democratic opinions, but loved by the Commons, was elected Mayor in 1272. Fresh ordinances for the regulation of various crafts were drawn up, and to these the Mayor, on his own responsibility, attached the city seal. When his year of office expired these so-called charters were called in question, and in 1274 they were examined in the Hustings before all the people and declared void.[313]

The craft gilds were supposed to be defeated, but this was not really so, for the merchants found that the struggle between the trade gilds and craft gilds was an unequal one. They therefore with much worldly wisdom joined the latter, and gradually gained an ascendency in them.

Mr. Ashley affirms that from the reign of Edward II. the gild system was no longer merely tolerated, but it was fostered and extended.[314]

The years which followed the Peace of Bretigny, until war broke out afresh in 1369, witnessed the reorganisation of many of the trade and craft gilds.[315]

In 1376 the gilds wrested for a time from the wards the right of electing members of the city's Council. The gilds continued to elect until 1384, when the right of election was again transferred to the wards.

The names of the representatives of the gilds forming the first Common Council of the kind are placed on record in Letter Book H, ff. *46b*, 47.

The year 1388-1389 was an important one in the history of gilds. The writs of 12 Ric. II. had important effects, and the returns form the chief substance of Mr. Toulmin Smith's *English Gilds*. There were two distinct writs: (*a*) the writ for returns from the social gilds; (*b*) the writ for returns from craft gilds. Toulmin Smith printed the writs with these side-notes: (*a*) 'The Sheriffs of London [and of every shire in England] shall, by authority of the Parliament that lately met at Cambridge, make proclamation calling on the master and wardens of all the social gilds [all gilds and brotherhoods whatsoever] to send up returns before the 2nd day of February A.D. 1388-9.

(*b*) 'The Sheriffs of London [and of every shire in England] shall, by authority of the Parliament that lately met at Cambridge, make proclamation calling on the masters, wardens and overlookers of all gilds of crafts holding any charter or letters-patent to send up before the second day of February 1388-9 copies of such charters and letters upon penalty of forfeiture.'

The original writs were returned by the London sheriffs with this endorsement: 'When and by whom proclamation was made in London and the suburbs—Fleet Street in the suburbs; the Standard, in Westcheap; the Ledenhall, Cornhill; St. Magnus Church, Bridge Street; St. Martin's Church, Vintry; Southwark.'

In Mr. Toulmin Smith's book only three of the returns relate to London, and these are not from craft gilds. They are the Gild of Garlekhith, the Gild of St. Katherine, Aldersgate, and the Gild of SS. Fabian and Sebastian, Aldersgate. It is not necessary to give extracts from these returns, but we can obtain a good idea of the objects of these gilds from Mr. Toulmin Smith's side-notes, which are as follows:—

Garlekhith.—'The gild was begun in 1375 to nourish good fellowship. All bretheren must be of good repute. Each shall pay 6s. 8d. on entry. There shall be wardens, who shall gather in the payments and yield an account thereof yearly. A livery suit shall be worn. The bretheren and sisteren shall hold a yearly feast. Two shillings a year shall be paid by each. Four meetings touching the gild's welfare shall be held in each year. Free gifts by the bretheren. Ill-behaved bretheren shall be put out of the gild. No livery-suit shall be sold within a year. On death of any, all the rest shall join in the burial service and make offerings under penalty. In case of quarrel, the matter shall be laid before the wardens. Whoever disobeys their award shall be put out of the gild and the other shall be helped. Weekly help to all seven-year bretheren in old age and in sickness, and to those wrongfully imprisoned. Newcomers shall swear to keep the ordinances. Every brother chosen warden must serve or pay 40s.'

St. Katherine.—'These are the ordinances of the gild: Oath on entry, and a kiss of love, charity and peace. Weekly help in poverty, old age, sickness, or loss by fire or water, etc. Payments by bretheren and sisteren. Members of the gild shall go to church and afterwards choose officers. Burials shall be attended. The gild shall bear charge of burials. Any brother dying within ten miles round London shall have worshipful burial. All costs thereof shall be made good by the gild. Loans to gild-bretheren out of the gild stock on pledge or surety. Wax lights to be found and used at times named. Further services after death. Newcomers by assent only. Four men shall keep the goods of the gild, and render an account yearly. Assent of all the gild to new ordinances. The goods of the gild are a "vestement, a chalys and a mass-book, pris of x marks." '

SS. Fabian and Sebastian.—'Oath on entry, and a kiss of love, charity and peace. Weekly help in poverty, old age, sickness, or loss by fire or water, etc. The young to be helped to get work. Payments by bretheren and sisteren. Four days of meeting in the year, when all must attend under penalty. Burials shall be attended. The gild shall bear charge of burials. Those dying within ten miles round London shall be fetched to London for burial. Loans to gild-bretheren out of the gildstock on pledge or surety. Wax lights to be found and used at times named. Ill-behaved bretheren shall be put out of the gild. Entry of new bretheren. Four men shall keep the goods of the gild and render an account yearly. Assent of all the gild to new ordinances. Grant of a house in Aldersgate worth £4, 13s. 4d. a year, less quit rent of 13s. a year, the profits of which are applied in aid of the gild.'

These regulations with their general likeness and slight divergencies help us to understand the gild life of the Middle Ages, which, it will be seen, was essentially practical and helpful to the growth of good feeling among those who were brought together in constant intercourse.

The rules of the gilds were often very strict, and men of evil life were put out of the fraternity. Moreover, idlers and ne'er-do-weels were not to expect to be relieved from the funds of the gild. From the ordinances of the Gild of St. Anne in the Church of St. Lawrence Jewry, we learn that 'if any man be of good state, and use hym to ly long in bed; and at rising of his bed ne will not work but go to the tavern... and in this manner falleth poor... and trust to be holpen by the fraternity: that man shall never have good, ne help of companie, neither in his lyfe nor at his dethe; but he shal be put off for evermore of the companie.'

Mr. Toulmin Smith's returns are taken from the originals in the Public Record Office, and, as has already been noted, by some fatality there are no records of the craft gilds.

The next great point in the history of gilds is connected with their abolition by the Act of 1 Edw. VI. cap. 14 (1547), a most iniquitous measure. Miss Toulmin Smith tells us how her father's indignation was roused by his researches into the story of the fate of the gilds:—

'In a MS. note he remarks that for the abolition of monasteries [there was] some colour, and after professed inquiries as to manners; moreover, allowances [were] made to all ranks. But in case of gilds (much wider) no pretence of inquiry or of mischief, and no allowance whatever. A case of pure wholesale robbery and plunder, done by an unscrupulous faction to satisfy their personal greed, under cover of law. No more gross case of wanton plunder is to be found in the history of all Europe; no page so black in English history.'[316]

Of course there is another side to the question, and Mr. Ashley, who discusses very fully the consequences of the Act of Edward VI., thinks that it has been unfairly condemned. He says that, so far as the companies were concerned, the Bill did not propose to take from them anything more than the revenues actually used for religious purposes; and further, that the Statute neither 'abolished' nor 'dissolved' nor 'suppressed' nor 'destroyed' the companies, but left all their corporate powers and rights intact, except so far as religious usages were concerned.[317]

We must remember, however, that Mr. Toulmin Smith's indignation was roused not so much by the forfeiture of certain trusts in the hands of the livery companies as by the robbery of the small gilds all over the country.

The early history of most of the city companies is rather disconnected, and, owing to the loss and destruction of documents, the mode by which the craft gilds were amalgamated with the livery companies is not very easy to follow. Still, the likeness between the two institutions is so marked, and their duties so similar, that there is no difficulty in acknowledging the fusion. To take a single instance, it may be mentioned that the original gild of Goldsmiths had exactly similar public duties to perform that are now performed by the present Goldsmiths' Company. This connection has usually been taken for granted, but it is necessary to allude to the question here, because Mr. Loftie, a high authority on the history of London, has strongly disputed this connection. In 1883 Mr. Loftie wrote: 'The identification of the adulterine guilds with the later companies is scarcely possible'[318]; and again in 1887: 'The Weavers' Company is not the only one which claims to represent directly an ancient guild, but it is the only one whose claim has anything so like a reasonable foundation.'[319] These are, however, only casual remarks, but in his latest work he has elaborated his attack in the following terms:—

'Popular errors are very difficult to deal with effectually. One of the most persistent is that which confounds the city guilds with the city companies. Here two widely different things are inextricably confused, and that, too, not in mere catchpenny popular books, but in books pretending to more or less authority. In the common run of London histories, guild means company, and company means guild.... To begin with, there are now no guilds in London. By an Act passed in 1557 all religious guilds were abolished and all guildable property was confiscated. But as there were no guilds not religious, and as the property of guilds was held in trust to provide burials, masses, and sometimes chantries for deceased members, the guilds and their land, and their money and their priestly vestments, and their illuminated manuscripts, all ceased to exist absolutely; and not only so, but it became penal to revive them. A city company which calls itself a guild renders itself liable to forfeiture—a penalty which would, of course, be rather difficult to enforce.'[320]

There are two statements here which may be challenged—one that all gilds were religious, and the other that all gilds were abolished by Act of Parliament.

Certainly the gilds which were not instituted for purposes of trade protection have often been styled religious, but Mr. Toulmin Smith preferred to class them as social gilds, and I think wisely. As already stated, their objects were entirely practical and social. Mr. Toulmin Smith writes: 'The gilds were lay bodies, and existed for lay purposes, and the better to enable those who belonged to them rightly and understandingly to fulfil their neighbourly duties as freemen in a free state.'

Religious duties were performed, but these were only incidental to the life of the time, and consisted mostly of services connected with the serious occasions in the life of laymen, which were general in the periods that have been styled 'ages of faith.'

As to the second point, a reference to the Statute 1 Edw. VI. cap. 14, will show us that the craft gilds are exempted from its operation. In the *Statutes of the Realm* one of the side-notes to the 'Act whereby certain chantries, colleges, free chapels, and the possessions of the same, be given to the King's Majesty,' runs as follows: 'All brotherhoods or guilds and their possessions, except companies of trade vested in the King.' The text is 'other then suche corporations, guyldes, fraterniteis, companyes and felowshippes of misteryes or craftes.'

I think we must allow that the terms of this Act strongly corroborate the general belief that the old craft gilds and the later companies were so closely connected as to be practically the same. Having dealt with the general question of gilds, we can now pass on to consider the influence of the different trades upon London life.

The origin of the companies seems to have been largely connected with the result of a combination of the numerous sections of a particular trade. Some trades were so important that they could stand alone; thus the Goldsmiths' Gild became the Goldsmiths' Company; but most of the other companies were formed by the union of more than one gild.

A marked feature of the old trades of London was the minute subdivisions which took place among them: thus there were hatters, cappers, chapelers (makers of caps), and hurers. The latter were makers of hures, or rough hairy caps. The hurers and cappers were united to the hatters by charter of Henry VII. in the sixteenth year of his reign, and again united in the following year to the haberdashers by the King's licence under his great seal.

The Company, subsequently known and chartered as the Clothworkers', was first incorporated by letters-patent of Edw. IV. in 1482, as the 'Fraternity of the Assumption of the Blessed Virgin Mary of the Shearmen of London.' The fullers were taken into union in 1528, thereby constituting the Clothworkers' Company.

A convincing proof of the connection of the gilds with companies, and the natural succession of the latter from the former, is seen in this case of the Clothworkers' Company. It appears from a deed dated 15th July 1456 that John Badby did remise, etc., unto John Hungerford and others, citizens and sheremen of London, 'a tenement and mansion-house, shops, cellars and other the appurtenances, lying in Minchin Lane, and their heirs for ever.' This is the site of Clothworkers' Hall, the Clothworkers' Company being the natural heirs of the Gild of Shearmen.[321]

There is much interest connected with the occupation of the shearman, who sheared the nap of wool. Woollen clothes in the Middle Ages were expected to last a lifetime. When new the nap was very long, and as the clothes became shabby it was customary to have them shorn, a process which was repeated as long as the stuff would bear it. In the delightful old ballad reprinted in Percy's *Reliques*, 'Take thy old cloak about thee,' the old cloak that had been in wear for forty-four years was likely to be a sorry clout at the end of that time, which would hold out neither wind nor rain. Well might the husband resolve:—

'For once I'le new appareld bee,
To-morrow I'le to towne and spend,
For I'le have a new cloake about mee.'

But the wife's plea for thrift, and her statement—

'Itt's pride that putts this countrye downe,'

succeeds in the end, and the ballad ends,—

'As wee began wee now will leave,
And I'le take mine old cloake about mee.'

The aid of the shearman was not merely called in by the poor, for we learn that the Countess of Leicester (Eleanor, third daughter of King John, and wife of Simon de Montfort) in 1265 sent Hicque the tailor to London to get her robes re-shorn.[322]

The date of the ballad was probably early, although the King alluded to in the printed text is King Stephen, in that of the Scotch version Robert, and in the Percy MS. a vague King Henry. The ballad must have had a wide popularity, for Shakespeare alludes to it twice. Iago quotes a whole stanza (*Othello*, act ii.), and Trinculo evidently alludes to it when he says:—

'O King Stephano, O Peere: O worthy Stephano,
Looke what a wardrobe here is for thee.'
(*Tempest*, act iv. sc. i.).

The number of trades connected with clothing were singularly numerous. Besides the shearman (or tondour) there were the feliper, pheliper or fripperer, who dealt in second-hand clothes, and the furbur or furbisher of old clothes.

Dr. Brentano points out that in all manufacturing countries, in England, Flanders and Brabant, as well as in the Rhenish towns, the most ancient gilds were those of the weavers; and Mr. Ashley writes that the first craft gilds to come into notice were the weavers and fullers of woollen cloth. No weaver or fuller might go outside the town to sell his own cloth, and so interfere with the monopoly of the merchants; nor was he allowed to sell his cloth to any save a merchant of the town.[323]

The London Gild of Weavers was recognised by Henry I., and the first charter of incorporation was granted by Henry II. in 1184, when the seal of Thomas à Becket was affixed to the document. The special privileges given to this trade created a strong jealousy among the citizens, and John was induced to suppress the gild.[324] As it had been accustomed to pay the King eighteen marks per annum, he bargained that the citizens should pay twenty marks so that he might not be out of pocket.

The suppression did not continue for long, and in the reign of Henry III. we find the feud between the citizens and the gild again in full force. When the authorities of the gild feared that the citizens would overpower them, they delivered their 'charter into the Exchequer, to be kept in the treasury there, and to be delivered to them again when they should want it, and afterwards to be laid up in the treasury.'[325]

Mrs. Green says that in 1300 the Mayor had gained the right to preside in the weavers' court if he chose, and to nominate the wardens of the gild.[326] In the fourteenth year of Edward II. (A.D. 1320-1321) the privileges of the weavers came before a court of law. In spite of the distinguished position that the Gild of Weavers held in its early days, the present Weavers' Company only stands forty-second in the order of the livery companies.

Many of the old trades of London have been entirely lost sight of, and their names only exist among the patronymics of the people.

The great feud between the victualling and clothing trades of London was one of the most remarkable features of the fourteenth century. Some allusion has been made to this in chapter viii. on the governors of the city, but a reference must also be made here in connection with the history of the London companies.

After the Peasants' Revolt, London was the battlefield of rival factions. The friends of the King (Richard II.) were found among the great merchants of the victualling trades. In one year sixteen of the twenty-five aldermen were grocers, and Nicholas Brembre was chief of them. The fishmongers, of whom Sir William Walworth was the leader, were scarcely less powerful.

The victuallers were very unpopular, and the public have always specially resented any advance in the price of food. Complaints were rife in the chief cities of the country of the abuses of the victuallers, and an Act (12 Edw. II. cap. 6) was passed to the effect that "no officer of a city or borough shall sell wine or victuals during his office."

This Act was frequently evaded, and another Act was passed in 1382 (see *ante*, p. 236). In the end the Act of Edward II. was repealed (3 Hen. VIII. cap. 8, 1511-1512).[327]

John of Northampton, when he became Mayor, took advantage of this Act, and began a policy of aggression directed against the victualling interest. He turned all his enemies off the governing body, and victuallers were forbidden to hold office in the city. These feuds were very serious, and the two leaders were unfortunate in their ends. Brembre was executed in 1388, and John of Northampton was sent to the Tower and imprisoned in Tintagel Castle.

A few words may be said here about the classes of trades represented by the gilds and companies commencing with—

The Bakers.—The price of bread was regulated by law, according to the price of wheat, and the Mayor had the right to levy a ½d. for every quarter of corn sent to the mill. This tax was called pesage from pisa, a corruption of mediæval Latin *pensa*, a weight. The right was called in question at the *Iter* held in the Tower in 1321, but the matter was adjourned for the consideration of the King and his Council.[328]

The fraudulent baker had a bad time, for he was sometimes carried about in a tumbrell, and at other times he was put in the pillory. For his first offence the culprit was drawn upon a hurdle from Guildhall through the most populous and most dirty streets, with the defective loaf hanging from his neck. On a second occasion he was drawn from the Guildhall 'through the great streets of Chepe' to the pillory, which was usually erected in Cheap or Cheapside, and there he was exposed for one hour. For the third offence he was again drawn on the hurdle, his oven was pulled down, and he was compelled to forswear the trade in London for ever. The use of the hurdle was discontinued in favour of the pillory in the reign of Edward II. Another offence punished by exposure in the pillory, besides short weight and bad quality was the putting of iron in a loaf of bread to increase its weight.[329]

In the famine of 1258, when the Earl of Cornwall's sixty cargoes of grain arrived, the first thing the King had to do was to issue an ordinance against the greed of the middlemen, known as forestallers and regrators.

No words appear to have been found too strong to hurl at these unfortunate middlemen, but the regratresses or female retailers who bought bread at the markets, and delivered it from house to house, were contented with a small profit. These dealers were privileged by law to receive thirteen batches for twelve, hence the expression 'a baker's dozen.' This seems to have been the extent of their profits. It was once the practice of the baker to give to each regratress who dealt with him sixpence on Monday morning by way of *estrene* or present, and threepence on Friday as *curtasie* money, but this was forbidden by public ordinance, and the bakers were ordered to let all such payments in future go towards increasing the size of the loaf, 'to the profit of the people.'[330]

Corn used to be stored by the city and the companies against times of scarcity, but the origin of the practice is obscure, and no obligation to provide corn appears to have been imposed upon any of the companies by the terms of their charters. Sir Simon Eyre, Mayor in 1435, formed a public granary in Leadenhall. Stow and Fuller eulogise Sir Stephen Brown, who, in 1438, was energetic in his endeavours to get corn stored in the city granaries. In 1578 the farmers of the Bridge House divided the store into twelve equal parts, and the same by lots were appropriated to the twelve companies, to each of them an equal part for the bestowing and keeping of the said corn.

Pannier (or Panyer) Alley, leading from Newgate Street to Paternoster Row, was once the standing place for bakers with their bread panniers. The bakers of London were divided into white bakers and brown or tourte bakers (turturarii), who made a coarse bread of unbolted meal. No maker of white bread was allowed to make tourte, nor a tourte baker to make white bread. House bread was prepared by the bakers of household bread, while hostellers, by whom it was exclusively used, were forbidden to make it. Similar trades were the pastellers, who made pies and other kinds of pastry, pie-bakers and cooks.

Butchers.—The sale of butchers' meat seems to have been somewhat limited during the Middle Ages in comparison with the population, although the number of butchers within the city walls were quite sufficient to create a considerable nuisance. Smithfield was then the great cattle market, as it remained until our own time. Lean swine were sold there, probably with the purpose of fattening them in the town. The chief meat markets within the city walls were Stocks Market and the flesh shambles of St. Nicholas, in Newgate Street and its vicinity. A lease of the latter place to the butchers, in 1343, is recorded in Riley's *Memorials*. The shocking condition of Newgate Street is indicated by such names as Stinking Lane, St. Nicholas's Shambles, and Blowbladder Street. There was a Butchers' Bridge on the Thames side, near Baynards Castle, to which the offal was brought from Newgate Street through the streets and lanes of the city, by which 'grievous corruption and filth have been generated.' The evil, in fact, was so great that a royal order was issued in 1369 for the removal of Butchers' Bridge.

The 'foreign' butchers, or those who did not possess the freedom of the city, brought their meat to shambles just outside the civic boundary. On the west, near St. Clement's Church in the Strand, there was a Butcher Row, and in the east, immediately beyond Aldgate, was another Butcher Row. This last still exists as 'Aldgate Market,' and consists of a row of butchers' shops on the south side of the High Street. Formerly imported animals were killed behind the shops.

The unfortunate tradesmen had to submit to public enactment, by which the exact price of the commodities they sold was fixed. In the reign of Edward I. the carcase of the best ox was sold for 13s. 4d., of the best pig for 4s., of the best sheep for 2s. The ill-treated butcher had no redress, for a provision was added to the order that if any person should withdraw himself from the trade by reason of the said ordinance he should lose the freedom of the city, and be compelled to forswear the trade for ever.[331]

These instances of interference with trade continued for centuries, and we learn that in 1533 it was enacted that butchers should sell their beef and mutton by weight—beef for ½d. a pound, and mutton for 3/4d. Stow, in relating this, adds that at this time, and not before, 'foreign' butchers were allowed to sell their flesh in Leadenhall Market.

Fishmongers.—The information relating to the sale of fish in the City Records proves how largely the population of London in the Middle Ages depended upon its ample supply. There was great variety, and a large number of enactments were made as to the sale. The fish mentioned in the *Liber Albus* as being sold in the London market are: Sturgeon, cod, ray, herring, bass, conger, sole, mackerel, sur-mullet, turbot, porpoise, haddock, sea-ling, sprats, salmon, shad, eels, pike, barbel, roach, dace, dabs, flounders, lampreys, smelts, stickelings, oysters, mussels, cockles, whelks, scallops, and stock fish (imported from Prussia). Of these, sprats, herrings, mussels, whelks and oysters are most often mentioned, but lobsters, crabs and shrimps are not alluded to.

Fish was not allowed to be sold retail upon the quays. The stalls in Stocks Market were occupied by the fishmongers on fish days, and by the butchers on flesh days. Other retail markets for fish were held by the wall of St. Margaret's Church, New Fish Street, by the wall of St. Mary Magdalen's in Old Fish Street, and in Westcheap. Stow writes of the first of these places: 'In this Old Fish Street is one row of small houses, placed along in the midst of Knightrider Street which row is also off Bread Street ward. These houses, now possessed by fishmongers, were at the first but moveable boards or stalls set out on market days to show their fish there to be sold; but procuring license to set up sheds, they grew to shops, and by little and little to tall houses of three or four stories in height.' Salmon, cod, and herrings are mentioned in the *Liber Albus* as being sold in the shops in the neighbourhood of Queenhithe.

Old Fish Street, and Old Fish Street Hill which run from it to the Thames, with Queenhithe as their landing-quay, formed the chief fish market of London before Billingsgate supplanted Queenhithe.

A curious regulation is found in a royal ordinance in existence as early as the reign of Henry III., by which the first boat in the season with fresh herrings from Yarmouth was forced to pay double custom at the quay.

Fishmongers selling fish in large quantities to their customers were to sell by the basket, such basket to be capable of containing one bushel of oats, and, if found deficient, to be burnt in open market. Each basket was also to contain one kind of sea-fish, and the fishmongers were warned not to colour their baskets; or, in other words, not to put good fish on the top and inferior beneath. Very stringent regulations were also made with respect to the size of nets used for fishing in the Thames, and any such which were contrary to these regulations were ruthlessly destroyed.

The trade of the Stock fishmonger was quite distinct from that of the ordinary fishmonger, and these belonged respectively to two separate companies. They were united in 1537. Thames Street was formerly known as Stockfishmonger Row. The Abbot of St. Alban's enjoyed the privilege of buying fish directly of the fishermen, for which he paid the bailiff of the market a fee of one mark per annum. The monks, however, appear to have taken an undue advantage of their privilege, and an order was issued by the Hallmote of the Fishmongers, *temp.* Edward I., 'that good care be taken that the buyers of the abbey take out of the city fish for the use of the abbot and convent only.'[332]

Poulterers.—Many of the streets of London must have been almost impassable from the stalls of the traders and the chaffering of the buyers and sellers. This evil grew, and the complaints of obstruction were great. Endeavours were made to provide covered markets, but so many of the trades had special stands appropriated to them, as we see on all sides by the names of the streets, that it was impossible to dislodge them.

Free poulterers had several special localities appropriated to their use. One was Cornhill—they were ordered to stand at the west side of St. Michael's Church, and were strictly forbidden to sell to the east of the Tun, the site of which and the Conduit are now marked by an unused pump, nearly facing No. 30 Cornhill. Another standing was close by, and still retains the name of the Poultry. Stow tells that it was once known as Scalding Alley, because the poultry which the poulterers sold was scalded there. Still another standing was in Newgate Street, close by the butchers' shambles. 'Foreign' poulterers were ordered to sell their wares at the corner of Leadenhall, known as the Carfukes (or Carfax).

The articles dealt in by poulterers were rabbits, game, eggs and poultry. Eggs were brought to market in baskets on men's backs, and poultry upon horses. The prices of poultry, like those of other food, were assessed by the Mayor from time to time, and duly proclaimed. In the reign of Edward I. the best hen was sold for 3d., the best rabbit, with the skin, for 5d., and without for 4d., 100 eggs (120 to the hundred) for 8d., a partridge for 3d., a plover for 2d., and eight larks for 1d.[333]

The body of London citizens suffered from one great evil in marketing, and that was that lords and great people were allowed the pick of the market. It was a common practice for the purveyors and servants of these great people to visit the various markets between midnight and prime (6 a.m.), after which hour the poorer classes were allowed to market. It is thus ordered by a proclamation of Edward I., that no poulterer, fishmonger or regrator shall buy any kind of victuals for re-sale until prime has been run out at St. Paul's, 'so that the buyers for the King and the great lords of the land and the good people of the city may make good their purchases, so far as they shall need.'[334]

Grocers.—The grocers (properly 'grossers,' or wholesale sellers in gross) were for some time the chief of the victualling companies. They were originally known as the pepperers of Soper Lane, and the apothecaries were associated with the grocers until they were incorporated as a distinct company in 1617.

By various charters and ordinances the company of grocers was entrusted with the examining, sorting and passing of spices and drugs. They were empowered to enter the shops of grocers, druggists, confectioners, tobacconists and tobacco cutters within the city and three miles around it, to seize and confiscate adulterated and unwholesome goods, and to fine and, in default of payment, imprison delinquent dealers.

Brewers and Vintners.—A passing allusion must be made to the sale of drink in London, which has always been very considerable. Mr. Riley tells us that there is no mention of milk as an article of sale or otherwise in the *Liber Albus*, and butter must have been of very inferior quality, for it was sold by liquid measure. The ale tavern, or ale-house, was a distinct establishment from the wine tavern. In 1309 the number of taverns in London was 354, whilst the number of brewers amounted to no less than 1334.[335]

The ale brewed was a very different product from what we understand by the term now, as malt liquor was not hopped in those days. Hops were not used in the making of beer until the early years of the sixteenth century. Mr. Riley says that the best ale was no better than sweet wort, and so thin that it might be drunk in potations 'pottle deep,' without danger to the head. The smallest measure mentioned in the *Liber Albus* is the quart, so that it was evidently drunk in large quantities. It was used immediately after being made, as may be inferred from the fact that, according to the *Domesday of St. Paul's*, the brewings at the Cathedral brewery took place twice a week throughout the year. Immediately after a brewing was finished it was the duty of the brewer (or rather brewster, for the business was almost entirely in the hands of women until the beginning of the sixteenth century) to send for the ale-conner of the ward in order to taste the ale. If this officer was not satisfied with its quality, he, with the assent of his alderman, set a lower price upon it, which upon sale thereof was not to be exceeded. Fine, imprisonment, and even punishment by pillory was the result of reiterated breaches of the Assize. The Assize price of ale varied at different periods. At one time it was 3/4d. per gallon and no more, but later the price was 1½d. for the best, and 3/4d. to 1d. for the second quality.[336]

The vintners were an important body, and were mostly located in the Vintry, a district which has kept its name to the present time. The Vintners' Company consisted of *vinetarii*, or wine importers and merchants, and *tabernarii*, tavern keepers, or retailers of wine.

The public taste in wine was not a very refined one in the Middle Ages, or possibly the liquor did not keep very well, as new wine was preferred to old. It was enacted that after the arrival of new wine at a tavern none of it should be sold before the old was disposed of. There is no allusion in the *Liber Albus* to bottles or flasks, and all the wine seems to have been drawn from the wood. Taverners who sold sweet wines were forbidden to deal in other kinds. The sweet wines enumerated are Malvesie, the modern Malmsey, a Greek wine sold in the reign of Richard II. at 16d. per gallon; Vernage (Vernaccia), a red Tuscan wine, sold at 2s.; Crete, sold at 1s; and wine of Provence, sold at the same price, probably a kind of Roussillon. By royal writ of 39 Edw. III., only three taverns for the sale of sweet wines were in future to be permitted within the city,—in Cheap, Walbrook, and Lombard Street. In the class of non-sweet wines were Rhenish, sold in the reign of Richard II. at 8d. per gallon, and Red (Vermaille) at 6d. Other wines came from Gascony, Burgundy, Rochelle, and Spain.

No wine was permitted to be sold till it had been submitted to a scrutiny, and been duly gauged. In the reign of Edward III. four vintners were chosen yearly to assess the prices of wine. King's Prisage, or Custom, was taken according to a certain scale on all imported wines. The wine taverns were furnished with a pole projecting from the gable of the house, and supporting a sign, or a bunch of leaves at the end (the bush of the proverb, 'Good wine needs no bush'). In one ordinance it is stated that the poles of the taverns of Cheapside and elsewhere were of such a length as to be in the way of persons on horseback, and so heavy as to cause the risk of greatly damaging the houses; in consequence of this it was enacted that from thenceforth no sign-pole should be more than seven feet in length.[337]

No ale or wine tavern was allowed to remain open after curfew.

The clothing trades are well represented among the city companies. The Mercers head the list of the 'Twelve,' and the freemen were originally 'chapmen in small or mixed wares,' that is, those articles which were sold retail by the little balance or small scale, in contradistinction to those things sold by the beam, or in gross, and they did business in the Mercery, Cheapside. Wadmal, a coarse woollen stuff, lake or fine linen, fustian, felt, etc., were among these smallwares. Gradually the mercers of Cheap extended their dealings, became vendors of silks and velvets (*temp.* Henry VI.), and formed a mixed body of merchants and shopkeepers, leaving the smallwares, or mercery proper, to the haberdashers. Sir William Stone held the position of mercer to Queen Elizabeth, and supplied her with her wardrobe.

The Haberdashers imported a cloth at first styled *halberject*, and in the fourteenth century *hapertas*, from which, as Mr. Riley suggests, the term 'haberdasher' probably originated. Subsequently the Hurers and the Hatters joined them.

The Merchant Taylors and Linen Armourers are in some documents styled 'Mercatores Scissores,' 'Scissors of London,' 'Scissors and Fraternity of St. John Baptist,'—titles alike pointing to their being anciently both tailors and cutters, and also making the padding and interior lining of armour, as well as manufacturing garments. Tailors made dresses for both sexes, their prices, as usual, being regulated by public enactment. By ordinance of the reign of Edward III. it is declared that 'Tailors shall henceforth take for a robe, garnished with silk, 18d.; for a man's robe, garnished with thread and buckram, 14d.; also a coat and hood, 10d.; also for a lady's long dress, garnished with silk and cendale, 2s. 6d.; also for a pair of sleeves for changing, 4d.'[338]

The Drapers' Company is the third on the list of the twelve great companies, and the second of the clothing companies, the Mercers being the first. Henry Fitz-Ailwin, the first Mayor of London, was a freeman of the Drapers' Gild, to which he left by will an inn, called the Chequer, in the parish of St. Mary Bothaw.

The Skinners represented the trade that dealt with furs. The furs mentioned in the *Liber Albus* as imported are, marten skins, rabbit skins, dressed woolfels, Spanish squirrel skins, and grysoevere or grey work. In the reign of Edward I. an enactment was made that 'no woman, except a lady who is in the habit of using furs, shall have a hood furred with dressed woolfel' (pelure). Women of ill-fame were forbidden at one period to wear minever or other furs, though at a later date they were permitted to use lambs' wool and rabbit skin. No mixed work, formed of different kinds of skins, was allowed to be made, and no new fur was to be worked up with the old.[339]

'The skynner unto the feeld moot also,
His hous in London is to streyt and scars
To doon his craft; sum tyme it was nat so.
O lordës, yeve unto your men hir pars
That so doon, and acqwente hem bet with Mars,
God of bataile; he loueth non array
That hurtyth manhode at preef or assay.'
(*The Regement of Princes*, by Thomas Hoccleve, II. 477-483.)

The Clothworkers' Company, formed by a junction of the Gilds of Shearmen and Fullers, has already been alluded to.

The minor companies connected with the clothing trades require some notice here. The Cordwainers held a prominent position, but in the reign of Edward I. (1303) there were public complaints of frauds and irregularities brought against them, and charges were made that they mixed inferior with the superior leathers. They were continually at feud with the Cobblers, and every endeavour was made to keep the two trades distinct. The cordwainers were forbidden to mend shoes and the cobblers to make them. Moreover, throughout the thirteenth, fourteenth and fifteenth centuries there were fixed regulations not only that cordwainers should use new leather in making shoes, but that cobblers should be restricted wholly to the use of old leather in mending them. The latter were even punished for having new leather in their possession.[340]

In the reign of Edward III. the prices fixed for boots and shoes were: a pair of shoes made of cordwain, 6d.; made of cow leather, 5d.; a pair of boots made of cordwain, 3s, 6d.; made of cow leather, 3s.[341] This shows that boots were then very dear.

In Edward IV.'s reign the cordwainers stood up for the defence of their trade against the decree of the Pope. They were decidedly in the wrong, but one cannot but admire their pluckiness. The story is told in William Gregory's *Chronicle of London*, which is thus paraphrased by Dr. James Gairdner, the editor: 'The Pope issued a Bull that no cordwainer should make any pikes [at the toes of the shoes] more than two inches long, or sell shoes on Sunday, or even fit a shoe upon a man's foot on Sunday, on pain of excommunication. Neither was the cordwainer to attend fairs on a Sunday under the same penalty; for not only were fairs held on that day, but the cordwainer's services, it must be supposed, were required at the fairs to adjust the dandy's *chaussure*, just as much as, in a later age, the barber's aid was necessary to dress his wig. The papal Bull was approved by the King's

Council and confirmed by Act of Parliament; and proclamation was consequently made at Paul's Cross that it should be put in execution. Yet, with all this weight of authority against a silly fashion, the dandy world had its own ideas upon the subject, and some men ventured to say they would wear long pikes in spite of the Pope, for "the Pope's curse would not kill a fly." The cordwainers, too, had a vested interest in the extravagance, though some of their own body had been instrumental in getting the Pope's interference. They obtained privy seals and protections from the King to exempt them from the operation of the law, which soon became a dead letter; and those who had applied to the Pope to restrain their practices were subjected to much trouble and persecution.'[342]

The Leathersellers had still more to do with leather than the cordwainers, and the same complaints were made against them for passing off inferior for superior leather. In the fourteenth and fifteenth centuries several ordinances were issued regulating the trade of the leathersellers in the City of London, and for the prevention of deceit in the manufacture and sale of their wares.

Pursers or Glovers were incorporated with the leathersellers in 1502, but in 1638 a new company of glovers was formed.

The Girdlers made belts or girdles for men and women. They were also called Ceinturiers and Zonars. In 1217 (1 Hen. III.) Benedict Seynturer was one of the sheriffs of London. The company still exists, although it cannot be said that the calling survived the reign of Charles II.

The Goldsmiths' Company stands almost alone, on account of the great services to the State which it performs in connection with the important trade it represents, and also in connection with the tryal of the gold and silver coins in the Pyx of His Majesty's Mint, a service which has been performed without intermission, at any-rate since the year 1281. This history also contains a strong argument in favour of the received opinion that the companies are the lineal descendants of the gilds, for the craft of goldsmiths performed by Statute the same duties of assaying vessels of gold and silver that the present company does. The Act (28 Edw. I., cap. 20) recites that: 'The wardens of the craft shall go from shop to shop among the goldsmiths to essay if their gold be of the same Touch that is spoken of before.'

According to Stow's *Chronicle* a variance fell between the fellowships of Goldsmiths and Taylors in 1268, 'causing great ruffling in the city and many men to be slain, for which riot thirteen of the captains were hanged.'

By the first charter (1 Edw. III., 1327), 'the company were allowed to elect honest, lawful and sufficient men, but skilled in the trade, to enquire of any matters of complaint, and who might, in consideration of the craft, reform what defects they should find therein, and punish offenders. It states that it had been theretofore ordained that all those who were of the goldsmiths' trade should sit in their shops in the High Street of Cheap; and that no silver or plate ought to be sold in the City of London except at the King's Exchange, or in the said street of Cheap amongst the goldsmiths, and that publicly, to the end that the persons of the said trade might inform themselves whether the sellers came lawfully by such vessel or not; whereas of late not only the merchants and strangers brought counterfeit sterling in the realm, and also many of the trade of goldsmiths kept shops in obscure turnings and by-lanes and streets, but did buy vessels of gold and silver secretly, without enquiring whether such vessel were stolen or lawfully come by, and melting it down, did make it into plate, and sell it to merchants travelling beyond seas, that it might be exported; and so they made false work of gold and silver, which they sold to those who had no skill in such things. These abuses and deceptions this charter provides against by ordaining that no gold or silver shall be manufactured to be sent abroad but what shall be sold at the King's Exchange, or openly amongst the goldsmiths; and that none, pretending to be goldsmiths, shall keep any shops but in Cheap.'

The King's Exchange for the receipt of bullion was situated in the street leading from Cheapside to Knight-riders Street, known from the early part of the seventeenth century as Old 'Change. The London goldsmiths chiefly inhabited Cheapside, Old 'Change, Lombard Street, Foster Lane, St. Martin's-le-Grand, Silver Street, Goldsmiths' Street, Wood Street, and the lanes about Goldsmiths' Hall. That part of the south side of Cheapside from Bread Street to the Cross was called Goldsmiths' Row. It was described in enthusiastic terms by Stow as 'the most beautiful frame of fair houses and shops that be within the walls of London or elsewhere in England... the same was [re]built by Thomas Wood, goldsmith, one of the Sheriffs of London, in the year 1491. It containeth in number ten fair dwelling-houses and fourteen shops, all in one frame, uniformly built four storeys high, beautified towards the street with the goldsmiths' arms and the likeness of Woodmen, in memory of his name, riding on monstrous beasts, all which is cast in lead, richly painted over and gilt: these he gave to the goldsmiths, with stocks of money, to be lent to young men having those shops. This said front was again new painted and gilt over in the year 1594; Sir Richard Martin being then Mayor and keeping his mayoralty in one of them.'

Sir Walter Prideaux, in his valuable *Memorials of the Goldsmiths' Company*, says that the native and the foreign goldsmiths appear to have been divided into classes, and to have enjoyed different privileges. First, there were the members of the company who were chiefly, but not exclusively, Englishmen; their shops were subject to the control of the company; they had the advantages conferred by the company on its members, and they made certain payments for the support of the fellowship. The second division comprised the non-freemen, who were called 'allowes,' that is to say, allowed or licensed. There were 'allowes Englis,' 'allowes Alicant,' 'Alicant strangers,' 'Dutchmen,' 'Men of the Fraternity of St. Loys,' etc. All these paid tribute to the company, and were also subject to their control.

All the livery companies possessed a class of young unmarried members called 'The Bachelors,' and in the Goldsmiths' Company a special place was reserved for their lodging. This was known as Bachelors' Alley or Court, and was situated between Foster Lane and Gutter Lane. The lodgings were supplied at 'very small and easy rents,' the greatest not to exceed 8s. per annum. The tenants could continue as long as they were unmarried, but difficulties arose by reason of attempts at underletting without authority, and disorderly persons gave much trouble. In 1595 an order was promulgated 'that from henceforth no goldsmith shall have his dwelling in any of the tenements in Bachelors' Alley before he be admitted by the wardens for the time being; and that everyone so admitted shall forthwith enter into a bond to deliver to the wardens, at his departure, the key of his tenement, and quietly to quit possession of the same.'

Sir Walter Prideaux states that at the early period of the first charter the goldsmiths acted as bankers and pawnbrokers. They received pledges not only of plate, but of other articles, such as cloth of gold and pieces of napery. Saint Dunstan was the patron saint of the company, and feasts were held on his day, when also bells were set ringing. This saint's likeness in wood (gilt) formed the figure-head of the company's barge. There was also a Chapel of St. Dunstan in St. Paul's Cathedral which was attached to the company.

In the foregoing remarks there are some references to the livery companies, but these are introduced more particularly on account of the light thrown by them upon the trade of London. The work of the gilds was devoted to the trades which they represented, but in course of time many of the companies lost touch with the trades whose names they bore. This largely came about in a quite natural way, and the privilege of introduction to a company by patrimony caused the addition to the list of freemen of a large number of those who were engaged in other occupations.

The relative position in precedence of the various companies have continually altered, and there is no information to show how the twelve chief companies have attained that commanding position.

The feuds between the trades continued to comparatively late times. Pepys relates, in 1664, how there was a fray in Moorfields between the butchers and the weavers, between whom there had ever been a competition for mastery. At first the butchers knocked down all the weavers that had green or blue aprons, but at last the butchers were fain to pull off their sleeves that they might not be known, and were soundly beaten out of the field.[343]

Some note must be made here of the Jews and of the Italian moneylenders who for so long carried on the financial business of the country.

One of the many hardships which the Jews suffered in this country was that wherever they might dwell they were compelled to bury their dead in London. This regulation was abolished by Henry II. in 1177.

The cruel calumny that the Jews at Lincoln crucified a Christian child brought them into great trouble, and in 1256 one hundred and two Jews were brought from Lincoln to Westminster charged with this crime. Eighteen of them were hanged, and the remainder lay in prison for a long time.

Clipping of money became very general about 1278, and the Jews were supposed to be the chief culprits. Those who were suspected, with their Christian accomplices, were arrested, and at the end of the trial 300 Jews were condemned to be hanged as well as three Christians. Nearly all the goldsmiths and moneyers escaped the death penalty. In 1290 came the final blow, when every Jew was expelled from England. It is difficult to understand Edward I.'s motive in banishing a class of men who were so useful to him. In Stow's *Chronicle* it is said that as their houses were sold 'the King made a mighty mass of money,' but the action certainly added to his difficulties, and drove him to resort to the Italian financiers, who were no more popular with the citizens than the Jews. The expulsion was ascribed to the instigation of the King's mother, Eleanor, widow of Henry III., but it certainly expressed the will of the nation. Stow gives the number of Jews banished as 15,060, but this is probably an exaggeration. The number of London Jews is estimated at 2000.

The Old Jewry was originally the Ghetto of London, and the burial-place of the Jews was on the site of Jewin Street. Mr. Joseph Jacobs, who compiled a valuable account of the Old Jewry, is of opinion that the Jews no longer lived in this place at the time of the expulsion. There was a Jewry within the Liberty of the Tower in the thirteenth century, and there is still a Jewry Street, Aldgate.

The republics of Italy during the Middle Ages were the home of finance, and had advanced far before the other states of Europe in wealth and civilisation. The necessities of the great countries of Europe, caused by the Crusades of the eleventh and twelfth centuries, were the opportunity of companies of moneylenders, who acted as the Pope's collectors.

Before the close of the reign of Henry III. the Italians had gained a firm footing in England as merchants and moneylenders. Citizens of Sienna, Lucca and Florence came here, and fought with the Jews for the financial control of the country.

Matthew Paris relates that Roger, Bishop of London, anathematised the Caorsins and banished them from his diocese in 1235 in spite of the support of 'judges that were servants (*familiaribus*) to the Caorsins, whom they had elected for their will.'[344]

In the early years of Edward I.'s reign, there were four companies of merchants of Sienna acting under the title of 'Campsores Papæ.' In his ninth year the keepers of the Exchange delivered £10,000 to Lombard merchants (as they are styled in the record) in part payment of sums they had lent to the King. It is recorded that between the twenty-third and twenty-seventh years of his reign Edward I. contracted a debt to the Friscobaldi alone of not less than £15,800.[345]

The King wanted much money for his wars, and, as he could no longer look to the Jews he was forced to apply for aid to the Italians. These loans grew so formidable that they caused considerable financial embarrassments in the reign of Edward II.

There were a large number of companies such as the Ricciardi, the Bardi, the Peruzzi, and the Spini, but the Friscobaldi, of which family there were several companies, occur most frequently in London history. Amerigo de' Friscobaldi was constable of Bordeaux in the first year of Edward II.'s reign.

Here are two entries from the city records:—

'14 Feb. 1299-1300.—Thursday after the Feast of St. Valentine came John de Pounteysse, goldsmith, and acknowledged himself bound to Faldo Jamiano, of the society of Frescobaldi, in the sum of £8 and 45d. sterling, to be paid at Easter next.'[346]

'2 Feb. 1305-6.—Andrew le Mareschal acknowledged himself indebted to Bettinus Friscobalde and his partners, merchants of the company of Friscobaldi, in the sum of £102, 13s. 4d.'[347]

The loans in the reign of Edward III. were very considerable, and the unpopularity of the Italians was great. In 1376 a petition was presented to the King by the Mayor, Aldermen and Commons of the City of London against usurious foreign moneylenders dwelling in London, asking that the Lombards might be forbidden from dwelling in the city, or acting as brokers and buying and selling by retail which they alleged to be against their ancient franchises. The King answered the petition to the effect that if the citizens would put the city under good government for the future no foreigner should be allowed to dwell, act as broker, or sell by retail in London or the suburbs save and except the merchants of the Hanse towns.[348]

On the whole we must extend our sympathy to the Italians, for the King was not very prompt in paying his debts, and he considered it immoral to have promised any interest. The effect was that he ruined many of these unfortunate foreigners. The name of Lombard Street occurs in the city books in 1382, and was in common use at the beginning of the fourteenth century. It is a remarkable fact that the locality in which the Italian financiers first settled in London should obtain a name which has continued to the present day as a synonym of finance, and was used by the late Mr. Bagehot as the title of his great work.

Matthew Paris tells us that the houses which the Italian moneylenders built for themselves were so costly that, although at one period the Italians were anxious to leave the kingdom to escape the persecutions they suffered from, they were constrained to remain by the loss they feared to incur by deserting their houses.[349]

In 1456 a serious attack was made upon the houses of the Lombards by the mercers and other crafts led by William Cantelowe, alderman and mercer, who was summoned before the King's Council and imprisoned. We learn also from the Paston Letters that two of the men who joined in the attack were hanged (ed. J. Gairdner, 1872, vol. i. p. 387). In Gregory's *Chronicle* it is said that the Lombards were compelled to quit London and take up their residence in Southampton and Winchester. Dr. James Gairdner writes of this outbreak: 'The withdrawal of the Lombard merchants in all probability produced a sensible effect upon the commerce of the city; for they made a bye-law among themselves that no individual merchant of Northern Italy should henceforth go to London and trade there.' This ordinance the Signory of Venice ratified by a decree of the Senate, and prohibited, under a heavy fine, all Venetian vessels from visiting the port of London.[350]

In spite of all this turmoil affairs settled down again, and the foreigners appear to have returned to their London houses.

In connection with the introduction of Italian bankers into London, the popular derivation of bankrupt from a broken bench is naturally called to mind, and I have tried to find some allusion in the city records to a broken bench in Lombard Street, but without success.

In Florio's *A New Worlde of Wordes*; or, *Dictionarie in Italian and English* (1598), we find the following entries:—

'Banca, a bench or a forme.'

'Bancarotta, a bankrupt.'

In Torriano's edition of Florio (1650) we come upon these amplified entries—

'Banca-rotta, a bankrout merchant, one that hath broken his credit.'

'Banca fallito, a bank broken, a merchant's credit crackt.'

This is the explanation that commends itself to Dr. Murray (*New English Dictionary*), who writes that he cannot trace the reference to a broken bench earlier than that of Dr. Johnson, who introduced the suggestion with the formula 'it is said.'

There is, however, an early note bearing on this derivation in Sir John Skene's remarkable little book, *De Verborum Significatione* (1641),[351] where we read under the words 'Dyour, Dyvour' this explanation: 'In Latine, *cedere bonis*, quhilk is most commonly used amongst merchandes to make bankrout, bankrupt or bankrompue; because the doer thereof, as it were, breakis his bank, stalle or seete quhair he used his traffique of before.'

No earlier date for the use of the word than the reign of Henry VIII. has been found by Professor Skeat or Dr. Murray, but surely an earlier reference must be lurking somewhere. In the First Folio of Shakespeare the word is printed 'bankeroute' (pronounced as four syllables), but this was altered in later editions to bankrupt. There can be no doubt that the word is directly derived from *bancarotta*, and that the form bankrupt is an afterthought of the learned to connect it with the Latin language.

The point that has to be accounted for is the strange appropriation of an expression meaning broken bench or broken bank to the individual whose credit is broken. This one would naturally expect to be a secondary meaning.

In concluding this chapter it is necessary to make an allusion to the Statute merchant (11 Edw. I.) for the recovery of debts. The first two Letter Books of the City of London are chiefly concerned with recognisances of debts, and they are of great value as illustrating the commercial intercourse of the citizens of London in the thirteenth and fourteenth centuries with Gascony and Spain, more especially in connection with wine and leather.

By the Statute of Acton Burnel (11 Edw. I.) it was enacted (*inter alia*) that recognisances of debts should be taken before the Mayor and a clerk appointed by the King. Nevertheless within a very short while after the passing of this Statute and notwithstanding its express provision to the contrary, we find the Mayor, sheriffs and aldermen declaring that such recognisances should be made before the city chamberlain, who might, if he liked, receive, as he frequently did, the recognisances at his own house instead of at the Guildhall.[352]

It was ordered that the recognisances should bear 'the debtor's seal and also the King's seal,' to be provided for the purpose. This latter seal appears to be no longer in existence. From impressions of it preserved at King's College, Cambridge, and elsewhere, it is found to have been circular, and nearly three-quarters of an inch in diameter, with the King's bust between two castles, with a lion of England in base. Legend—'S+ Edm Reg+ Angl+ ad recogn Debitor+.'[353]

The following entry from Letter Book A forms an interesting illustration of the contents of these books:—

'Laurence de Gisors acknowledged before H. le Galeis the Mayor that he owed Sir Philip le Taylor a cask of wine to be delivered on a certain love day (*diem amoris*) because the said Laurence killed a dog belonging to him.'

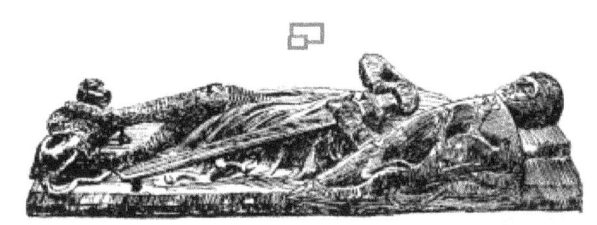

SIR WILLIAM MARSHAL, EARL OF PEMBROKE, TEMPLE CHURCH.

CHAPTER XI

The Church and Education

THE influence of the Church during the mediæval period was great. In London the Dean and Chapter of St. Paul's (secular canons) held the first place after the bishop, then came other bodies of secular and regular canons, followed by the monks and friars and officers of the hospitals, etc. Last in rank, but most esteemed by the people, came the rectors and vicars of the various parishes. Here was a large army of persons forming the officials of the Church, and the buildings of the Church occupied a very large portion of the city and of the land beyond its walls.

Between the secular and the regular clergy a great feud always existed. During the Saxon period the number of religious houses was few, but a great increase occurred almost immediately after the Conquest. Monasteries grew in number rapidly during the Norman period, but in time the monks having grown rich and lazy the need of a revival became evident. The great movement of evangelisation which took place during the early Plantagenet period when the friars came from Italy to England caused a religious revolution.

Poverty and humility were the great principles of the friars, but these were soon forgotten, and in the fourteenth and fifteenth centuries all the regulars became equally obnoxious to the reformers. Wycliffe and his followers preached against them, and writers with such different views as Langland and Chaucer had little but evil to say of them. Chaucer condemns monks and friars alike, and reserves his praise for the poor parish priest.

We must first deal with the bishop and the secular clergy, and then consider the conditions relative to the establishment of the regulars, ending with a note on education in London during the Middle Ages.

The Cathedral Church of St. Paul's is of great antiquity, and was established in the first period of Saxon Christianity. There have been three buildings on the same site, and the first was erected in the earliest years of the seventh century by Mellitus the missionary bishop and Ethelbert, King of Kent. Although this church existed for nearly five centuries no record whatever remains of it. Sir Gilbert Scott wrote: 'I am not aware that we have any information as to the Cathedral built by the companions of Augustine (Mellitus and Justus) at London and Rochester. Curiously enough there continues to this day at Rochester, and continued to the seventeenth century in our own St. Paul's equally as at Canterbury, a crypt beneath the elevated sanctuary, no doubt the lineal successor and representative of those erected by these missionary bishops, in imitation of the great basilica at Rome, whence they had been sent to evangelise this distant region.'[354]

Erkenwald, whose shrine stood at the back of the high altar in the oldest church, was the fourth bishop (A.D. 675-693), and it was at his house in London that Archbishop Theodore, the organiser of the Church of England, was reconciled to Bishop Wilfrid after their long estrangement.[355] Aelfun, or Alhunus, was Bishop of London in 1012, and performed the burial service over Aelfah (or Alphage), Archbishop of Canterbury, who was murdered by the Danes and buried in St. Paul's.

William, the chaplain of Edward the Confessor, was consecrated in 1051. He was driven from England with the other foreign prelates in the following year, but returned to his See and died in 1075. It was he who was addressed as 'William Bishop' in William the Conqueror's charter to the citizens of London.

The first Church of St. Paul's was destroyed by fire at the end of the eleventh century, but the exact time is not certain as Matthew of Westminster and Roger of Wendover give conflicting dates for the rebuilding. There seems to be no doubt that the second cathedral was commenced by Bishop Maurice, and as he was not consecrated until 1085 the date given by Dugdale, 1083, must be wrong. Probably the received date of 1087 (the last year of William the Conqueror's reign) is more correct. Fire again did great damage in the year 1136, but the work of rebuilding proceeded slowly, and in 1221 the steeple was finished; the choir was rebuilt and the whole building was nearly completed by 1283.

Old St. Paul's was a very grand building, which took a prominent position among the cathedrals of the country. It was longer than Winchester, and the height of the choir was the same as Westminster; that of the nave was rather less.[356]

The crowning glory of old St. Paul's was its elegant spire, but the building itself had many beauties, the magnificent rose window at the east end of the Lady Chapel, with the beautiful seven-light window beneath, being among these. This grand building, therefore, standing on a hill in the most prominent position of city, was for several centuries the great ornament of London, bringing in harmony all the picturesque elements of the mediæval town.

In the year 1314 the cross fell, and the steeple of wood being ruinous, was taken down and rebuilt with a new gilt ball. Many relics were found in the cross, which were replaced in the new cross, and the new pommel or ball was made of sufficient size to contain ten bushels of corn. A Chronicle in Lambeth Palace Library contains an account of the solemn dedication of these relics, which is quoted by Canon Benham: 'On the tenth of the calends of June 1314, Gilbert, Bishop of London, dedicated altars, namely those of the Blessed Virgin Mary, of St. Thomas the Martyr, and of the Blessed Dunstan, in the new buildings of the Church of St. Paul, London. In the same year the cross and the ball, with great part of the Campanile of the Church of St. Paul, were taken down because they were decayed and dangerous, and a new cross, with a ball well gilt, was erected; and many relics of divers saints were, for the protection of the aforesaid Campanile, and of the whole structure beneath, placed within the cross, with a great procession, and with due solemnity, by Gilbert the bishop, on the fourth of the nones of October, in order that the Omnipotent God and the glorious merits of His saints, whose relics are contained within the cross, might deign to protect from all danger of storms.'[357]

In 1444 the spire was nearly destroyed by lightning and was not repaired until 1462. In the severe fire of 1561 the spire was destroyed and never rebuilt, although the rest of the Cathedral was restored in 1566. The great height of the steeple gave point to many a proverb, and in Lodge's *Wounds of Civil War* (1594) a clown talks of the 'Paul's steeple of honour,' meaning by that phrase the highest point that could be attained.[358] The choristers ascended the spire to a great height on certain saints' days, and chanted prayers and anthems, a custom still observed in the tower of Magdalen College, Oxford, on May Day. The last observance of the custom at St. Paul's is said to have taken place in the reign of Mary I.[359]

The western front was originally a plain Norman façade of great size, which was flanked by two strong stone towers. The one on the north was connected with the Bishop's Palace, while that on the south was called the Lollards' Tower, and was used as the Bishop's prison 'for such as were detected for opinions in religion contrary to the faith of the Church' (Stow's *Survey*).[360]

St. Paul's Churchyard was formerly an enclosure, and not a thoroughfare. The public route to Cheapside from Ludgate Hill passed up the Old Bailey and along Newgate Street. The Cathedral Close is thus described by the late Dr. Sparrow Simpson: 'The wall erected about 1109, and, by letters-patent of Edward I., greatly strengthened in 1285, extends from the N.E. corner of Ave Maria Lane, runs eastward along Paternoster Row to the north end of Old 'Change in Cheapside, thence southward to Carter Lane, and on the north of Carter Lane to Creed Lane, back to the

Great Western Gate. There are six entrances to the enclosure. The first is the Great Western Gate, by which we have just entered; the second, in Paul's Alley in Paternoster Row, leading to the postern gate of the Cathedral; the third at Canon Alley; the fourth, or Little Gate, where S. Paul's Churchyard and Cheapside now unite; the fifth, S. Augustine's Gate, at the west end of Watling Street; the sixth, at Paul's Chain.'[361]

The great western gate spanned the street towards the ends of Creed Lane and Ave Maria Lane. On entering the gate the west front of the Cathedral came in view. The old Church of St. Gregory adjoined the main building at the south-west corner. It stood in the same position to the first Cathedral, and within its walls the body of St. Edmund, king and martyr, was preserved for a time before it was carried to Bury St. Edmund's for honourable burial. The early history of this church is lost, and it is not known whether it was destroyed with the first Cathedral, and rose again from its ashes like the second Cathedral, or whether it continued for a time in its original state. It was pulled down before 1645, and not rebuilt. On the northern side of the nave of the Cathedral stood the Bishop's Palace, a large and gloomy building.[362]

Still further to the north (past the palace and its grounds) was the cemetery, called Pardon Church Haugh. Here was a cloister painted with the subjects of the Danse Macabre or Dance of Death, commonly known as the Dance of Paul's. John Lydgate translated out of French the old verses that explained these paintings. Over the east quadrant of the cloister was the Cathedral Library, built by Walter Sherington,

PAUL'S CROSS.
(*From an original drawing in the Pepysian Library, Cambridge.*)

Chancellor of the Duchy of Lancaster in Henry VI.'s time, and Canon Residentiary. At one time the library was 'well furnished with fair-written books in vellum.'

In the midst of the churchyard was a chapel, first founded by Gilbert, the father of Thomas à Becket, and rebuilt by Dean More in the reign of Henry V. Near by was Minor Canons' Hall, and the College of Minor Canons, or Peter's College. The Charnel House, with a chapel over it, stood at the north-east, not far from Paul's Cross.[363] This building existed in the reign of Edward I., and the chapel contained some monuments and alabaster figures. Among the historians of St. Paul's there is some little confusion respecting these various chapels.

Paul's Cross holds a very prominent position in the history of the religious life of the Middle Ages and for many years after. In ages when the voice of the people was largely inarticulate the preacher has often been the man to make it heard. Stow describes the Cross as having 'been for many ages the most solemn place in this nation, for the greatest divines and most eminent scholars to preach at,' and Carlyle calls it a kind of *Times* newspaper. It is worthy of remark that the position of Paul's Cross was near the place where the ancient folkmoots were held, and the former continued the traditions of the latter.

At the east end of the Cathedral was St. Paul's School, founded by Dean Colet, and the famous Bell Tower, formed of wood covered with lead, and containing the common bell, which called the people to their folkmoots, and afterwards four bells, known as the Jesus Bells, because they specially belonged to Jesus Chapel, in the crypt of the Cathedral. As the open space at the east end was claimed by the citizens as a place for their assemblies in folkmoots, so the space at the west end was reserved for the military displays in connection with the appearance of Fitz-Walter as Bannerer of the city.

On the south side of the close, and to the west of the transept, was the old octagonal Chapter House, with its own two-storeyed cloister (built in 1332). This was a small but beautiful building.[364]

Close by stood the house of the Chancellor. On the south-west is the Deanery, first built by Ralph de Diceto, and more westward various houses for the use of the canons. On the south side of the Cathedral also stood the dormitory, refectory, kitchen, bakehouse and brewery of the college. The brewhouse became subsequently the Paul's Head tavern.

This brief list of the buildings in the old Cathedral Close will give some idea of the arrangement of the College of Secular Canons, and the houses which they occupied.

Having walked round the close we may now enter the Cathedral church at the western end where were three gates or entries. The middle gate had a massive pillar of brass, to which the leaves of the great door were fastened. In the nave were twelve noble Norman bays with Norman triforium and pointed clerestory windows. It is probable that originally the roof of the nave was a flat painted ceiling, but Mr. Ferrey supposes that a vaulted roof was

INTERIOR OF OLD ST. PAUL'S.

added in 1255; apparently this was originally of wood, but that stone vaulting was intended may be inferred from the flying buttresses in some of the pictures of the Cathedral.

The view along the nave, as represented in Hollar's engraving is very fine, and reminds one of the noble nave at Ely. Both the nave and choir had twelve bays counting from the west door. The second bay of the north side contained the Court of Convocation, and close by was the font near which Sir John Montacute desired in his will (1388) to be buried. 'If I die in London, then I desire that my body may be buried in St. Paul's, near to the font wherein I was baptized.' In the tenth bay was the Chantry Chapel of Thomas Kempe, bishop of the diocese (1448-1489), and rebuilder of Paul's Cross.

In the eleventh bay, on the south side, was the tomb of Sir John Beauchamp, K.G. (d. 1358), Constable of Dover Castle, and son to Guy Beauchamp, Earl of Warwick. This tomb was commonly called after Duke Humphrey, and the nave of the church from this misnomer went by the name of Duke Humphrey's Walk. On May Day watermen and tankard-bearers came to the tomb early in the morning, strewed herbs upon it and sprinkled it with water. At the foot of this tomb was the image of the Virgin, before which a lamp was kept perpetually burning, and every morning after matins a short office was said before it. A taper was also kept burning before the Great Crucifix, near to the north door, fabulously said to have been discovered by King Lucius, A.D. 140. Richard Martin, Bishop of St. David's in the reign of Edward IV., had a special veneration for this crucifix, and left an annual gift to the choristers that they might sing before it *Sancte Deus fortis*.[365]

In the north aisle was the famous *Si quis* door, on which notices were fixed; originally these were probably purely ecclesiastical, but in course of time all classes made their wants known there. Decker writes: 'The first time that you venture into Paul's, pass through the body of the church like a porter, yet presume not to fetch so much as one whole turn in the middle aisle, no, nor to cast an eye to *Si quis* door, pasted and plastered up with serving-men's supplications, before you have paid tribute to the top of Paul's steeple with a single penny.'

Bishop Hall, in his *Satires*, shows that Churchmen could be hired there too—

'Sawst thou ever *Si quis* patched on Paul's church door,
To seek some vacant vicarage before?'

This practice is alluded to by Chaucer:—

'He sette not his benefice to hyre,
And leet his sheepe encombred in the myre,
And ran to Londoun unto Saint Paules,
To seken hym a chaunterie for soules.'
(Prologue to *Canterbury Tales*.)

Passing from the nave to the transept we notice that the central tower was treated as a lantern internally, and was open to the base of the spire. The choir was cut off by a screen with a central archway; on each side of the entrance were four canopies with figures beneath them. An ascent of twelve steps took the worshipper to the level of the choir pavement.

The choir was naturally the most gorgeous portion of the Cathedral. The architecture was pure and noble, and the carved woodwork of the canons' stalls was famous for its beauty. The reredos and high altar, dedicated in honour of St. Paul, formed the chief attraction of the choir. There was also an altar to the north, dedicated in honour of St. Ethelbert, king and confessor, and one to the south, dedicated to St. Mellitus. Six more steps led to the sanctuary, from which the worshipper could pass behind the altar screen. Eastward of the screen was the famous shrine of St. Erkenwald. Mention has already been made of the original tomb in the first Cathedral. Legend reports that in the fire of the eleventh century the saint's resting-place alone remained unharmed. On 14th November 1148 his bones were transferred to a more noble tomb. Gilbert de Segrave laid the first stone of a still more magnificent shrine in 1314, in which the body of the saint was placed on 1st February 1326. This was for a long period the most famous of the tombs of old St. Paul's, to which pilgrims flocked from distant parts, and riches of all kinds were lavished upon it. A canon of the church, Walter de Thorpe, gave to it all his gold rings and jewels; the Dean and Chapter in 18 Edward II. presented a rich store of gold and silver and precious stones; in the 31st of Edward III. three goldsmiths were engaged upon it for a whole year, at wages of 8s. a week for one and 5s. a week for each of the others. King John of France, when he was a prisoner in England, made an offering of twelve nobles, and Richard de Preston, citizen and grocer, presented a remarkable sapphire in the reign of Richard II. This stone was supposed to cure infirmities of the eyes, and the donor directed proclamation to be made of its great virtues. Dean Evere in 1407 provided an endowment for the lights which burned before the shrine.[366]

The choir was full of tombs and brasses, many of them of great importance. On the north side stood the stately tomb of John of Gaunt, Duke of Lancaster (d. 1399), with recumbent figures of the Duke and his second wife, Constance of Castile. Special offices were performed at several of the shrines, especially those of St. Erkenwald and St. Thomas of Lancaster, as the grandson of Henry III. was popularly styled, although he was never canonised. On the 28th of June 1323 Edward II. sent a letter to Stephen Gravesend, Bishop of London, commanding him to prohibit the reverence paid to Thomas of Lancaster in the Cathedral.[367]

The high altar was the scene twice a year of a strange custom, which was kept up for several centuries. Sir William le Band in 1275 commenced to give yearly a doe in winter and a fat buck in summer to be offered at the altar and then distributed to the resident canons. These were given in lieu of twenty-two acres of land lying within the lordship of Westlee in Essex, to be enclosed within his park of Toringham, so that the knight appears to have made a very good bargain. The reception of the buck and doe was 'till

Queen Elizabeth's days solemnly performed at the steps of the quire by the canons of this Cathedral, attired in sacred vestments, and wearing garlands of flowers on their heads, and the horns of the buck carried on the top of a spear in procession round about within the body of the church, with a great noise of horn-blowers.'[368]

As already stated the choir was rebuilt early in the thirteenth century, and in 1255 it was considerably extended. Previously a street ran close to the east end, from Watling Street to Cheapside, and here stood the old Church of St. Faith. The exact site of the houses was marked by nine wells in a row which were found by Wren. When this street was built over and the church pulled down the parishioners were provided with a church in the Crypt. About the middle of the north side of the choir was a low-arched door, and from this six-and-twenty steps led down to St. Faith's, at the eastern end of which was the Jesus Chapel.[369]

We have now traced the principal features of the exterior and interior of old St. Paul's, and a few words may be said of the body who governed the Cathedral.

Bishop Stubbs, in the remarkable Preface which he added to the Master of the Rolls' edition of the *Historical Works of Ralph de Diceto*, Dean of London, at the end of the twelfth century, has given a vivid picture of the ecclesiastical greatness of London during the reigns of Henry II. and Richard I. Ralph was the friend of Fitz-Stephen, the biographer of Becket, and before he became dean he had held the office of archdeacon.

Stubbs writes: 'The fact that the Cathedral of Canterbury was in the hands of a monastic chapter left St. Paul's at the head of the secular clergy of southern England. It was an educational centre too, where young statesmen spent their leisure in something like self-culture. London with its 40,000 inhabitants had 120 churches all looking to the Cathedral as their mother. The resident canons had to exercise a magnificent hospitality, carefully prescribed in ancient Statutes; twice a year each of them had to entertain the whole staff of the Cathedral and to invite the Bishop, the Mayor, the sheriffs, aldermen, justices and great men of the Court.'

The dean was a capable head, and his government stands out in history as one of the most successful during a very difficult period.

'Early in 1187 Ralph lost his old friend and patron, Bishop Foliot, and the See of London was not filled up for nearly three years. Within a few weeks after Foliot's death he had to receive the Archbishop of Canterbury, Baldwin, who visited the church on mid-Lent Sunday, and he took advantage of the opportunity to obtain from him an injunction forbidding the persons who were in charge of the temporalities of the See to interfere with the spiritual officers in the discharge of their duties.'

DOORWAY, ST. HELEN'S, BISHOPSGATE.

How important a body the Chapter of St. Paul's really was may be inferred from the remarkable fact stated by Serjeant Pulling in his work on *The Order of the Coif* that among the canons in the reign of Henry III. were as many as ten of the Judges at Westminster Hall.

The early history of the parishes of London is one of great difficulty and complexity. Although some of the parishes must be of great antiquity, we have little authentic information respecting them before the Conquest. The dedications of many of the churches indicate their great age, but the constant fires in London not only destroyed the buildings but also the records within the buildings. The original churches appear to have been very small, as may be judged from their number. It is not easy, however, to understand how it was that when the parishes were first formed so small an area was attached to each. Mr. Loftie is of opinion that there is no proof that London was divided into more than three or four parishes until the time of Alfred, or, indeed, till much later.[370]

ST. HELEN'S, BISHOPSGATE.

He has written a very instructive chapter on 'the Church in London' in his *London* (Historic Towns, 1887), but he is not able to give any very definite information. Moreover, he doubts whether it is wise to take for granted the early dedications of, for instance, such churches as are named in honour of Sts. Alphage, Magnus and Olave, or of Sts. Ethelburga and Osyth.

The parish church of which we have the most authentic notice before the Conquest is St. Helen's, Bishopsgate, in existence many years before the Priory of the Nuns of St. Helen's was founded. In 1010 the remains of St. Edmund, King and Martyr, were removed from Edmundsbury in order that they might not fall into the hands of the Danes, and deposited in the Church of St. Helen, where they remained three years. Many of the London churches were small, but some were of considerable size. When the religious houses were dissolved the churches of some of these became the most important of the parish churches.

The Church of St. Mary le Bow in Cheapside (better known as Bow Church) is named from having been the first in London built on arches of stone, and the Norman Crypt is of great interest. When Wren built his church he used these arches of the old churches to support his own superstructure. This crypt also gives its name to the Court of Arches which was held here.

In the *Liber Albus* there is a chapter on the periodical visits of the Mayor to various churches on certain saints' days, such as to St. Thomas's at the Feast of All Saints (November 1), to St. Peter's on Cornhill on the Monday in the Feast of Pentecost, and to St. Bartholomew's and St. Michael le Quern on other occasions.[371]

The position of the parish priest was a good one in the eyes of the parishioners, who looked up to him as a friend, and resented the interference with his duties by monks and chantry priests. Among the parish priests the highest rank was conceded to the rector of St. Peter's, Cornhill. The mediæval writers, who are mostly vituperative when speaking of monks and friars, have little but good to say of the parson.

The great evil of lay rectorship, which has done so much to injure the Church, was largely introduced by the monasteries.

BOW CHURCH CRYPT.

Bishop Stubbs, in his Introduction to the Historical Works of Ralph de Diceto, writes: 'S. Paul's stood at the head of the religious life of London, and by its side, at some considerable interval, however, S. Martin's-le-Grand, S. Bartholomew's, Smithfield, and the great and ancient foundation of Trinity, Aldgate.'[372]

CHURCH OF ST. BARTHOLOMEW THE GREAT.

Besides the Chapter of St. Paul's, there were several other bodies of secular canons. One of these was at the Collegiate Church of St. Martin-le-Grand, within Aldersgate, which church was founded about A.D. 1056, and its privileges confirmed by William the Conqueror. It had special rights as a royal free chapel, and its privileges of sanctuary were given by Henry VIII. to the Abbot and Convent of Westminster. Others were the College of St. Michael, Crooked Lane, founded by William Walworth in 1380; Barking College, Holmes's College, and several other colleges in London, besides the Collegiate Chapel of St. Stephen, Westminster.

The canons regular of the Order of St. Austin occupied the Priory of Christ Church or Holy Trinity, the Priory of St. Bartholomew in Smithfield; the Priory of St. Mary Overy, in Southwark, and many hospitals.

These canons were less strict than monks, but lived under one roof, had a common dormitory and refectory. They were well shod, well clothed, and well fed. Monks always shaved, but canons wore beards, and caps on their heads.

The chief rule of the canons regular was that of St. Augustine (or Austin), Bishop of Hippo, A.D. 395. The Order was little known until the tenth or eleventh centuries, and was not brought to England until after the Norman Conquest, and the designation of Austin canons was not adopted until some years afterwards.

The Priory of Christ Church or the Holy Trinity within Aldgate was a house of the first importance in London, and the Pope absolved it from all jurisdiction. Norman, the first prior, was the first canon regular of his Order in England.

The priory was founded in 1108 by Queen Maud, and in 1125 the land and soke of Cnichten Gild (now Portsoken Ward) were assigned to it. The prior became an alderman of London by reason of possessing the soke without the port or gate called Aldgate, an honour continued to his successors till the dissolution of the religious houses, when the church was surrendered and the site of the priory granted by Henry VIII. to Sir Thomas Audley, Lord Chancellor.

The great Benedictine monastery of Black Monks was situated at Westminster, away from the city, as was usual. This was the only monastic house subject to the rule of St. Benedict in the neighbourhood of London, but the houses of nuns, of which there were many dotted over the suburbs of London, were governed by the rule of St. Benedict. Among these may be mentioned the nunneries of Barking, Clerkenwell, Halliwell at the eastern extremity of Finsbury Fields, St. Helen's, Bishopgate, Kilburn and Stratford at Bow.

As time proceeded there was a widespread desire for a stricter rule among the monks, and reforms of the Benedictine rule were instituted at Cluni (A.D. 910), Chartreux (about 1080), and Citeaux (1098). All these reforms were represented in London.

Cluniac Order.—This reform was begun by Bernon, Abbot of Gigni, in Burgundy, and perfected by Odo, Abbot of Cluni. The first charter of the Order was dated A.D. 910. The Order was first brought to England by William, Earl of Warren, son-in-law to William the Conqueror, who built the first house at Lewes, in Sussex, about 1077. The Priory of Bermondsey, in Surrey, was founded by Aylwin Child, citizen of London, about 1082. The manor of Bermondsey and other revenues were granted by William Rufus. The original priories were subject to the heads of the parent foreign houses, but John Attilburgh, prior of Bermondsey, having procured the erection of his priory into an abbacy, himself became the first of the abbots in 1399.

If we are to believe the word of the satirist, we may judge that the rule of the Cluniac Order was hard, for we are told that—

'When you wish to sleep they awake you,'

and

'When you wish to eat they make you fast.'

There were cells attached to the Cluniac house of Bermondsey at Aldersgate, Cripplegate and Holborn.

Carthusians.—Bruno first instituted the Order at Chartreux, in the diocese of Grenoble in France, about 1080. The rule was confirmed by Pope Alexander III. about 1174. This was the most strict of any of the religious Orders. The monks never ate flesh, and were obliged to fast on bread, water and salt one day in every week. No one was permitted to go out of the bounds of the monastery except the priors and procurators or proctors, and they only upon the necessary affairs of their houses. When the Order was brought to England in 1178 the first house was started at Witham, in Somersetshire. In all there were nine houses of the Order in England. One of these was the Charterhouse of London, which was not founded until 1371 by Sir Walter Manny, K.G.

Until Henry II. founded the Carthusian house at Witham it is said that there was no such thing known in England as a monk's cell, as we understand the term. It was a peculiarity of the Carthusian Order, and when it was first introduced it was regarded as a startling novelty for any privacy or anything approaching solitude to be tolerated in a monastery. The Carthusian system never found much favour in England.

Cistercians.—The Cistercian Order was named after Cistertium or Cîteaux, in the bishopric of Chalons in Burgundy, where it was founded in 1098 by Robert, Abbot of Molesme, in that province. St. Bernard was a great promoter of the Order, and founded an abbey at Clairvaux about 1116, and after him the members of the Order were sometimes named Bernardines.

It was usual to plant these monasteries in solitary and uncultivated places, and no other house, even of their own Order, was allowed to be built within a certain distance of the original establishment. This makes it surprising to learn that there were two separate houses of this Order in the near neighbourhood of London.

A branch of the Order came to England about 1128, and their first house was founded at Waverley in Surrey. Very shortly after (about 1134) the Abbey of Stratford Langthorne, in Essex, was founded by William de Montfichet, who endowed it with all his lordship in West Ham.

It was not until two centuries afterwards that the second Cistercian house in the immediate neighbourhood of London was founded. This was the Abbey of St. Mary Graces, East Minster or New Abbey, without the walls of London, which Edward III. instituted in 1350 after a severe scourge of plague (the so-called Black Death.)

The two great military Orders—the Knights Hospitallers of St. John of Jerusalem and the Templars—followed the Augustinian rule, and both were settled in London. The Knights Hospitallers were founded about 1092 by the merchants of Amalfi, in Italy, for the purpose of affording hospitality to pilgrims in the Holy Land. The Hospital or Priory of St. John was founded in 1100 by Jordan Briset and his wife, Muriel, outside the northern wall of London, and the original village of Clerkenwell grew up around the buildings of the knights. A few years after this the Brethren of the Temple of Solomon at Jerusalem, or Knights of the Temple, came into being at the Holy City, and they settled first on the south side of Holborn, near Southampton Buildings. They removed to Fleet Street or the New Temple in 1184, when, as Spenser terms it, 'they decayd through pride,' and the Order after much persecution was suppressed in England, as it had been in other countries, by command of the Pope. The house in Fleet Street was given in 1313 by Edward II. to Aymer de Valence, Earl of Pembroke, at whose death, in 1323, the property

THE TEMPLE CHURCH—THE ROUND.

passed to the Knights of St. John, who leased the New Temple to the lawyers, still the occupants of the district.

The Templars wore a long flowing white mantle with a red cross on the left breast. The Knights Hospitallers originally wore a black robe with a cross, but subsequently, when the Order was reconstructed on the model of the Templars, they wore a red mantle with a white cross on the shoulder. After Palestine was lost the original body passed (1) to Acre, (2) to Cyprus, (3) to Rhodes, and (4) to Malta.

The Templars left their beautiful church to continue for centuries one of the most interesting architectural relics of a past age. The buildings of the Knights Hospitallers at Clerkenwell passed through more vicissitudes, and when the religious houses were suppressed by Henry VIII. these were mostly destroyed. The gateway which was completed in 1504 by Prior Docwra still stands, but no portion of the church or other buildings remain above ground.

Friars

The enthusiasm which brought the great religious movement after the Conquest and produced the numerous monastic institutions of the country had cooled by the beginning of the thirteenth century, when the remarkable evangelical revival instituted almost simultaneously by St. Dominic and St. Francis swept over Europe.

The distinctive characteristics which at first marked them off from the monks were poverty and care for others. The monks lived apart from the world in order to attend first to their own souls, while the friars placed care for others first of all duties. They preached to and visited the masses; hence, instead of living in retired spots, they settled in the heart of the cities. In their humility they called themselves brothers rather than fathers, but in course of time they fell far short of the ideals of their founders. Their property increased, and their houses grew to be as rich as those of the monks, and in consequence they became singularly unpopular. Mr. Trevelyan writes in his *Age of Wycliffe* that, while the monks were despised by the reformer, the friars were hated.

Black Friars.—The Spaniard, St. Dominic, founded the Order of Preaching Friars at the beginning of the thirteenth century. Their rule, which was chiefly that of St. Augustine, was approved of by Pope Innocent III. in the Lateran Council, A.D. 1215, by word of mouth and by the Bull of Pope Honorius III., A.D. 1216. They were called Dominicans from their founder, Preaching Friars from their office to preach and convert heretics, and Black Friars from their garments. In France they were known as Jacobins from having their first house in the Rue St. Jacques in Paris. This name gained a portentous meaning in the eighteenth century from the French Revolutionists who met in the disused friary. At first the friars used the same habit as the Austin Canons, but about the year 1219 they took another, viz., a white cassock with a white hood over it, and when they went abroad, a black cloak with a black hood over their white vestments. They came to England in 1221, and their first house was at Oxford. Shortly after this they came to London, settled in Holborn near Lincoln's Inn, where they remained for more than fifty years. In 1276 they removed to the neighbourhood of Baynard Castle, where they erected a magnificent house with the help of royal, clerical and other noble benefactors which has given a name to a London district that it still retains. The place is thus described by Stevens, the monastic historian: 'This monastery enjoyed all the privileges and immunities that any religious house had; and having a very large extent of ground within its liberty, the same was shut up with four gates, and all the inhabitants within it were subject to none but the King, the superior of the monasteries and justices of that precinct; so that neither the Mayor nor the sheriffs, nor any other officers of the City of London, had the least jurisdiction or authority therein. All which liberties the inhabitants preserved some time after the suppression of the monastery.' Thomas Lord Wake is said to have intended to bring Dominican nuns into England, and he had the King's license for this purpose, but he does not appear to have carried out his intention. The nuns of Dartford, in Kent, are supposed to have been of this Order at one time.

Grey Friars.—The Italian, St. Francis, was the founder of this Order, whose rule he drew up in 1209. It was approved of by Pope Innocent III. in 1210, and by the Lateran Council in 1215. His followers were called Franciscans from their founder, Grey Friars from their clothing, and Minor Friars from their humility.

Nine Grey Friars landed at Dover in the eighth year of Henry III. (1223-1224), five of them settled at Canterbury, and there founded the first house of the Order in England. The remaining four established themselves in London, lodging for fifteen days with the Dominicans in Holborn. These four, we learn from a Cottonian MS. (Vitellius, F. xii., 13, fol. 45) were (1) Richard Pugworth, an Englishman, priest and preacher; (2) Richard Senonef, English, clerk acolyte, a youth; (3) Henry Detrews, by nation a Lombard, lay brother; (4) Monachetus, also a lay brother.

These four men founded the great London house of Grey Friars. They removed to Cornhill, where they erected cells, made converts, and acquired the goodwill of the Mayor and citizens. John Ewin, mercer, appropriated to the use of the friars a piece of ground within Newgate. Here a noble building was erected by the help of numerous distinguished persons, which contained a church, a chapter house, a dormitory, a refectory, an infirmary, etc. The district was long known as Greyfriars, and afterwards as Christ Church or Christ's Hospital.

The habit of the friars was a loose garment of a grey colour reaching down to their ankles, with a cowl of the same, and a cloak over it when they went abroad. They girded themselves with cords and went barefoot.

In connection with the Franciscans were the nuns of the Order of St. Clare, founded at Assisi by St. Clare about 1212. The nuns observed St. Francis's rule and wore the same coloured habit as the Franciscan Friars. They were called Poor Clares and also Minoresses.

About the year 1293 Blanche, Queen of Navarre, wife to Edward, Earl of Lancaster, Leicester and Derby, founded a house for the Minoresses on the east side of the street leading from the Tower to Aldgate without the walls of the city. This street is still known as the Minories. There were only three other houses of this Order in England, viz.: at Waterbeche and Denny in Cambridgeshire, and Brusyard in Suffolk.

Austin Friars.—The history of the foundation of the Friars Eremites of the Order of St. Augustine has not been given with any fulness, and its origin is somewhat uncertain. They came to England from Italy about 1250, and a house in Broad Street ward was founded by Humphrey Bohun, Earl of Hereford and Essex, in the year 1253. The habit of the Austin Friars was a white garment and scapulary when they were in the house, but in the choir and when they went abroad they had over the former a sort of cowl and a large hood, both black; round their waist they had a black leather girdle fastened with an ivory bone.[373]

White Friars.—The origin of the Friars of the Blessed Virgin of Mount Carmel is not very clear. Their rule, which was chiefly that of St. Basil, is said to have been given them by Albert, Patriarch of Jerusalem about 1205, and to have been confirmed by Pope Honorius III. in 1224. They were driven out of Palestine by the Saracens about 1238, and they then sought refuge in Europe. They were brought into England by John Vasey and Richard Gray, and had their first houses at Hulne in Northumberland and Ailesford in Kent. At the latter place they held their first European charter A.D. 1245.

The London house of the Carmelites or White Friars was founded in 1241 by Sir Richard Grey on land situated between Fleet Street and the Thames which was given by Edward I. The garments of the friars at first were white, but having been obliged by the infidels to change them to parti-coloured ones, they continued these for fifty years after their coming into England, but about the year 1290 they returned to the use of white again.[374]

Of the four chief Orders of mendicant friars, the Carmelites ranked last, and in official processions had to give place to the Dominicans, Franciscans and Austin Friars.

The district which originally contained the house of the White Friars continues still to be known by the old name. After the dissolution of the religious houses, the privileges of sanctuary were still allowed to the inhabitants, and in consequence the place, generally known as Alsatia, gained a most unenviable notoriety. Other places in London obtained an evil repute from the same cause, but Whitefriars was far beyond all others in disgraceful associations. It is known from old records that the bad repute of the district dates back to a period long before the suppression of the friary.

From a Close Roll of the 20th Edw. III., it appears that persons of ill-repute had for a considerable time made their abode so close to the friary that the friars could not celebrate divine service in their church in consequence of the continual clamours and outcries by which the district was disturbed, and the Mayor and aldermen of London were ordered, in the King's name, for the tranquility of the prior and brethren, to remove the nuisance.

Mr. Trevelyan writes: 'Twenty years before Wycliffe's attack was made Fitz-Ralph, Bishop of Armagh, had laid a famous indictment against the four Orders before the Pope at Avignon. It made a great stir at the time, but came to nothing, for the friars were under the Pope's special protection. The bishop chiefly complained of their competition with his secular clergy in the matter of confession and absolution.[375]

Besides the four chief Orders, several other Orders of friars were settled in London. First in importance of these were the Crutched Friars, from the cross forming part of the staff carried by them, which was styled a crutch. This was afterwards given up, and a cross of red cloth was placed upon the breast of the gown. The Order is said to have been instituted by Gerard, Prior of St. Mary of Morella at Bologna, and confirmed in 1169 by Pope Alexander III., who brought them under St. Austin's rule. They came to England in 1244, and had their first house at Colchester. It was not until about 1298 that these friars came to London, and the house in the parish of St. Olave, Hart Street, was founded by Ralph Hosier and William Sabernes. The memory of the friary is kept alive in the name of the street that marks its site.

Other Orders in London were the Friars of the Penance of Jesus Christ, or *de Sacco*, and the Friars de Areno.

The Friars of the Sac, according to Stow, first settled in a house near Aldersgate, outside the gate. This was about the year 1257. When the Jews were banished from England by Edward I., these friars were given the synagogue on the south side of Lothbury, at the north corner of the old Jewry.

The tenements which the prior and friars held in the street 'called Colcherdistrete' were in the parishes of St. Olave in the Jewry and of St. Margaret de Lothebury.

The friars of the Order of St. Mary de Areno were settled at Westminster at a house near Charing Cross, given to them by Sir William de Arnaud or Amand, 51 Henry III., and here the small house remained until the death of Hugh de Ebor, the last friar, 10 Edw. II.

Bishop Stubbs refers to a cemetery near St. Clement's Danes, which once belonged to the Pied Friars, a small order of mendicants which had been suppressed in 1278.

In the revised edition of Dugdale's *Monasticon*, by Caley, Ellis and Bandinel, there is a notice of the house of the Fratres de Pica or Pied Friars at Norwich, from Blomefield's *History of Norfolk*, but no mention is made of any house in London. Tanner says that there is no mention of these friars in any public record, and Taylor, in his *Index Monasticus*, gives no new information concerning them. Blomefield says that the friars were called from their outward garment, which was black and white like a magpie.

At Hounslow there was a House of Trinitarian or Maturine Friars for the Redemption of Captives. The earliest record known of this priory is a charter dated 1296.

Besides the religious houses, there were during the Middle Ages many hermitages over the country, and several of these were to be found in London. One was in Monkwell Street, Cripplegate, which was founded by the widow of Sir Eymer de Valence, Earl of Pembroke, who was killed in a tournament in 1324. This was Mary de Castillon, daughter of Guy, Count of St. Pol, third wife of the earl, and the foundress of Pembroke Hall, Cambridge, who established the hermitage for the good of the soul of her husband.

London was so full of religious houses, both within and without the walls, that when the great dissolution took place in Henry VIII.'s reign, large portions of the town were left desolate. Doubtless the time had come for this great revolution, or, otherwise, even that King could never have carried it through.

The popular feeling which held these great establishments in disfavour had gradually grown. Still the number of those who were dependent upon the religious houses was very considerable, and great evils followed the dissolution. Multitudes were thrown out of their regular employment, and the poor who were dependent upon the alms bestowed upon them at the gates of the monasteries had to be considered and provided for in some other way. The difficulties of this position certainly formed one of the causes of the institution of the Poor Law in the reign of Henry's daughter Elizabeth.

Most of the relics of the various religious houses which occupied so large a portion of London and its environs have been entirely swept away.

In the eighteenth and the beginning of the nineteenth centuries many remains existed. There were then vestiges of St. Helen's Priory, and the old hall of the Nunnery was not pulled down until 1799. Relics of Bermondsey Abbey were standing in 1807.

THE CRYPT, ST. JOHN'S, CLERKENWELL.

The grand Crypt built soon after the foundation of the house of the Priory of St. John at Clerkenwell, which was added to and afterwards made to form an undercroft to the choir, is now one of the most interesting of the remains of mediæval buildings in London. It is below the Church of St. John, Clerkenwell, and has been restored with loving care to much of its original beauty. Other portions of the old buildings of the Priory are to be seen in the cellars of some of the houses round about.

The position of the old Charterhouse buildings can still be traced, although little of the old monastery exists, but the east and south walls of the Chapel and Washhouse Court can be seen. The latter was built by the monks to accommodate the lay brothers who acted as servants to the convent. The walls of the monastic refectories surround the present Brothers' Library. Beneath this is the Monks' Cellar.

The friaries situated within the walls of old London have left little but their names to tell the Londoner of to-day of their existence. Still even here something of the past remains. The Church of Austin Friars is left to us, and the position of the choir of the great Franciscan house of Grey Friars is marked by the present Christ Church, Newgate Street. Some traces of the buildings of the Whitefriars have also been found underground.

Sanctuary.—One of the privileges of the Middle Ages, which continued on into comparatively modern times, was that of sanctuary, and in its belated form this caused many gross scandals. There are numerous stories connected with the College of St. Martin's-le-Grand, which was under the jurisdiction of the Abbot of Westminster. One of these relates to Richard III. and Lady Anne. When the Duke of Gloucester desired to marry Anne, the betrothed of the late Edward Prince of Wales, son of Henry VI., her brother-in-law Clarence objected and hid her away. Richard discovered her in London, disguised as a kitchen-maid, and placed her in sanctuary at St. Martin's-le-Grand.[376]

In 1416 a man was sentenced to the pillory for slandering an alderman, but he escaped and found sanctuary at the monastery of St. Peter's, Westminster.[377]

Mr. G. M. Trevelyan, in his work on the *Age of Wycliffe*, gives a full account of the great scandal which occurred in 1378, when two prisoners escaped from the Tower and sought sanctuary in Westminster Abbey. The governor of the Tower, with his soldiers, entered the nave and attempted to drag one of the prisoners, who was attending Mass, out of sanctuary. He fled for his life, and his pursuers chased him twice round the choir. He was stabbed to death, and one of the attendants of the church, interfering to save him, was killed in the scuffle.

Archbishop Sudbury excommunicated the governor of the Tower (Sir Alan Buschall) and all his aiders and abettors. Richard II. ordered the reading of the excommunication to be stopped and the church to be reconsecrated. The abbot refused to allow the place to be hallowed, and the services ceased for a while. There was now an open quarrel between Church and State, which continued till the Parliament met at Gloucester in October, 'when the whole question of sanctuary was brought up in all its issues.'

Mr. Trevelyan sums up the case in these words: 'In vain Wycliffe argued, in vain the Commons petitioned and the Lords hectored. From all the mountains of talk in the discussions at Gloucester there came forth the most absurd legislative mouse in the shape of a Statute passed at Westminster by the next Parliament in the spring of 1379. By this Act the fraudulent debtor taking sanctuary was to be summoned at the door of the church once a week for 31 days. If at the end of that time he refused to appear, judgment was to go against him by default, and his goods, even if they had been given away by collusion, might be seized by his creditors. This mild measure, which was scarcely an interference with the right of sanctuary itself, was accepted even by the staunchest adherents of the Church.'

If a felon succeeded in taking sanctuary in a church or other privileged place before capture, he was free from the clutches of the law for the space of forty days. He was allowed to be supplied with food, but he was sufficiently guarded to prevent his escape. If he elected to abjure the realm an oath was administered to him.[378]

There seem to have been special privileges of sanctuary in the city, for we learn that at the end of the thirteenth century it was ordered by the aldermen that no robber, homicide, nor other fugitive in the churches should be watched. This ordinance was for the purpose of giving a fugitive a chance of escape out of sanctuary. In 1321 a royal pardon was granted to the city for neglecting to keep watch on those who had fled for sanctuary to the city churches. This was granted, however, on the distinct understanding that in future a watch was to be kept on such fugitives in the same manner as in other parts of the realm.[379]

In 1334 the Mayor was roundly taken to task, and made to do penance by the Archbishop for allowing a felon to escape from the Church of Allhallows', Gracechurch.[380]

The sanctuary men were marked by a badge representing cross keys.

Education.—Mediæval London was well supplied with facilities for education. We know that there were many schools in various parts of the city, although we still require more definite information. The Church supplied the public well with schools, although for a time these fell into decay, and then it was that lay schools came into existence.

Bishop Stubbs writes: 'Over against the many grievances which modern thought has alleged against the unlearned ages which passed before the invention of printing it ought to be set to the credit of mediæval society that clerkship was never despised or made unnecessarily difficult of acquisition. The sneer of Walter Map, who declared that in his days the villains were attempting to educate their ignoble and degenerate offspring in the liberal arts proves that even in the twelfth century the way was open. Richard II. rejected the proposition that the villains should be forbidden to send their children to the schools to learn "clergie"; and even at a time when the supply of labour ran so low that no man who was not worth twenty shillings a year in land or rent was allowed to apprentice his child to a craft, a full and liberal exception was made in favour of learning; "every man or woman"—the words occur in the Petition and Statute of Artificers passed in 1406—"of what state or condition that he be, shall be free to set their son or daughter to take learning at any school that pleaseth them within the realm." ' Again: 'Schools were by no means uncommon things; there were schools in all cathedrals; monasteries and colleges were everywhere, and wherever there was a monastery or a college there was a school. Towards the close of the Middle Ages, notwithstanding many causes for depression, there was much vitality in the schools.'[381]

The larger English abbeys about the country not only had schools within their own precincts, but others dependent upon them in the neighbouring towns.

Fitz-Stephen, in his description of London as preserved in the city's *Liber Custumarum* (vol. i. p. 5), particularises the Church of St. Martin-le-Grand as one of the principal churches of London which had ancient and prerogative schools,[382] the others being St. Paul's and Holy Trinity, Aldgate. In other texts of Fitz-Stephen's work the names of the churches are not mentioned, and Stow, overlooking the text in the city archives, gives the three schools as attached to St. Paul's, St. Peter's Westminster, and St. Saviour's.[383]

Fitz-Stephen's patron, St. Thomas of Canterbury, received his early education at one of the London schools after leaving the school of the canons regular at Merton, and before proceeding to the university.

In 1447 four parish priests, in a petition to Parliament, begged the Commons to consider the great number of grammar schools 'that sometime were in diverse parts of the realm beside those that were in London, and how few there be in these days.' They asked leave to appoint schoolmasters in their parishes, to be removed at their discretion. King Henry VI. granted the petition, but subjected the priests' discretion to the advice of the Ordinary. During this King's reign nine grammar schools were opened in London alone.

CHARING CROSS.
(From the Crace Collection, British Museum.)

CHAPTER XII

London from Mediæval to Modern Times

MEDIÆVAL London was almost entirely within the walls; but outside the walls, to the west, there was a connecting line of mansions on the river front leading to the village of Charing and on to Westminster, which is almost of equal antiquity with London itself. When the body of Queen Eleanor arrived at its last stage the funeral procession stopped a fair way from Westminster Abbey. One might have expected that the body would have remained under the shadow of its last resting-place, and we are, therefore, led to inquire why the village of Charing was chosen. The only answer to the question that can be given is, that here, on the site of Northumberland House, now occupied by Northumberland Avenue, there then stood a Hospital and Chapel of St. Mary, belonging to the Priory of Rouncevall (Roncesvalles), or De Rosida Valle, in the diocese of Pampelon, in Navarre. At the death of Eleanor this house was a comparatively recent establishment, having been founded by William Marshal, Earl of Pembroke, in the reign of Henry III., but it probably afforded sufficient accommodation for the funeral procession for one night. The house was suppressed as an alien priory in the reign of Henry V., but restored in that of Edward IV. for a fraternity. In the Year Books of Henry VII. the master, wardens, brethren and sisters of Rouncevall are mentioned, and these continued until the general suppression.

The Cross, which gives its name to the place, was erected in the years 1291-1294, and is supposed to have been the handsomest of the series. As good a copy of the original as our imperfect information allows is to be seen within the railings of the South-Eastern Railway terminus. Westminster is of unknown antiquity, and was long known, from its wild growth of underwood, as Thorney, before the Abbey and the Palace arose to give the place a name which marked its position in relation to London and St. Paul's. There is but little authoritative history before Edward the Confessor and the consecration of the Abbey Church in 1065, but the history since that time is so considerable, and of so important a character, that it is impossible to do more than refer in these few words to what is universally acknowledged by all Englishmen to be the most hallowed building in the country.

On the opposite shore of the Thames is Lambeth, where is situated the Manor House of the Archbishops of Canterbury (now called Lambeth

Palace). The site was originally given to the See of Rochester by the Countess Goda, sister of Edward the Confessor, and wife of Eustace, Count of Boulogne, but in the year 1197 the Bishop of Rochester made an exchange with the Archbishop of Canterbury of this place for other property, and Lambeth has ever since been the London residence of the Archbishops. From here we pass over Lambeth Marsh to Southwark, a place whose history has been intimately associated with that of the City of London, and is now an integral part of the county.

The chief glory of the borough is the grand church of the Augustinian Priory of St. Mary Overy, dating from the beginning of the twelfth century, and now known as St. Saviour's.

Southwark has been from the earliest times the chief thoroughfare to and from London and the southern counties and towns, and the cities of the Continent. From this cause it was for centuries the quarter for famous old inns, beginning in order of importance with the Bear at the Bridge Foot, the Tabard of Chaucer, and following on with the King's Head, the White Hart, and the George—a portion of the latter hostelry only remaining to the present day.

"The Gatehouse & Church Tower
Lambeth Palace"

Southwark was also notorious for its prisons—the King's Bench, the Marshalsea, the White Lion, the Borough Compter and the Clink. The last-named was on the Bankside, so intimately associated from the earliest times with the rough sports of the Londoners, and in Elizabeth's reign the chief home of the dramatic displays of that great period. The "Bank" was then a long straggling street, extending from the manor of Paris Garden on the west to the liberty of the Clink on the east. Near Paris Garden was the Falcon Inn, which was once supposed to have been the resort of Shakespeare. This apparently is an error, for at the time of the great dramatist's death there appears to have been no inns on the Bankside. Little or nothing actually exists now that was there in the sixteenth century, but the contour of the street and nearly every name have lasted in their integrity, and probably will last for many a long year more.

Although during the reigns of the Tudor sovereigns the Renascence became triumphant, the men and women of London still continued to live in a town which retained its mediæval characteristics.

Two striking scenes in the history of London during the reign of Mary I. may be alluded to here.

When the Queen made known her intention of marrying Philip of Spain, the discontent of the nation found vent in the rising of Sir Thomas Wyat, and the city had to prepare itself against attack. Wyat took possession of Southwark, and expected to have been admitted into London, but finding the gate of the Bridge closed against him and the drawbridge cut down he marched to Kingston. Having restored the bridge there, which had been destroyed, he proceeded towards London. In consequence of the break down of some of his guns he imprudently halted at Turnham Green. Had he not done this he might have obtained possession of the city. He planted his ordnance on Hay Hill, and then marched by St. James's Palace and Charing Cross. Here he was attacked by Sir John Gage with a thousand men, but he repulsed them, and reached Ludgate without further opposition. He was disappointed at the resistance which was made, and after musing a while "upon a stall over against the Bell Savadge gate," he turned back. His retreat was cut off, and he surrendered to Sir Maurice Berkeley.

To picture another striking scene, we must move from the west side of London to the north. Outside Cripplegate was built a barbican or watch-tower, as an outwork for observance, and the little village, with its Fore Street, which grew up outside the walls, was sheltered behind it. The care of this important position was naturally given to trustworthy persons. Edward III. appointed Robert Ufford, Earl of Suffolk, Keeper of the Barbican, and from him it descended, in course of time, to Catherine, daughter of William Lord Willoughby de Eresby, who married, firstly, Charles Brandon, Duke of Suffolk; and secondly, Richard Bertie. Bertie and his wife were Protestants, and in Queen Mary's reign their lives were in such danger that they were forced to arrange in secrecy for their flight.

Between four and five o'clock in the morning of 1st January 1554-1555 the Duchess began her adventurous journey in a thick fog. She could place no confidence in the bulk of her dependants, and there was great difficulty in arranging for company and baggage. As she was leaving, one Atkinson, a herald, issued from the house bearing a torch in his hand, and evidently bent on discovering the cause of the unusual bustle at this early hour. Fearing to be discovered as she stood up under a gateway, she moved on quietly and left her baggage at the gatehouse. Finding that the herald still followed, she bade her servants to hasten onwards to Lion Key, where she proposed to embark. Taking with her only two servants and her child, "she stept into Garter House, hard by."[384] She dared not pass into the city through Cripplegate but walked on to Moorgate. Thence she proceeded across the town to the port of embarkation. Eventually she joined her husband, who had preceded her, in Flanders. Soon after her escape she gave birth to a son at Wesel. He was named Peregrine, from the circumstance of his being born in a foreign land and during the wandering of his parents. This name was long continued in the family. The child grew up to be one of Queen Elizabeth's greatest generals, popularly known as the "brave Lord Willoughby."

"But the bravest man in battel
Was brave Lord Willoughby."

There is a special fascination to us now in a picture of Elizabethan London, for with its history are bound up some of the most interesting incidents in the lives of the statesmen and other great men of the spacious days of the great Queen; and have we not Shakespeare and Ben Jonson among those who have portrayed the various places for us.

London has always appealed to the imagination of the adventurous country youth to be the home of golden promise. If he can only get there he believes that his successful career has commenced, but it appears that in Elizabeth's reign there was pretty much the same difficulty in obtaining employment as there is now. This is illustrated by a curious account of the early life of John Sadler, a native of Stratford-on-Avon, and one of Shakespeare's contemporaries, which has come down to us. "He joined himself to the carrier, and came to London, where he had never been before, and sold his horse in Smithfield, and having no acquaintance in London to recommend him or assist him he went from street to street, and house to house, asking if they wanted an apprentice, and though he met with many discouraging scorns and a thousand denials he went on till he lighted on one Mr. Brokesbank, a grocer in Bucklersbury, who, though he long denied him for want of sureties for his fidelity, and because the money he had (but ten pounds) was so disproportionate to what he used to receive with apprentices, yet upon his discreet account he gave of himself and the motives which put him upon that course, and promise to compensate with diligent and faithful service whatever else was short of his expectation, he ventured to receive him upon trial, in which he so well approved himself that he accepted him into his service, to which he bound him for eight years."

The outdoor life of his time, with the men and women who frequented the streets, is brought vividly before our eyes in Ben Jonson's plays. The useful and useless members of society pass across the stage. The water-carriers who congregate around the conduits are represented by Cob in *Every Man in His Humour*.

Before Sir Hugh Myddelton made the New River and brought to men's houses, all water that was wanted had to be fetched from the conduits. The men who supplied the town drew off the water into large wooden tankards, broad at the bottom, but narrow at the top, which held about three gallons. This vessel was borne upon the shoulder, and to keep the carrier dry two towels were fastened over him, one to fall in front and the other to cover his back.

The narrowness of the old London streets is strikingly shown in *The Devil is an Ass*, where the lady and her lover speak gentle nothings to each other from the windows of two contiguous buildings.

All the fashions of his time—the rapier fighting of the gallants, the smoking madness of all classes at a time when tobacco was supposed to be the panacea for all the ills of human nature, the custom of garnishing conversation with oaths—are introduced into the books of Ben Jonson. The poet's love of good liquor and social intercourse made him a frequenter of inns. His acquaintance with the two rival taverns of Cheapside—the Mermaid and the Mitre—must have commenced early, because the names of both occur in the first quarto of *Every Man in His Humour* (1601); in the later folio edition the Mitre is changed to the Star and the Mermaid to the Windmill. The ever-memorable Mermaid was situated on the south side of Cheapside, between Bread Street and Friday Street. From the mention of this tavern in the first draft of *Every Man In His Humour* it may be inferred that Jonson was a frequenter before the famous club, consisting of Shakespeare, Jonson, Beaumont, Fletcher, Carew, Donne, Selden and others, was established by Sir Walter Raleigh in 1603.

The Mitre was a rival house, and some writers tried to write it up at the expense of the Mermaid. Thus Middleton has the following dialogue in his comedy, *Your Five Gallants* (1608):—

"*Goldstone.* Where sup we, gallants?

Pursenet. At Mermaid.

Gold. Sup there who list, I have forsworne the house.

Pur. Faith! I'm indifferent.

Bungler. So are we, gentlemen.

Pur. Name the place, Master Goldstone.

Gold. Why, the Mitre, in my mind, for neat attendance, diligent boys, and—Push! excels it far.

All. Agreed. The Mitre then."

The Windmill, in the old Jewry, which occupies so prominent a position in the revised edition of *Every Man in His Humour*, was a house with a long history. It was first of all a synagogue for the Jews of the neighbourhood; then it was granted by Henry III. to the prior and brethren of the Order of friars called the Fratres de Sacca, and in 1439 it was occupied by Lord

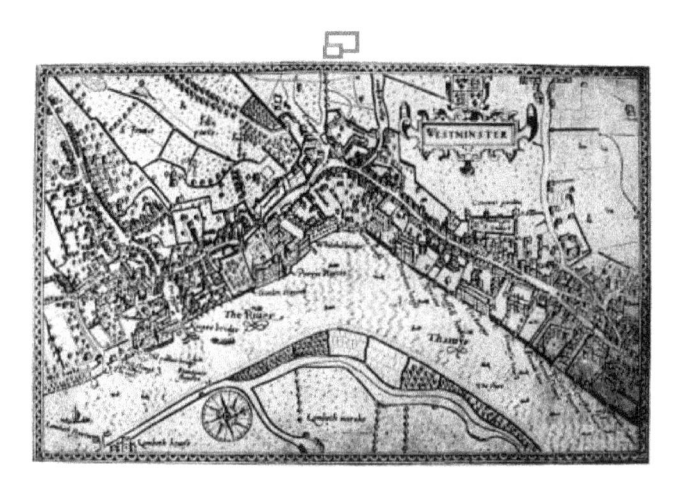

Mayor Robert Large. In 1492 Sir Hugh Clopton, the worthy who built Clopton Bridge at Stratford-on-Avon, kept his mayoralty in the mansion, which, a hundred years afterwards, was turned into a tavern.

The Devil, in Fleet Street, was one of the most famous of the places of entertainment of the time. It is not known when Ben Jonson started the "Apollo" Club here, but it was probably not long before 1616, when the *Devil is an Ass* was acted.

Herrick, in his well-known ode, mentions several other taverns to which Ben and "his sons" resorted:—

"Ah, Ben!
Say how or when
Shall we thy guests
Meet at those lyric feasts
Made at the Sun,
The Dog, the Triple Tun?
Where we such clusters had
As made us nobly wild, not mad;
And yet each verse of thine
Outdid the meal, outdid the frolic wine."

It was in Jonson's day that the suburbs, which (as previously referred to) had long been treated with disfavour, were gradually asserting themselves, and the poet was particularly at home in the understanding of their peculiarities. Of the northern suburbs the fullest mention is to be found in *A Tale of a Tub*, where we read of Totten Court, Kentish Town, Maribone, Kilborne, Islington and Belsize, and the fields near Pancras.

If we look for Hoxton in a modern map of London we shall find it near Old Street, St. Luke's, not far from the centre of the present London, but in Jonson's time it was a country place, cut off from the city by Moorfields. Knowell's house (*Every Man in His Humour*) was at Hogsden, which was then, according to Stow, "a large street with houses on both sides." Master Stephen describes his uncle's property as "Middlesex land," and he himself is called a country gull, in opposition to Master Matthew, the town gull. Ben had reason to remember Hoxton, for it was in the fields close by that he fought and nearly killed Gabriel Spenser. Moorfields remained for several years in an almost impassable condition, but in 1511 regular dykes and bridges of communication over them were made, in order partially to drain the rotten ground.

In the play so frequently referred to we find Turnbull mentioned by Bobadil, among other disreputable places, as one of the "skirts of the town." Turnbull, or, more properly, Turnmill Street, was situated near Clerkenwell Green, and was known as the haunt of ruffians, thieves and disorderly persons. Justice Shallow boasted to Falstaff of the wildness of his youth and the feats he had done in Turnbull Street.

On the west the Oxford Road, commencing at the village of St. Giles, was in the country, and where Stratford Place now stands was a cottage among trees and hedges called the Lord Mayor's Banqueting House, which was used by the city magnates when they hunted at Bayswater and Hyde Park. This is alluded to in *The Devil is an Ass*:—

"But got the gentlewoman to go with me
And carry her bedding to a conduit-head,
Hard by the place towards Tyburn which they call
My Lord Mayor's banqueting house."

"Eastward for Ratcliff!" is a cry in the *Alchemist*. Ratcliff, which Stow remembered as a highway, with fair elm trees on each side, in later times became the synonym of all that is dangerous and disreputable in London streets.

The actor William Kemp, in describing his remarkable morris dance from London to Norwich (1600), writes: "Being past Whitechappel and having left fair London, multitudes of Londoners left not me, eyther to keepe a custome which many holde, that Mile-end is no walke without a recreation at Stratford Bow with cream and cakes, or else for love they beare towards me, or perhaps to make themselves merry if I should chance (as many thought) to give over my morrice within a mile of Mile-end."

Shakespeare lived outside the city walls, and although we cannot exactly tell the position of his houses it is pretty certain that he lived both in the parish of St. Helen, Bishopsgate, and in the Clink on the Bankside.

Stuart London followed Tudor London, but with the death of James I. in 1625 the older history may be said to close, for there was a considerable change during the reign of Charles I. The upper classes moved westward to Lincoln's Inn and Great Queen Street and Covent Garden. The great architect, Inigo Jones, built houses for them in both these districts.

There was a certain stagnation in the movements of the population during the period of the Commonwealth, but at the Restoration of Charles II. a new life came into existence. The exiled Cavaliers returned to their country and found their fathers' houses in the City of London either occupied by others or unfitted for their reception. In consequence, they migrated to a district far from the city. The builders were busy in covering fields with houses, and Pall Mall, where the game of that name had been played, was planned out as a fine street, which it remains to the present day. Lords Clarendon, Burlington and Berkeley erected mansions in Piccadilly, and Lord St. Albans created St. James's Square. Many others followed the example of these leaders of Society, and the upper classes were completely cut off from the city. The contemptuous references to the traders of London, which are first noticed in Elizabeth's reign, became common. The cits were laughed at, and the courtiers poured out a torrent of abuse upon all those who lived in the east.

The Great Fire of 1666 made an enormous change in the topography of London, and caused great misery, but it is supposed to have been a blessing in disguise as it cleared out many a centre of plague and disease.

When we read of the heroism of the homeless Londoner we must feel proud of our ancestors. They had lost everything, but they did not sit down and wring their hands. When the streets were destroyed by fire the river became more than ever a highway, and boats filled with the goods of the sufferers covered the waters. Moorfields formed a handy open space, and soon streets of huts were raised to shelter the homeless families. Wren, England's greatest architect, John Evelyn, the most accomplished man of his time and the model of a Royalist gentleman, and Robert Hooke, the great philosopher, were all three, ready within a few hours of the fire with plans for the rebuilding of the city, but none of the plans were adopted although all had their good points, and Wren's especially would certainly have given us fine avenues and convenient thoroughfares.

The difficulties in carrying out these schemes would no doubt have been very great, and it is useless now to regret that a great opportunity was lost.

Wren and Hooke were appointed to superintend the progress of the work of making London arise anew out of its ashes. The Act of Parliament passed to regulate the work of rebuilding was a very practical, and altogether excellent, statute. In fact, the way in which all concerned in the complicated business of raising a new city worked in unison is worthy of every praise. At the same time that they proceeded with their labours they did not allow the trade and business of the countr

y's

centre to fall out of gear, and this does the greatest credit to all concerned, both governors and governed.

While the burnt town remained a waste there must have been overwhelming inconveniences, but no time was allowed to be lost, and in the end a new city arose infinitely superior in comfort and convenience to that which had gone before, although certainly it was not so picturesque.

Before passing on to take a rapid view of the later periods of London life some mention may be made of a few of the interesting buildings that escaped the fire and have not previously been alluded to in these pages.

Outside the confines of the city to the west grew up from early times a district with many various associations. Curious traditions and odd customs gather round the history of the parish of St. Clement Danes, where Westminster and London met, which still suggest many points of special interest well worthy of fuller investigation than they have as yet received.

The accompanying view shows Temple Bar and the old-world houses of Butcher Row. The first mention of Temple Bar is in a grant of land "extra barram Novi Temple" in 1301. At that time there was no building, but merely posts, rails and chain to mark the extent of the liberties of London. In course of time a gate was erected, and the one which existed at the time of the Great Fire was pulled down, and a new gate was erected in 1670-1672 from the designs of Sir Christopher Wren. This, after existing for two centuries as one of the best-known objects in London, was removed in the winter of 1878-1879. The stones remained exposed to the weather for ten years before Temple Bar was re-erected at the entrance to the late Sir Henry Meux's private grounds at Theobalds, Waltham Cross. The erection was completed on 3rd December 1888, and the gate in its new position and restored condition presents a very handsome appearance, showing it to be worthy of its great architect.

The history of Butcher Row is crowded with incidents in the lives of authors and the unfortunate hangers-on to literature. The timber-framed house, with projecting upper storeys and barge-boarded gables, the front decorated with *fleurs-de-lis* and coronets, was known as Beaumont House, and it is said that Sully, then Marquis of Rosny, supped and slept there on his arrival in London (1603) as Ambassador to James I.

Butcher Row was pulled down in 1813, and Pickett Street was erected in its place. This street was pulled down to make way for the new Law Courts, and now nearly the whole northern portion of St. Clement's parish has been cleared away. A great improvement has been made, but in order to obtain this many picturesque houses of interest have had to be destroyed.

Returning within the Bar to the city, and walking up Chancery Lane, we come to Lincoln's Inn Gateway, one of the three historical gateways of importance in London; the other two being St. John's Gate, Clerkenwell, and the entrance to St. James's Palace. This gatehouse of brick was built by Sir Thomas Lovell, K.G., son of the executor of Henry VII., and bears the date upon it of 1518. This interesting building, although perfectly sound and in good condition, was shored up a few years ago when old chambers by the side of it were pulled down and rebuilt, and it then narrowly escaped destruction. Efforts were successfully made to save the gate, and it is to be hoped that it may remain to give distinction to Chancery Lane for many years. Returning to Chancery Lane, and crossing Holborn, we come to Gray's Inn. The fine hall, which is full of associations of the deepest interest, was built between the years 1555 and 1560. Of the hall which it replaced there is no record, save that in 5 Edw. VI.

LINCOLN'S INN GATEWAY, CHANCERY LANE.

(1551), it "was seiled with fifty-four yards of wainscot, at 2s. a yard."

GRAY'S INN HALL

The present hall has the great distinction, according to Mr. Halliwell-Phillipps, of being "one of the only two buildings now remaining in London in which, so far as we know, any of the plays of Shakespeare were performed in his own time."[385] The other, of course, being the Middle Temple Hall, where *Twelfth Night* was acted on February 2, 1601-2.

The Comedy of Errors was played on the evening of Innocents' Day (December 28), 1594, in the hall, before a crowded audience; some of the guests from the Inner Temple created a disturbance because they were not properly accommodated, and this led to an official inquiry. Mr. Sidney Lee thinks it probable that Shakespeare himself was not present, as he was acting on the same day before the Queen at Greenwich. Another performance of the play was given in the hall by the Elizabethan Stage Society on December 6, 1895.[386]

George Gascoigne's *Jocasta*, adapted from the Phœnissæ of Euripides, was acted in the Refectory in 1566. Gray's Inn was famous for its masques and revels, and on July 7, 1887, in honour of Queen Victoria's Jubilee, the Benchers of Gray's Inn presented in the hall, to a distinguished audience, the *Masque of Flowers*, which had been performed before James I. on Twelfth Night, two hundred and sixty-four years before.

Gray's Inn had a brilliant roll of members in the sixteenth and seventeenth centuries, but it is Bacon's spirit that seems to haunt the whole place. He helped the students in preparing their revels, probably wrote a masque or masques, and planted trees in the gardens, the arrangement of which he is believed to have super-intended. His name remains in Verulam Buildings.

Returning to Holborn, and walking a little to the west, we come to the impressive front of Staple Inn, the most remarkable street front of old houses still in existence in London. The origin of the place is unknown, and nothing satisfactory has been discovered respecting the meaning of the name, or as to what it was before it came into the occupation of the Inn of Chancery. There is a tradition that it originally belonged to the merchants of the Staple. It was purchased by the Benchers of Gray's Inn in 1529, and in Elizabeth's reign there were 145 students in term, and 69 out of term. It was bought in 1884 by the Prudential Assurance Company for £68,000, and the Holborn front was restored and cleared from plaster covering the timber beams.

There are now very few old street fronts of interest in London, one or two in the Strand, and some in the great roads out of London, but a few years ago there were many still remaining in the Whitechapel and Mile End Roads, and in Bishopsgate Street Without. In the latter street (No. 169) there was until lately the remains of the mansion of Sir Paul Pindar, an eminent English merchant (who died in 1650), distinguished for his love of architecture, and the magnificent sums he gave towards the restoration of old St. Paul's Cathedral. In 1617-1618 the house was occupied by the Venetian Embassy. In its last days it was used as a public-house, with the sign of "Sir Paul Pindar's Head." When it was pulled down the front was obtained for the South Kensington Museum, where it was re-erected.

The London of Johnson and Hogarth was not a handsome city, but it was a social one, and we owe to these two men many vivid pictures of the life lived in it. They were both true Londoners, but they were not alone in their love for their city, for a marked feature in the character of the eighteenth-century Londoner was his intense feeling that here only was life to be lived with true enjoyment. Much of the life was frivolous, and some of it worse than that, but among the respectable classes the opportunities for social intercourse were greater than now, when large numbers of the workers live out of London, some in the north, and some in the south, and it takes as long to get from Hampstead to Croydon as to travel a hundred miles into the country.

During the eighteenth century London continued to grow, but it became uglier every day. The original growth was along the course of the river, but near the middle of the century a little building was commenced to the north of Oxford Street, when Cavendish Square and the surrounding streets were laid out. Soon afterwards the New Road from the Angel at Islington to the Edgware Road (now re-named Pentonville, Euston, and Marylebone Roads) was planned. The opening of this road greatly facilitated the locomotion of the town, but it was disliked by the dwellers in what was then thought

Sir Paul Pindar's House

to be the north of London, who had their view of the country cut off. When Queen Square was built in the reign of Queen Anne it was left open to the north, as it has remained to this day, in order to enable the inhabitants to have a view of Hampstead and Highgate. The gardens of Bedford House, which stood on the north side of Bloomsbury Square, had an uninterrupted view of the country, and the Duke of Bedford strongly opposed in the House of Lords the Bill for making the New Road. On this opposition Horace Walpole cynically remarked to Conway (March 25, 1756): "A new road through Paddington has been proposed to avoid the stones; the Duke of Bedford, who is never in town in summer, objects to the dust it will make behind Bedford House, and to some buildings proposed, though if he was in town he is too short-sighted to see the prospect."

The gardens of Bedford House were famous for their beauty and for the trees which flourished there, "the ancient stems" of "the light and graceful acacia" being specially mentioned by Walpole.

Behind Montagu House (now the British Museum) was Capper's Farm, which extended to Tottenham Court Road. The old farmhouse still exists behind Messrs Heal & Son's shop, No. 195 Tottenham Court Road.

Near where University College in Gower Street now stands was a wild district known as the Field of Forty Footsteps, which had a bad repute as the scene of a sanguinary duel about the time of the Monmouth Rebellion between two brothers who were both killed.

No grass would grow over the footsteps trodden by the duellists, which were said to be recognisable until the year 1800 when the ground was built over.

A little further east, where Cromer Street now stands, was a wayside inn named "The Boot," which is made by Dickens in his *Barnaby Rudge* the meeting-place of the Gordon Rioters of 1780.

The site of this inn is still occupied by a public-house with the same sign.

Even after these fields were built upon, the air continued so good that the gardens round about produced excellent fruit. When Lord Eldon lived at No. 42 Gower Street at the beginning of the nineteenth century his peaches and vegetables were famous. Nectarines were grown at 6 Upper Gower Street in 1800, and grapes were also successfully cultivated there.

The district north of the New Road is of a clayey soil and without a sufficient water supply, so that the ground remained unbuilt upon until at the beginning of the nineteenth century several new Water Companies came into existence and the building operations were commenced. Since that time the suburbs have continued to increase, and a great start was given to the increased growth of the town after the holding of the Great Exhibition of 1851. Before the middle of the nineteenth century the growth of London had been continually increasing, but it was not until after 1851 that the abnormal growth set in.

The Commissioners of the Exhibition of 1851 bought a large property at Brompton and the district of South Kensington sprang into existence. The glass and iron forming the Exhibition buildings were transferred to Sydenham, and the Crystal Palace was erected there. Soon this rural district, where gipsies once told fortunes, was covered with houses.

This was the beginning of the onward march of bricks and mortar, which is going on still so rapidly that on all sides we have to travel by rail for miles before we get out of the labyrinth of buildings.

When we see on all sides of us modern buildings where interesting old buildings once stood, we are apt to jump to the conclusion that all signs and relics of Mediæval London have passed away, but this is not so, for there is still much to see in out-of-the-way places if we go about the search with intelligence. From what we see we may reconstruct much of the old topography in our mind's eye. The first thing to do is to follow the course of the wall, and mark out the position of the gates. This can easily be done by studying an old map. Some remains of the wall are still to be seen.

Many most interesting remains of Roman London will be found in the Guildhall Museum.

There are few remains left of the Saxon period, but some bits are to be seen at Westminster. Of Norman buildings we have portions of the Tower, of Great St. Bartholomew's Church, the 'Round' of the Temple Church, and the Crypt of Bow Church, Cheapside.

Of later ages there are a few relics of the religious houses which have already been referred to. All the churches which escaped the ravages of the Great Fire have their points of interest. Lambeth Palace, although much of it is comparatively modern, has a most venerable appearance and is certainly one of the most important relics of past ages that the present London has to boast.

Westminster Hall, Abbey, Church and School are of transcendent interest, and some relics of the old Abbey buildings still exist in connection with the School.

Of secular buildings there are Crosby Hall, Middle Temple Hall, Gray's Inn Hall, and some others.

It is impossible to print a detailed list of all the places that should be visited, but these few notes will give some slight indication of what little is left of Mediæval London.

FOOTNOTES:

[1] Journal, Anthropological Society, vol. v. pp. lxxi.-lxxx.

[2] *Lake Dwellings in Europe*, 1890, pp. 460-464.

[3] Elton, *Origins of English History*, p. 360.

[4] Rev. W. Sparrow Simpson, *Chapters in the History of Old St. Paul's*, 1881, p. 3.

[5] *Archæologia*, vol. xxxii. pp. 298-311.

[6] *Norman Conquest*, vol. i. pp. 44-46.

[7] The Treaty was really made at Chippenham.

[8] *See* Earle's edition of the Saxon Chronicle. Mr Charles Plummer, who edited a new edition of *Two of the Saxon Chronicles, Parallel* (Oxford, 1892-99), does not altogether agree with Earle in these views. He holds that no distinction was meant between Lunden and Lundenburh.

[9] Quoted in *Archæologia*, vol. xxxix. p. 56.

[10] *Heimskringla*, done into English out of the Icelandic by William Morris and Eirikr Magnusson, vol. ii. p. 14.

[11] *Norman Conquest*, vol. i. p. 418.

[12] This device of Cnut's is one of great interest, although we have no details of how it was carried out. The late Sir Walter Besant contended that it was not the great work which some had supposed, and he made an elaborate plan of his suggestion as to its construction. (See *South London*, 1899, p. 40.)

[13] A very instructive article on 'The Conqueror's Footprints in Domesday,' which contains an account of his movements after the Battle of Senlac, between Enfield, Edmonton, Tottenham, and Berkhamsted, was published in the *English Historical Review*, vol. xiii. (1898), p. 17.

[14] *See* Dr. Reginald Sharpe's *London and the Kingdom*, to the contents of which valuable work I am pleased to express my great obligations.

[15] *Archæologia*, vol. xxxii. p. 305.

[16] Riley's Introduction to *Liber Albus* (Rolls Series), 1859, vol. i. p. cx.

[17] *Political Poems and Songs*, ed. T. Wright (Rolls Series), 1861, vol. ii. pp. 157-205.

[18] *See* Riley's *Memorials*, pp. 21, 93; also *Liber Albus*, p. 240.

[19] Records of St. Giles's, Cripplegate (1883).

[20] It is scarcely creditable to the city authorities that no mark of the position of the other gates has been set up. To place these memorials would be an easy thing to do, and this attention to historical topography would be highly appreciated by all Londoners. The mark of Aldgate should take the form of a statue of Chaucer, who lived at that gate for some years. The Corporation would honour themselves by doing further honour to the great Englishman, who was also one of the greatest of Londoners, if they placed at the great eastern entrance to London a full length effigy of the son of one of London's worthy merchants. This would be in addition to the gift of a bust to Guildhall by Sir Reginald Hanson. The line of the wall should also be marked, but this would be a more difficult operation.

[21] *Liber Albus*, p. 603.

[22] William Fitz-Stephen's invaluable work has been printed several times both in the original Latin and in an English translation. The most convenient form is the reprint in Thoms's edition of Stow's *Survey*, 1842 or 1876.

[23] Riley's *Memorials*, p. 79.

[24] Riley's *Memorials*, p. 489.

[25] *History of English Law before Edward I.*, vol. i. p. 633.

[26] Riley's *Memorials*, p. 479.

[27] Stow's *Chronicle*, ed. 1615, p. 300.

[28] Quoted in Turner's *Domestic Architecture in England*, vol. i. p. 18.

[29] Quoted in Turner's *Domestic Architecture in England*, vol. i. p. 22.

[30] Riley's Introduction to *Liber Albus*, pp. xxxiii., xxxiv.

[31] Riley's Introduction to *Liber Albus*, p. xxxii.

[32] Riley's Introduction to *Liber Albus*, p. xxxiii.

[33] Translation of the *Liber Albus*, p. 263, and Riley's Introduction to *Liber Albus*, p. lix.

[34] Letter Book B, p. i.

[35] Riley's *Memorials*, p. 54.

[36] *Ibid.*, p. 86.

[37] *Ibid.*, p. 458.

[38] Riley's Introduction to *Liber Albus*, p. lii.

[39] From an 'Anominalle Cronicle,' once belonging to St. Mary's Abbey, York. The original apparently has been lost, and the copy now existing is a late sixteenth-century manuscript of this portion of the Chronicle in the handwriting of Francis Thynne. It is now preserved in the British Museum (Stowe MS. 1047), and was one of the Duke of Buckingham's MSS. in the library at Stowe, Bucks, which came into the possession of the Earl of Ashburnham, and was sold by his son to the nation. It was published by Mr. G. M. Trevelyan in the *English Historical Review*, vol. xiii. (1898), p. 509. It is a curious circumstance, that it may be referred to as the 'Stowe MS.,' because it comes from the Stowe collection, or as the 'Stow MS.,' because it was used by the historian, John Stow.

[40] Trevelyan, p. 226.

[41] Trevelyan, p. 227.

[42] Trevelyan, p. 227.

[43] Trevelyan, p. 234.

[44] Trevelyan, p. 240.

[45] Stow's *Chronicle*, ed. 1615, p. 288.

[46] *English Historical Review*, xiii. p. 519.

[47] Stow's *Chronicle*, p. 288.

[48] *Second Part of King Henry VI.*, act iv. sc. i

[49] *Three Fifteenth Century Chronicles*, ed. J. Gairdner (Camden Society), 1880, p. 94.

[50] Stow's *Chronicle*, ed. 1615, p. 391.

[51] Rendle and Norman's *Inns of Old Southwark*, 1888, p. 134.

[52] *Historical Collections of a Citizen of London*, ed. Gairdner (Camden Society), p. 191. The chief contents of this volume consist of the valuable 'Chronicle of William Gregory, Skinner' (1189-1469).

[53] *Ibid.*, p. xxii.

[54] Vernon Text (A), ed. Skeat, pp. vi., 60.

[55] *Piers Plowman* (Text C), ed. Skeat, pass. xvii. II. 286-296.

[56] There was another Cock Lane near Shoreditch (now Boundary Street), which may be the one connected with Langland.

[57] *Piers Plowman*, part iv. sect. ii. p. xliii.

[58] It is scarcely possible to keep within bounds one's enthusiasm for the magnificent edition of *Piers Plowman*, which Professor Skeat has placed in our hands. I feel, having watched the work from its inception in 1866, when 'Parallel Extracts from 29 Manuscripts' was published, that if the Early English Text Society had published nothing else it would have worthily justified its existence. The labour bestowed on the work by its editor is immense, and the result is that we have for the first time a perfect text of one of the most influential works in English literature, with all the illustrative notes necessary to exhibit its vast effect upon English history.

[59] Hoccleve's Works, vol. i. Minor Poems, ed. by F. J. Furnivall (Early English Text Society, Extra Series), p. 61, 1891. The editor has gathered much fresh material for the biography of Hoccleve.

[60] *Gower's Complete Works*, ed. G. C. Macaulay, Oxford, 1899, vol. i.

[61] Of these especial honour is due to Dr. Furnivall, who has for years sought ceaselessly and with the greatest success for documentary evidence of the facts of Chaucer's life.

[62] Chaucer at Aldgate, *Home Counties Magazine*, Oct. 1900, p. 259.

[63] Chaucer at Aldgate (*Folia Litteraria*, 1893, p. 87).

[64] *Folia Litteraria*, pp. 88, 89.

[65] *Folia Litteraria*, p. 100.

[66] *Scrope and Grosvenor Roll*, vol. i. p. 178 (translated from French).

[67] *See* letter of Prof. J. W. Hales, *Athenæum*, Aug. 9, 1902, p. 190.

[68] The Tabard was one among many inns from which travellers started on their journeys along the road to Canterbury and to the seaports of the South. The whole of the buildings which Chaucer knew were burnt in the great Southwark fire of 1676.

[69] Commune, p. 246. Further consideration is given to the condition of trade in London in the Middle Ages in chapter x.

[70] *Liber Custumarum*, ed. H. T. Riley, 1860, p. xxxvi.

[71] *Liber Custumarum*, p. cix.

[72] Inquis. 1 *Henr. V.*, quoted by Riley, p. cix.

[73] Riley's *Memorials*, p. 306.

[74] Riley's *Memorials*, p. 376.

[75] *Riley's Memorials*, p. 648.

[76] *Ibid.*, p. 215.

[77] *Ibid.*, p. 219.

[78] *Ibid.*, p. 220.

[79] Cal. Letter Book A, p. 187.

[80] Riley's *Memorials*, p. 509.

[81] *Chronicle of Mayors and Sheriffs*, pp. 146, 147, quoted in Cal. Letter Book C, p. 61 (note).

[82] Cal. Letter Book C, p. 133.

[83] *Ibid.*, p. 95.

[84] Cal. Letter Book B, p. 219.

[85] Cal. Letter Book A, pp. 178, 179.

[86] Stow's *Chronicle*, p. 681.

[87] W. B. Rye's *England as seen by Foreigners*, 1865, pp. 9, 192.

[88] *Liber Custumarum*, ed. Riley, 1860, p. ciii.

[89] Round's *Geoffrey de Mandeville*, 1892, pp. 328-346.

[90] *Mediæval Military Architecture*, 1884, vol. ii. p. 204.

[91] *Mediæval Military Architecture*, 1884, vol. ii. p. 205.

[92] *Mediæval Military Architecture*, 1884, vol. ii. p. 253.

[93] *Mediæval Military Architecture*, vol. ii. p. 271.

[94] 'Geoffrey de Mandeville.'

[95] *London and the Kingdom*, vol. i. p. 53.

[96] Stow's *Chronicle*, p. 193.

[97] Longman's *Edward III.*, vol. i. p. 179.

[98] Clark's *Mediæval Military Architecture*, vol. ii. p. 271.

[99] *Liber Custumarum*, pp. 407-409.

[100] Clark's *Mediæval Military Architecture*, vol. ii. p. 264.

[101] Riley's *Memorials*, p. 320.

[102] Stow's *Chronicle*, p. 896.

[103] Proclamation was made against playing at football in the fields near the city as early as 1314 during the mayoralty of Nicholas de Farndone, *Liber Memorandorum* (preserved at Guildhall), folio 66 (quoted in Riley's *Memorials*, p. 571 (note)).

[104] Riley's *Memorials*, p. 561.

[105] *Ibid.*, p. 571.

[106] Riley's *Memorials*, pp. 509-510.

[107] *Ibid.*, p. 510 (note).

[108] Stow's *Chronicle*, p. 208.

[109] Riley's *Memorials*, pp. 105-107.

[110] Jessopp's *Coming of the Friars*, etc., 1889, p. 177.

[111] Stow's *Chronicle*, p. 264.

[112] Stow's *Survey of London*, ed. by Strype, 1754, vol. i. p. 303.

[113] Gregory's *Chronicle* (*Historical Collections of a Citizen of London*, ed. J. Gairdner, Camden Society, 1876), p. 165. This *Chronicle* contains a full description of the coronation and of the banquet in Westminster Hall.

[114] This description is taken from Fabyan's *Chronicle*. The speeches in the pageant were by Lydgate, who also wrote a long poem on the 'Coming of the King out of France to London.'

[115] The particulars respecting the sermon on Edward IV.'s title were obtained by Dr. J. Gairdner from a Latin Chronicle, printed by the Camden Society (*Three Fifteenth Century Chronicles*, 1880, pp. xxii. 173), as also his sitting in the royal seat (*sedes regalis*), which Dr. Gairdner supposes to be the King's Bench.

[116] Stow's *Chronicle*, p. 416.

[117] Information on London pageants can be obtained from a small octavo volume published by J. B. Nichols & Son in 1831, and from Nichols's *Progresses of Queen Elizabeth and James I*.

[118] *Liber Custumarum*, p. 579.

[119] Riley's *Memorials*, p. 42.

[120] *See* Mr. Riley's Introduction to the *Liber Custumarum*, pp. xlviii.-liv.

[121] *Liber Custumarum*, p. xxxii.

[122] Glossary to *Liber Custumarum*, p. 795.

[123] Riley's Introduction to *Liber Albus*, pp. lv., lvii.

[124] Introduction to *Liber Albus*, p. lviii.

[125] In the compilation of this chapter I am much indebted to the kindness of my friend Mr. D'Arcy Power, who has not only helped me with information from his own great knowledge of the history of surgery and medicine, but who also drew my attention to and lent me books and pamphlets of which I should otherwise have been ignorant.

[126] *Coming of the Friars*, London, 1889, p. 6.

[127] *A History of Epidemics in Britain*, 2 vols. 8vo, Cambridge, 1891-1894.

[128] *Medical Times and Gazette*, November 18, 1881, p. 601.

[129] *Progress of Medicine at St. Batholomew's Hospital*, 1888, p. 5.

[130] *See* the *British Medical Journal*, 1902, vol. ii. p. 1176.

[131] In 'How Surgery became a Profession in London.' London, *Medical Magazine*, 1899.

[132] Dr. Poore has analysed the different points in Chaucer's description, and explained the various allusions of the statement that the doctor's line of study had little to do with the Bible. Dr. Poore writes: 'This line is frequently quoted to show that the scepticism with which doctors are often charged is of no modern growth. The point of the line is however to be found in the fact that Chaucer's doctor was certainly a priest, as were all the physicians of his time, and that the practice of medicine had drawn him away, somewhat unduly, perhaps, from the clerical profession, to which he also belonged.'—G.V. Poore, M.D. *London from the Sanitary and Medical Point of View*, 1889, p. 52.

[133] *Joannis Anglici praxis medica, Rosa Anglica dicta* (Augsburg, 1595, lib. ii. p. 1050), quoted by J. J. Jusserand (*English Wayfaring Life in the Middle Ages*, 1901, p. 180), and by J. Flint South (*Craft of Surgery*, 1886, p. 29.)

[134] D'Arcy Power's *How Surgery became a Profession in London* (1899), which valuable article contains a full account of the scheme.

[135] *Ibid.*, p. 9.

[136] D'Arcy Power's *How Surgery became a Profession in London*, p. 9.

[137] *Ibid.*, p. 1.

[138] He was born in 1307 (Sloane MS., No. 75).

[139] See *John Arderne and his Time*, by William Anderson, F.R.C.S., 1899 (reprinted from the *Lancet*, Oct. 23); J. F. South's *Memorials of the Craft of Surgery*, ed. by D'Arcy Power, M.A., F.R.C.S., 1886, pp. 30-45; also *London from the Sanitary and Medical Point of View*, by G. V. Poore, M.D., F.R.C.P., 1889, pp. 53-56.

[140] Riley's *Memorials*, p. 274.

[141] *How Surgery became a Profession in London*, pp. 3, 4.

[142] Riley's *Memorials*, p. 337.

[143] *Ibid.*, p. 519.

[144] *Ibid.*, p. 520.

[145] *How Surgery became a Profession in London*, p. 4.

[146] Riley's *Memorials*, p. 651.

[147] *How Surgery became a Profession in London*, pp. 2, 3.

[148] 'William Hobbes (appointed in 1461) was the first Serjeant Surgeon, a distinguished office which carried with it certain well-defined professional privileges. Thomas Morstede, William Bredewardyne, and John Harwe, who attended Henry V. in his French campaigns, did not receive this title, but are called simply "*Surgeons to the King*." '—D'Arcy Power, *The Serjeant Surgeons of England and their Office* (*Janus*, 1900, p. 174).

[149] *How Surgery became a Profession in London*, pp. 11, 12.

[150] *Annals of the Barber Surgeons of London*, by Sidney Young. London, 1890.

[151] *Ibid.*, p. 245.

[152] London, 1885.

[153] Dr. Norman Moore has printed the Cottonian MS. Life of Rahere in the *Bartholomew Hospital Reports*, vol. xxi., and copious extracts from the MS. had previously been given by Mr. J. Saunders in his articles on St. Bartholomew's in Knight's *London*, vol. ii.

[154] *Progress of Medicine*, 1888, p. 21.

[155] These documents are printed in the Appendix to *Memoranda relating to the Royal Hospitals of London*, 1836, pp. 1-49.

[156] Reprinted in Dr. Furnivall's edition of Thomas Vicary's *Anatomie of the Bodie of Man*, E. E. T. S., 1888, pp. 289-336.

[157] 'The Physicians and Surgeons of St. Bartholomew's Hospital before the time of Harvey,' St. Bartholomew's Hospital Reports, vol. xviii., 1882, pp. 333-338.

[158] 'The Serjeant-Surgeons of England and their Office,' by D'Arcy Power (*British Medical Journal*, 1900, vol. i. p. 583).

[159] The manuscript is dated 1392, but the handwriting of the copy used by Dr. Payne is of a much later date. Dr. Payne says that the *Anatomy* of Vicary is absolutely that of the fourteenth century, without any correction or addition to bring it up to the standard of his own day, 'On an unpublished English Anatomical Treatise of the fourteenth century, and its relation to the *Anatomy* of Thomas Vicary' (*British Medical Journal*, 25th January 1896, p. 208).

[160] *A History of Epidemics in Britain*, by Charles Creighton, M.D., 1891, vol. i. pp. 97, 98.

[161] *Ibid.*, p. 106.

[162] Creighton, vol. i. p. 97.

[163] *England in the Fifteenth Century*, 1888, p. 208 (note).

[164] Creighton, vol. i. p. 105.

[165] *Quarterly Review*, No. 388, p. 540.

[166] *Epidemics in Britain*, vol. i. p. 119. *See* also *The Great Pestilence*, by F. A. Gasquet, D.D., O.S.B., London, 1893.

[167] Riley's Introduction to *Liber Albus*, p. liv.

[168] Jessopp's *Coming of the Friars*.

[169] Riley's *Memorials*, p. 219 (note).

[170] *Ibid.*, p. 240 (note).

[171] *A History of Epidemics in Britain*, vol. i. p. 202.

[172] *Ibid.*, p. 228.

[173] Creighton, vol. i. pp. 313, 314.

[174] *Anatomie of the Bodie of Man*, ed. Furnivall, App. 161.

[175] *Ibid.*, pp. 163, 164.

[176] *Calendar of State Papers*, Venetian, vii. 749.

[177] Creighton, vol. i. p. 316.

[178] Vicary, App. iii. p. 166.

[179] Mr. Power refers me to the fact that isolated cases of plague and local epidemics occurred long after the Great Fire.

[180] In a broadside referring to '*The Plague of London*, printed by Peter Cole, at the printing office in Cornhill, near the Royal Exchange, 1665,' the number of deaths from plague in 1603, 1625 and 1636 are given as follows:—1603, 30,561 persons; 1625, 35,403; and 1636, 10,400. The numbers in 1593 are given as above.

[181] Mr Pearce gives some interesting facts in his *Annals of Christ's Hospital* (p. 207) respecting the effects of the plague in 1603 and 1665 on the condition of the Blue Coat School. During 1665 no more than 32 children of the total number of 260 in the house died of all diseases, although the neighbourhood was severely visited.

[182] Creighton, vol. i. p. 265.

[183] Creighton, p. 270.

[184] *Progress of Medicine*, 1888, p. 24.

[185] Creighton, vol. i. p. 44.

[186] *London (Ancient and Modern) from the Sanitary and Medical Point of View*, by G. V. Poore, M.D., F.R.C.P., 1889, p. 114.

[187] *Ibid.*, p. 31.

[188] Creighton, vol. i. p. 323.

[189] Stow's Chronicle, p. 212.

[190] Riley's *Memorials*, p. 67.

[191] Rymer's *Foedera*, vol. iii. p. 411.

[192] Creighton, vol. i. pp. 323, 324.

[193] Creighton, vol. i. p. 324.

[194] Riley's Introduction to *Liber Albus*, p. xl.

[195] Cal. Letter Book A.

[196] Riley's Introduction to *Liber Albus*, p. xli.

[197] Mr. Round conjectures that the 'Gosfregth Portirefan' of the Conqueror's Charter was the first Geoffrey de Mandeville.—*Geoffrey de Mandeville, a Study of the Anarchy*, 1892, p. 439.

[198] 'The acceptance of this view will at once dispose of the alleged disappearance of the portreeve, with the difficulties it has always presented, and the conjectures to which it has given rise. The style of the "portreeve"

indeed disappears, but his office does not. In the person of the Norman vicecomes it preserves an unbroken existence. Geoffrey de Mandeville steps, as sheriff, into the shoes of Ansgar, the portreeve.'—*Geoffrey de Mandeville*, p. 354.

[199] *Constitutional History*, chap, xi., note to par. 131.

[200] *Select Charters*, Oxford, 1884, p. 107.

[201] *Geoffrey de Mandeville*, 1892, p. 372

[202] *Geoffrey de Mandeville*, p. 373.

[203] *Constitutional History*, chap. xiii. par 165.

[204] *Ancient Charters prior to* 1200, edited by J. H. Round. Part I, p. 27, 1888 (Pipe Roll Society).

[205] *The Commune of London*, p. 98.

[206] Round's *Commune of London*, pp. 223, 224.

[207] 'A London Municipal Collection of the Reign of John,' part i., *English Historical Review*, July 1902, p. 480.

[208] 'Nunc primum in sibi indulta conjuratione, regno regem deesse cognovit Londonia, quam nec rex ipse Ricardus, nec prædecessor et pater ejus Henricus pro mille millibus marcarum argenti fieri permississet.'—*Richard of Devizes*, p. 416 (*Commune of London*, p. 223)

[209] Bishop Stubbs's *Historical Introductions*, pp. 200-309.

[210] *The Commune of London*, p. 224. The Beffroi of France was the symbol and pledge of independence. So was the bell-tower of St. Paul's, which is styled in documents *berefridum* or campanile, p. 234.

[211] *The Commune of London*, p. 225.

[212] *The Commune of London*, p. 228.

[213] *Ibid.*, p. 228.

[214] 1193. 'Sacramentum Commune tempore regis Ricardi quando detentus erat Alemaniam' (Add. MS., No. 14,252, f. 112 d.), 1205-1206. 'Sacramentum xxiiij factum anno regni regis Johannis vii°.' (Add. MS., No. 14,252, f. 110).—(*The Commune of London*, 1899, pp. 235-237.)

[215] *Commune of London*, p. 240.

[216] A curious point is that formerly the Leges Britolii were supposed to relate to Bristol, and the great English port obtained credit which it did not deserve.

[217] 'The Laws of Breteuil [Britolium],' *English Historical Review*, xv. (1900), pp. 73, 302, 496, 754.

[218] The seal is figured in '*Rotuli Curiæ Regis*. Rolls and Records of the Court held before the King's Justiciars or Justices, ed. by Sir Francis Palgrave,' vol. i., 1835 (plate 1), and is here reproduced.

[219] *Constitutional History*, chap. xiii. sec. 165.

[220] Cal. Letter Book B, p. 244.

[221] Cal. Letter Book A, pp. 89, 209.

[222] Rymer's *Foedera*, vol. i. pt. ii. p. 892.

[223] Cal. Letter Book C, pp. 27, 212, 213.

[224] *Constitutional History*, chap. xxi. sec. 486.

[225] Sharpe, *London and the Kingdom*, vol. i. p. 158.

[226] Letter Book F, fo. 44. Riley's Introduction to *Liber Albus*, 1859, pp. xcviii., xcix. (note).

[227] This church was destroyed in the Great Fire, and rebuilt after the designs of Sir C. Wren. It was cleared away in 1831 to make way for the approaches to the new London Bridge.

[228] Stubbs, *Constitutional History*, chap. xxi. sec. 487.

[229] Statutes at Large, ed. 1762, ii. 257.

[230] Riley's *Memorials*, pp. 473, 474.

[231] Riley's *Memorials*, pp. 415, 416.

[232] *Rotuli Parl.* iii. 227.

[233] Riley's *Memorials*, p. 494.

[234] *Ibid.*, p. 526.

[235] Cal. Letter Book A, p. 64.

[236] *Constitutional History*, chap. xxi. sec. 488.

[237] See Jewitt and Hope's *Corporation Plate*, 1895, vol. ii., pp. 446, 463.

[238] Riley's *Memorials*, pp. 604, 605.

[239] *Historical Collections of a Citizen of London*, 1876, pp. 222, 223.

[240] *London and the Kingdom*, i. 69. 'Cives vero Lundonie servierunt de pincernaria, et Cives Wintonie de Coquina.'—Roger de Hoveden, Bodl.

Laud., MS. 582, fo. 52. (*See* Wickham Legg's *English Coronation Records*, 1901, p. 50).

[241] 'Andrew the Mayor came to serve as butler with 360 cups, on the ground that the City of London is bound to serve in butlery to help the great butler (just as the City of Winchester serves in the kitchen to help the steward). The King said that no one ought to serve by right except Master Michael Belet, so the Mayor gave way and served the two bishops on the King's right hand. '*De Servitiis magnatum in die Coronationis Regis et Reginæ*, Red Book of the Exchequer, ed. by Hubert Hall, pt. ii., 1896, pp. 755-760 (Rolls Series). The germ of the Court of Claims will be found in this MS. *See* also Wickham Legg's *English Coronation Records*, 1901, pp. 60, 63.

[242] *English Coronation Records*, 1901, pp. 140, 159.

[243] *London and the Kingdom*, i. 275.

[244] 'Dinner being concluded, the Lord Mayor and twelve principal citizens of London, as assistants to the Chief Butler of England, accompanied by the King's cupbearer and assistant, presented to His Majesty wine in a gold cup; and the King having drank thereof, returned the gold cup to the Lord Mayor as his fee.'—L. G. Wickham Legg, *English Coronation Records*, 1901, p. 361.

[245] The Petition of the Mayor and Commonalty and Citizens of London, containing their claims fully set forth, is printed in *Coronation of King Edward VII. The Court of Claims. Cases and Evidence*, by G. Woods Wollaston, London, 1903, p. 52.

[246] *Constitutional History*, iii. 587.

[247] Cal. Letter Book C, p. 32.

[248] Riley's *Memorials*, p. 41.

[249] *Ibid.*, p. 46.

[250] *Ibid.*, p. 78.

[251] *Liber Albus*, trans. by Riley, p. 291.

[252] *Liber Albus*, p. 276.

[253] *The Aldermen of Cripplegate Ward*, by John James Baddeley, 1901, p. I (Calendar of Letter Book A, pp. 209, 226).

[254] Cal. Letter Book C, pp. 11, 12.

[255] In 1711 a return was made to the practice of nominating two persons only, followed in 1714 by 'an Act for reviving the ancient manner of electing aldermen'(13 Anne), which restored to the 'inhabitants their

ancient rights and privileges of choosing one person only to be their alderman.' These particulars respecting the election of aldermen are taken from *The Aldermen of Cripplegate Ward*, from 1276 to 1900, by Mr. Deputy John James Baddeley, who has collected in his valuable book a considerable amount of fresh information on the office of aldermen, etc.

[256] *Liber Albus*, translated by H. T. Riley, 1861, p. 29.

[257] Sharpe's *London and the Kingdom*, vol. i. p. 217.

[258] Riley's *Memorials*, p. 655.

[259] Cal. Letter Book A, p. 76. By the Local Government Act of 1888 the citizens of London were deprived of all right of jurisdiction over the county of Middlesex, which had been expressly granted by various charters.

[260] *Liber Albus*, English translation, p. 399.

[261] *The Aldermen of Cripplegate Ward*, 1900, p. 235.

[262] Mr. Baddeley continues the account of the changes in the mode of election up to the present time: 'From 1642 to 1651 the Mayor's claim to elect a sheriff was always contested. For the year 1652 and for some years afterwards the Mayor neither nominated nor elected a sheriff, but in 1662, when he would have elected one Bludworth as sheriff, the commonalty claimed their right, although they accepted the Mayor's nominee. The prerogative thus claimed by the Mayor, although frequently challenged, was exercised for the most part by subsequent Mayors down to 1674, when exception was taken to William Roberts, whom the Mayor had formally nominated (according to a custom which is said to have arisen in the time of Elizabeth) by drinking to him at a public banquet. In the following year and for some years later the Mayor exercised his prerogative of electing one of the sheriffs without opposition. In 1703 an Act was passed declaring the right of election of sheriffs to be in the liverymen of the several companies of the city in Common Hall assembled.' It was, however, lawful for the Lord Mayor to nominate for the office. 'By an Act of 1748 the Lord Mayor might continue to nominate to the extent of nine persons in the whole.' By an Act of Common Council in 1878 the right of election to the office of sheriff was vested in the liverymen of the several companies of the city in Common Hall assembled. The Lord Mayor nominating one or more freemen (not exceeding three in the whole) for the shrievalty.

[263] *The Aldermen of Cripplegate Ward*, by J. J. Baddeley, 1900, p. 218.

[264] Letter Book F, f. 206.

[265] Letter Book H, f. 46b (Baddeley's *Aldermen of Cripplegate Ward*, p. 215).

[266] *Corporation Plate and Insignia of Office of the Cities and Towns of England and Wales*, by Llewellyn Jewitt, ed. and completed by W. H. St. John Hope, 1895, vol. ii. p. 122.

[267] *Corporation Plate and Insignia of Office of the Cities and Towns of England and Wales*, p. 120.

[268] *Archæologia*, vol. v. pp. 211-213.

[269] See *Liber Custumarum* (Rolls Series), Introduction, p. lxxvi.

[270] Cal. Letter Book C, p. 71.

[271] Cal. Letter Book A, p. 222.

[272] *Dugdale's Baronage*, i. 220.

[273] Riley's *Memorials*, p. 178.

[274] Riley's *Memorials*, p. 236.

[275] *Ibid.*, p. 178.

[276] Cal. Letter Book A, p. 161.

[277] *Calendar of Charter Rolls*, vol. i. 1903, p. 163.

[278] *Liber Custumarum* (Rolls Series), vol i. p. 243.

[279] Calendars: Letter Book A, p. 128; Letter Book C, p. 116.

[280] Letter Book C, p. 157 (note).

[281] Letter Book B, pp. vi., xi.

[282] Riley's *Memorials*, p. 650.

[283] *Corporation Plate and Insignia of Office of the Cities and Towns of England and Wales*, by Llewellyn Jewitt, ed. by W. H. St. John Hope, 1895, vol. ii, pp. 100, 109.

[284] *Ibid.*, p. 91.

[285] Round's *Commune of London*, p. 246.

[286] *Calender of Documents preserved in France*, ed. by J. Horace Round, 1899, p. 502.

[287] No woollen cloth was allowed to be dyed black except with woad. See *Liber Custumarum*, Introd., pp. xl., xliii., quoted in Letter Book C, ed. Sharpe, pp. 135, 136 (note), from which this information is obtained.

The whole history of the cultivation and use of woad is one of great interest. It was cultivated in England from the earliest times, and the trade was ruined by the indigo growers as they in turn have been ruined in our own day by the manufacture in Germany of synthetic indigo.

[288] Sharpe's *London and the Kingdom*, vol. i. p. 215.

[289] Riley's *Memorials*, p. 444.

[290] Riley's *Memorials*, p. 345.

[291] *Calendar of State Papers*, 1611-1618, p. 369.

[292] Cal. Letter Book B, p. 236; Cal. Letter Book C, p. vii

[293] Cal. Letter Book B, p. 236.

[294] Letter Book A, p. 3; Letters-Patent for St. Botolph's Fair, 1298. Letter Book B, p. 219.

[295] *Liber Albus*, English translation, p. 473.

[296] *Liber Albus*, English translation, p. 228.

[297] Mr. W. J. Ashley writes of this town: 'The conquest of Calais furnished a place which combined the advantages of being abroad and therefore near the foreign market with that of being within English territory.'—Introduction to *English Economic History and Theory*, 1888-1893, p. 112.

[298] Starkey, *England in the Reign of Henry VIII.* (Early English Text Society), p. 173.

[299] Mr. W. J. Ashley notes that the earliest instance of the prohibition of the export of wool is found in the action of the Oxford Parliament of 1258. The barons then 'decreed that the wool of the country should be worked up in England and should not be sold to foreigners, and that every one should use woollen cloth made within the country,' and lest people should be dissatisfied at having to put up with the rough cloth of England they bade them 'not to seek over precious raiment.'—*English Economic History and Theory*, 1888-1893, part ii. p. 194.

[300] *Political Poems and Songs*, ed. T. Wright (Rolls Series), vol. ii. 1861, pp. 157-205.

[301] Letter Book C, p. 128 (note).

[302] *Liber Custumarum*, p. xxxix.

[303] Letter Book B, p. 94.

[304] *English Gilds*, p. xvi.

[305] *Ibid.*, p. lxxv.

[306] *Ibid.*, p. cvii.

[307] *English Economic History and Theory*, p. 67.

[308] *Ibid.*, p. 82.

[309] *English Historical Review*, No. 70 (April 1903), vol. xviii. p. 315. See also *Calendar of Charter Rolls*, vol. i. (1903), p. 407.

[310] *Twelve Great Livery Companies* (1834), vol. i. p. 24.

[311] *Chronicles of the Mayors and Sheriffs of London*, 1188-1274. Translated from the *Liber de Antiquis Legibus* by H. T. Riley, 1863, p. 59.

[312] *London and the Kingdom*, vol. i. p. 101.

[313] *Ibid.*, p. 108.

[314] *English Economic History and Theory*, p. 87.

[315] *London and the Kingdom*, vol. i. p. 200.

[316] *English Gilds*, p. xlii. (note).

[317] See *English Economic History and Theory*, 1888-1893, pt. ii. pp. 134, 148, 154.

[318] *History of London*, vol. i. p. 171 (note).

[319] *London* (Historic Towns), p. 50.

[320] *London Afternoons*, 1902, p. 88.

[321] I am indebted to Sir Owen Roberts, M.A., D.C.L., clerk to the Clothworkers' Company, for this information.

[322] Botfield's *Manners and Household Expenses of England*, 1841.

[323] W. J. Ashley, *English Economic History and Theory*, pp. 81, 83.

[324] Cal. Letter Book C, p. 35.

[325] Madox's *Firma Burgi*, p. 286.

[326] *Town Life*, vol. ii. p. 142.

[327] The reason given for the repeal of the Act of Edward II. excluding victuallers from the office of Mayor is that 'since the making of the Statute many and the most part of all cities, boroughs and towns corporate be fallen in ruin and decay, and not inhabited with merchants and men of such substance as they were at the time of making the Statute. For at this day the dwellers and inhabitants of the same cities and boroughs be

most commonly bakers, brewers, vintners, fishmongers, and other victuallers, and few or none other persons of substance.'

Mr. W. J. Ashley (Introduction to *English Economic History and Theory*, part ii. 1893, p. 53), observes that, 'without further proof it were hardly safe to build on the wide language of the preamble of a Statute a conclusion which seems in obvious conflict with what we know of the generic course of events.'

In London, evidently, little or no attention was paid to the original Act of Edward II., but in other places this was not the case. The Statute of Henry VIII. provided that when the Mayor was a victualler, two honest and discreet persons, not being victuallers, should be chosen to assist him in 'settling prices' of victuals.

[328] *Liber Custumarum*, vol i. p. 326-333.

[329] *Liber Albus*, Introduction by H. T. Riley, 1859, p. ci.

[330] *Liber Custumarum*, p. lxviii.

[331] *Liber Albus*, Introduction by H. T. Riley, p. lxxxi.

[332] *Liber Albus*, Introduction by H. T. Riley, p. lxxix.

[333] These prices, obtained from the *Liber Albus*, are of great interest. Of course, it is necessary to bear in mind the great difference in the value of money. It is impossible to fix a uniform standard of comparison, but we may put the present value broadly at between twelve and twenty times that of the reign of Edward I., the latter being more likely to be a true one. It will thus be seen that much food was dearer in the Middle Ages than at present. A rabbit and its skin are considerably less valuable now, as also a partridge.

[334] *Liber Albus*, Introduction by H. T. Riley, p. lxxxii.

[335] Cal. Letter Book D, p. xix.

[336] Riley's Introduction to *Liber Albus*, p. lxii.

[337] Riley's Introduction to the *Liber Albus*, p. lxv.

[338] H. T. Riley's Introduction to *Liber Albus*, p. lxxxviii.

[339] *Ibid.*, p. lxxxix.

[340] *Liber Custumarum*, ed. Riley, p. lxx.

[341] *Liber Albus*, p. xc.

[342] *Historical Collections of a Citizen of London in the Fifteenth Century* (Camden Society, 1876).

[343] Diary, July 26, 1664.

[344] Whitwell (Roy. Hist. Soc. Trans., xvii. p. 208).

[345] Extracts from the Liberate Rolls relative to loans supplied by Italian merchants to the Kings of England in the thirteenth and fourteenth centuries, with an Introductory Memoir by E. A. Bond (*Archæologia*, xxviii. (1839), pp. 207-326). There has lately been a revival of interest in this subject. In 1902 Mr. W. E. Rhodes published a paper on 'The Italian Bankers in England, and their Loans to Edward I. and Edward II.,' in *Historical Essays by Members of the Owen's College, Manchester*. Mr. R. J. Whitwell read his important paper on 'Italian Bankers and the English Crown' before the Royal Historical Society on March 19, 1903, which is published in the Transactions of that Society, N.S., xvii. pp. 175-233.

[346] Cal. Letter Book B, p. 94.

[347] *Ibid.*, p. 165.

[348] Longman's *Edward III.*, vol. ii. pp. 262, 263.

[349] *Archæologia*, vol. xxviii. p. 240.

[350] *Three Fifteenth Century Chronicles* (Camden Society, 1880), p. 9.

[351] '*De Verborum Significatione*. The Exposition of the Termes and difficill wordes contained in the foure buiks of Regiam Maiestatem and uthers. Collected and exponed by Master John Skene. London, 1641.'

[352] Cal. Letter Book A, ed. Dr. Reginald Sharpe, p. iv.

[353] *See* Jewitt and Hope's *Corporation Plate*, etc., vol. ii. p. 123 (Cal. Letter Book A, p. 79).

[354] Scott's *Lectures on Mediæval Architecture*, vol. ii. p. 29.

[355] Sparrow Simpson's *Chapters in the History of Old St. Paul's*, 1881, p. 19.

[356] The dimensions as given by Dugdale agree with those stated on a tablet which once hung in the Cathedral on a column near the tomb of John of Gaunt. They are:—

Length	690 ft.
Breadth	130 ft.
Height of roof of west part from floor	102 ft.
Height of roof of new fabric (viz., east from steeple)	88 ft.

Body of church	150 ft.
Height of tower steeple from the level ground	260 ft.
Height of the spire of wood, covered with lead	274 ft.
'And yet the whole, viz., tower and spire, exceedeth not'	520 ft.
Cross, 'length' above the ball	15 ft.
Cross, traverse	6 ft.

Ball contains ten bushels of corn.

Space on which the cathedral stands, 3½ acres, 1½ roods, 6 perches.

—(*Documents Illustrating the History of St. Paul's Cathedral*, Camden Society, 1880, p. 191.)

Mr. Edmund B. Ferrey, who worked on Hollar's plans, and made illustrations for Mr. William Longman's *Three Cathedrals of St. Paul* (1873), considers that Dugdale's figures are untrustworthy. His own figures are:—

Length (inclusive of end walls)	596 ft.
Breadth (including aisle walls)	104 ft.
Height of roof, west part (up to ridge of vaulting)	93 ft.
Height of roof (up to vault ridge) to 'choir proper'	101 ft. 6 in.
Height of roof at Lady Chapel	98 ft. 6 in.
External height (ground to ridge of outer roof to choir)	142 ft.
External height (ground to ridge of outer roof to nave)	130 ft.
Height of tower steeple from level ground	285 ft.
Height of the spire covered with lead	208 ft.

(or 204 ft. if calculated from top of tower parapet).

—(Longman's *Three Cathedrals dedicated to St. Paul in London*, 1873, p. 30).

It will be seen that Mr. Ferrey's figures, formed on careful calculations, not only differ considerably from those of Dugdale, but in the case of the relative heights of the nave and choir they are positively opposite. Mr. Ferrey came to the conclusion that the choir was decidedly higher than the nave.

[357] *Old St. Paul's Cathedral*, by Canon Benham, D.D. (Portfolio Monograph), 1902, pp. 6, 7.

[358] Simpson's *History of Old St. Paul's*, 1881, p. 64.

[359] Stow quoted in Longman's *Three Cathedrals*, p. 57.

[360] In 1633 Inigo Jones designed, at the expense of Charles I., a classic portico of some beauty in itself, but quite incongruous to the Gothic design of the rest of the building. The King, however, is said to have intended to rebuild the church, and of this scheme the portico was an instalment, but political events effectually prevented this from being carried out. After the Restoration, but before the Fire of London, it was proposed to rebuild the Cathedral in the style of the Renaissance, under the direction of Wren, who had no more liking for Gothic than Inigo Jones had.

[361] *History of Old St. Paul's*, 1881, pp. 62, 63.

[362] The name of London House Yard preserves the memory of the palace.

[363] Paul's Cross was pulled down in 1642, but its site was long marked by a tall elm tree. This mark passed away and the exact position was forgotten. In 1879, however, Mr. F. C. Penrose found the remains of the octagonal base, which are now to be seen at the north-east angle of the choir of the present Cathedral.

[364] During the Commonwealth it was proposed to turn the so-called Convocation House into a meeting-place for Mr. John Simpson's congregation. A plan (dated 1657) in the Public Record Office (Council of State Order Book, 1657-1658, p. 172) shows the remains of the pillars of the cloisters as they were then. This plan is reproduced in *Documents Illustrating the History of St. Paul's Cathedral* (Camden Society, 1880), p. 154.

[365] The amount of the offerings at St. Paul's during the Middle Ages must have been enormous; for instance, the receipts at the Great Crucifix, in May 1344, amounted to no less than £50 in the money of that day.—Dr. Sparrow Simpson's *History of Old St. Paul's*, p. 83.

[366] Simpson's *History of Old St. Paul's*, p. 90.

[367] The late Dr. Sparrow Simpson's Documents illustrating the History of St. Paul's Cathedral (Camden Society, 1880) contains a list of altars in old St. Paul's (p. 178), and a list of chapels (p. 181).

[368] Dugdale quoted in Longman's *Three Cathedrals*, p. 58.

[369] Simpson's *History of Old St. Paul's*, p. 91.

[370] *London* (Historic Towns), 1887, p. 158.

[371] *Liber Albus*, translated by Riley, pp. 24-27.

[372] Historical Introduction to the Rolls Series. Collected by Arthur Hassall, 1902, p. 77.

[373] In connection with the history of the Austin Friars the fact that the church of the friary still exists is one of great interest. At the dissolution a large portion of the friary was given to Lord St. John, afterwards Marquis of Winchester and Lord Treasurer. The church was reserved by the King, and the nave still remains.

[374] Dugdale (*Warwickshire*, ed. 1730, p. 186), says that the Patriarch Albert prescribed for the Carmelite Friars a parti-coloured mantle of white and red, and that Pope Honorius III., disliking this, appointed in 1285 that it should be all white.

[375] G. M. Trevelyan, *England in the Age of Wycliffe*, p. 139.

[376] *Dictionary of National Biography* (Anne), vol. i. p. 424.

[377] Riley's *Memorials*, p. 630.

[378] Cal. Letter Book B, pp. xiii.-xv.

[379] *Ibid.*, p. 215.

[380] In Gross's *Select Cases from Coroner's Rolls* (Selden Society, Introduction, p. xxx.), instances are given of the part played by the privilege of sanctuary in thwarting criminal justice.

[381] *Constitutional History of England*, chap. xxi. para. 496.

[382] Master Hugh de Whytington was master of the scholars of St. Martin-le-Grand in 1298 (Cal. Letter Book B, p. 73).

[383] *Survey*, ed. Thoms, pp. 27, 28.

[384] Foxe, *Acts and Monuments*, ed. 1597, p. 1885; Holinshed, p. 1142. This incident will be recognised as the groundwork of Mr. Weyman's delightful romance of *Francis Cludde*.

[385] *Outlines of the Life of Shakespeare* (seventh edition), 1887, vol. i. p. 124.

[386] *Life of William Shakespeare*, 1898, p. 70.

Milton Keynes UK
Ingram Content Group UK Ltd.
UKHW030903151124
451262UK00006B/1056